SECRET
LONDON
AN UNUSUAL GUIDE

Rachel Howard and Bill Nash

PHOTOGRAPHS
Stéphanie Rivoal, Jorge Monedero and Adam Tucker

JONGLEZ PUBLISHING

Rachel Howard is a journalist and copywriter who has lived in almost every borough in London. A regular contributor to *Conde Nast Traveller*, *National Geographic Traveler*, and the *Guardian*, Rachel writes mainly about travel, food, and the arts. She previously spent a decade writing speeches for the Greek foreign minister. But that's another story.

Bill Nash is an actor and writer, with family roots all across London. An obsession with the city's corners is the foundation for his contribution to this book. He lives in Brixton with his family and an ineffective cat.

We have taken great pleasure in compiling *Secret London – an unusual guide* and hope that through its guidance you will, like us, continue to discover unusual, hidden or little-known aspects of the city. Some entries are accompanied by historical asides or anecdotes as an aid to understanding the city in all its complexity.

Secret London - an unusual guide also draws attention to the multitude of details found in places that we may pass every day without noticing. We invite you to look more closely at the urban landscape and to see your own city with the curiosity and attention that we often display while travelling elsewhere…

Comments on this guidebook and its contents, as well as information on places we may not have mentioned, are more than welcome and will enrich future editions.

Don't hesitate to contact us:
E-mail: info@jonglezpublishing.com
Jonglez publishing, 25, rue du Maréchal Foch,
78000 Versailles, France

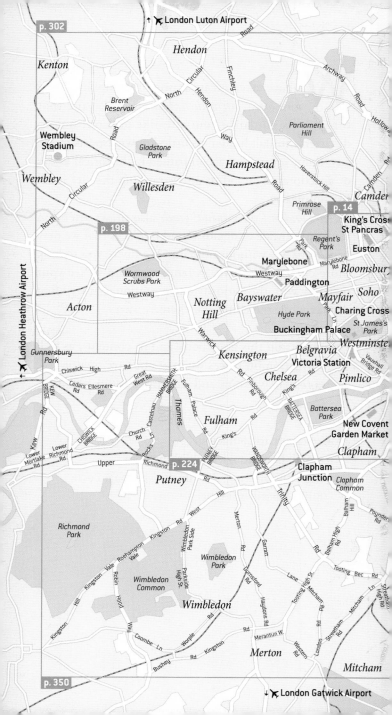

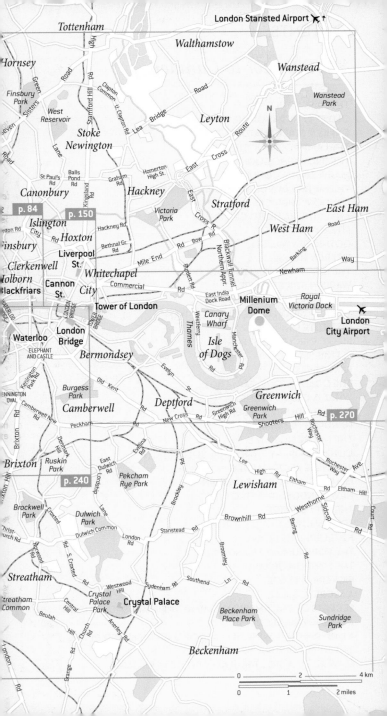

CONTENTS

Westminster to Camden

Temple to Angel

CONTENTS

Towerbridge to Shoreditch

Marylebone to Shepherd's Bush

CONTENTS

Westminster to Hammersmith

South Bank to Brixton

Whitechapel to Woolwich

CONTENTS

Greater London (North)

Greater London (South)

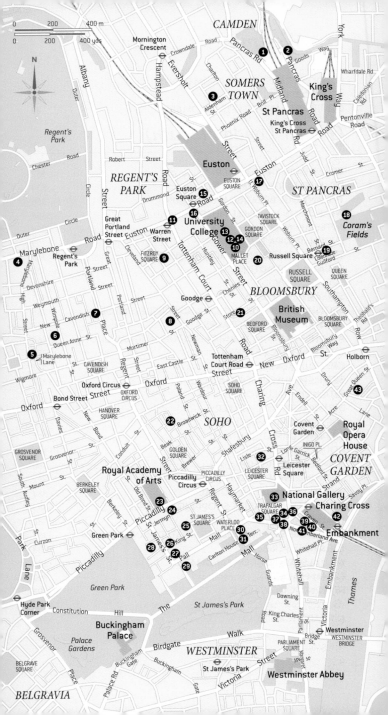

Westminster to Camden

THE HARDY TREE

Rearranging the dead

Old St Pancras Churchyard, Pancras Road, NW1 1UL
www.posp.co.uk/st-pancras-old-church
Admission free
King's Cross St Pancras tube/rail, Mornington Crescent tube

F amously gloomy 19th-century novelist Thomas Hardy may have had his distaste for the city confirmed by his involvement with this North London oddity. Hardy trained as an architect at King's College, and was apprenticed to Arthur Blomfield between 1862 and 1867, a time when railway networks in the UK were expanding rapidly. Blomfield was commissioned by the Bishop of London to supervise the exhumation of human remains and the dismantling of tombs in the churchyard at Old St Pancras to make way for the extension of the Midland Railway to its new terminus at King's Cross. Blomfield passed the job on to Hardy.

Hardy must have spent hours in the churchyard helping to oversee the removal of bodies and tombs from the land designated for the new railway. He would have been 25 when he took on the job. It must have made a deep impression on him – certainly, progress riding roughshod over tradition is a recurrent theme in his books.

The Victorians were obsessed by death and made a fetish of all its trappings. They had a particular horror of cremation, so the preservation of the physical remains of the dead was extremely important to them. The headstones carried less meaning for the Victorians than the corpses, and in most cases would have simply been discarded. However, some were stacked in a tightly packed circle around this ash tree. Over the years, the tree has grown around them and the mossy headstones are beginning to become part of it; they now look like a strange crop. What remains is an accidental and effective memento mori, which almost certainly inspired Hardy's poem, "The Levelled Churchyard":

> *We late-lamented, resting here,*
> *Are mixed to human jam,*
> *And each to each exclaims in fear,*
> *"I know not which I am!"*

Old St Pancras Graveyard

Charles Dickens describes Old St Pancras graveyard in *A Tale of Two Cities* as a sinister place where body snatchers used to "fish". Sir John Soane is among those buried in the churchyard, in a surprisingly understated (for him) tomb that provided the inspiration for Sir Giles Gilbert Scott's iconic red telephone boxes (see p. 54). Mary Wollstonecraft and William Godwin were originally buried here (there is a monument to her in the churchyard), though her remains now lie in Bournemouth. Wollstonecraft's daughter, Mary, author of *Frankenstein*, supposedly planned her elopement with the poet Shelley during clandestine meetings at her mother's grave.

CAMLEY STREET NATURAL PARK ②

Urban jungle

12 Camley Street, N1C 4PW
0207 833 2311
www.wildlondon.org.uk/reserves/camley-street-natural-park
Winter: Mon-Sun 10am-4pm, Summer: Mon-Sun 10am-5pm
Admission free
King's Cross tube/rail

The insurgence of property developers has sanitised King's Cross, which was one of the most squalid patches of London only a few years ago. Gone are the crack-heads and kerb-crawlers; in their place, a towering citadel of sterile flats, bland restaurant chains, and shiny office blocks. Paying lip service to public space, the estate agents have left a few pockets of loveliness, including Camley Street Natural Park.

Wedged between Regents Canal and the railway tracks of St Pancras, this two-acre wildlife sanctuary used to be a dumping ground for coal, before it was transported along the canal by barge. In 1981, the derelict land was earmarked as a lorry park by local authorities; luckily, a campaign led by London Wildlife Trust won out and a nature reserve was created instead.

As soon as you enter the narrow waterside park, serenity engulfs you. Insects buzz around as you wander the overgrown pathways, dragonflies shimmering through waist-high reeds. Frogs burble in the muddy depths of the pond. Everything is made from natural materials: hazel branch fences, salvage bird boxes, rough-hewn benches, log piles for creepy-crawlies.

If you listen carefully, you can still hear the twitter of warblers and kingfishers above the distant throb of pneumatic drills. There's a blackboard where you can record wildlife sightings and a sweet little community-run café.

One footpath peters out at Viewpoint, a wooden 'island' floating on the canal, where you can watch houseboats drift by and spot geese, moorhens, and joggers in fluorescent Lycra. A new pedestrian bridge across the canal, linking Camley Street Natural Park to Coal Drops Yard, will bring more footfall; but hopefully the cranes, construction workers, and roaring traffic will be kept safely at bay.

NEARBY
The lamp posts of St Nicholas ③

Built by the St Pancras House Improvement Society in the 1930s, St Nicholas Flats on Aldenham Street were designed as low-cost housing to replace the slums of Somers Town. St Nicholas is the patron saint of sailors, which explains the small fleet of ships marooned atop the lamp posts in the courtyard. The quirky ornamentation extends to the French windows, crowned with ceramic lunettes depicting fairy tales.

THE BROWNING ROOM

A shrine to forbidden love

St Marylebone Church, 17 Marylebone Road, NW1 5LT
0207 935 7315
www.stmarylebone.org
9am-5pm daily. The Browning Room is open by appointment
Admission free
Baker Street or Regent's Park tube

The Victorian poets Elizabeth Barrett and Robert Browning enjoyed one of literature's most chronicled courtships: they exchanged 573 love letters over a 20-month period. They wrote mutually appreciative – and increasingly passionate – letters for five months before they even set eyes on each other.

It was an unlikely union. She was an opium-addicted invalid confined to her bed at the family home on Wimpole Street, watched over by her puritanical father. He was an erudite and handsome poet from a humble family in Camberwell. She was a spinster of almost 40 – positively ancient by Victorian standards; he was already an over-ripe 36. But when they finally met in 1845, love blossomed.

Mr Barrett knew of Browning's visits to his daughter's bedroom, but believed they were exchanging literary pleasantries. On 12 September 1846, Elizabeth crept out of the house and headed for nearby St Marylebone Parish Church, where she and Robert were married in secret. A week later, the couple eloped to Italy, never to return. When Elizabeth's sister Henrietta broke the news to their father, he allegedly flew into such a rage that he flung Henrietta down the stairs and never spoke of his daughter Elizabeth again.

But these illicit lovers are commemorated today at St Marylebone Church, which still holds the couple's original wedding certificate. As you enter, the Browning Room is on the left. It is now only open when in use for church functions, primarily after Sunday services. Since some of Browning's original furniture was stolen, it stands fairly empty, but does contain two small reliefs of Barrett and Browning and a pretty stained glass window that memorialises their marriage. The room is usually locked, so call the verger or parish office to arrange a visit.

NEARBY

Marylebone conduit ⑤

St Marylebone was originally called St Mary-by-the-Bourne, after the Tybourne stream, which ran close by. The last remaining trace of this river – once the main source of water for the City of London – is a tiny white plaque inset into the wall at 50 Marylebone Lane, which reads: 'Conduit belonging to the City of London 1776.' Hidden beneath the gaudy photographs advertising the Depilex hair removal clinic, this little fragment of forgotten history is overlooked by most passers-by.

THE BRITISH DENTAL ASSOCIATION MUSEUM

Jaw-dropping instruments

64 Wimpole Street, W1G 8YS
0207 935 0875
www.bda.org/museum
Tues and Thurs 1-4pm
Admission free
Oxford Circus, Bond Street or Regents Park tube

This tiny little museum is an adjunct to the library of the British Dental Association, and as such is set up as an educational display.

Although the glass cases might be bright and clean, the room warmly lit, and every effort made to avoid any Chamber of Horrors or overly clinical undertones, the collection of tools, teeth and other odontological artefacts is still unsettling.

What is immediately striking is how lucky we are to have the dental service we do today. Dentists were only fully regulated in 1921; before this, anyone could have a go. Dental drills were adapted from carpenters' drills and had a similarly robust mechanical air, as the advertisement for 'Shaw's Dental Engine, Complete with Oil Can and Spanner' attests. Replacement teeth were usually made from hippo or walrus ivory. Dr Edward H. Angle's Head Gear, a fearsome brace attached to sieve-like headgear, is a testament to how far orthodontics has come. Possibly the most alarming exhibit is the extraction display case containing various dental keys – bolt-on handles that were used to twist teeth out of the mouth, and often resulted in the tooth breaking or jaw fractures.

Beautifully made dental tools with carved mother-of-pearl handles in custom-made cases are the centrepiece of the exhibition, but they are impossible to admire without a grimace as you imagine the pain they could inflict. There is also a computer loaded with dental health films that are terrifying and hilarious by turns: *Oral Surgery Part 2 1948* is like a short film made by Francis Bacon; *No Toothache for Eskimos* looks like a spoof; and *Came The Dawn*, from 1912, includes a mystifying sequence in which a fat soldier in a kilt and his friend laugh at a man with no front teeth for five minutes.

London's medical museums

There is a wide variety of medical museums dotted around London, including the Old Operating Theatre (see p. 264), the Alexander Fleming Laboratory Museum (p. 216), the British Optical Association Museum (p. 76) and the Bethlem Museum of the Mind (p. 372). See www.medicalmuseums.org for a full list.

ANAESTHESIA HERITAGE CENTRE ⑦

It's a knockout

21 Portland Place, W1B 1PY
0207 631 1650
www.medicalmuseums.org/Anaesthesia-Heritage-Centre/
Mon-Fri 10am-4pm. Visitors should call ahead
Email heritage@aagbi.org to make an appointment
Admission free
Oxford Circus, Regent's Park or Great Portland Street tube

Don't know the difference between a Boulitte oscillotonometer and nasopharyngeal insufflation? This is the place to find out. In the basement of a majestic Robert Adam building, on one of London's grandest streets, is a small museum that outlines the history of anaesthesia, resuscitation and pain relief. The collection includes over 4,500 objects, from primitive syringes to the high-tech equipment used to knock patients out today.

Glass cases contain ethers, vapours and "resuscitation bags" – giant bellows, which were squeezed to push air into the patient's lungs. "Soporific sponges" soaked in opium, mandragora and hemlock are a chilling reminder of early dentistry.

The oldest object is a Resuscitation Set designed by the Royal Humane Society in 1774, 'for affording immediate relief to persons apparently dead from drowning'. These clunky kits were strategically placed along the banks of the Thames so that volunteers could revive people who had fallen into the river.

In 1800, Humphry Davy, a young chemist and future president of the Royal Society, first explored the 'inebriating and pain-relieving properties of nitrous oxide'. The gas wasn't used initially for medical purposes, but became popular at parties, or 'ether frolics' – not much different from the balloons filled with laughing gas, inhaled at raves and festivals today.

The wordy captions are definitely geared towards medical professionals rather than squeamish trypanophobes. The archives and library are popular with medical students; otherwise, you're likely to have this ode to oblivion all to yourself.

The term anaesthesia, Greek for 'loss of sensation', wasn't coined in English until 1846, when ether was first officially used to relieve pain during an operation at Massachusetts General Hospital. The surgeon, John Collins Warren, announced: 'Gentlemen, this is no humbug.'

Previously, patients usually turned to religion, superstition, astrology or magic to alleviate the effects of cauterisation, dental extraction and even amputation. Mesmerism was a popular form of pain relief that used magnets and hypnosis.

In 1853, Queen Victoria was given chloroform during the birth of her eighth child. She gushed in her diary: 'Dr Snow gave that blessed chloroform and the effect was soothing, quieting and delightful beyond measure.'

FITZROVIA CHAPEL

Pocket-sized luxury

Fitzroy Place, 2 Pearson Square, W1T 3BF
www.fitzroviachapel.org
Wed 11am–6pm
Admission free
Goode Street tube

Tucked away in the heart of a new residential development north of Soho, Fitzrovia Chapel is a little golden jewel box of a building which is all that remains of the Middlesex Hospital.

Opened in the 1740s, the hospital evolved from a 15-bed operation to a leading teaching hospital, with the first dedicated AIDS wards in the UK. It finally closed in 2005 and was consolidated with University College Hospital round the corner on Euston Road.

Officially opened by the Bishop of London in 1892, the chapel was designed by John Loughborough Pearson, who was well known as an ecclesiastical architect at the end of the 19th century. Typically, he appears to have worked on a massive scale, designing Bristol and Truro Cathedrals, as well as St Augustine's, Kilburn, an overwrought barn of a church sometimes called the Cathedral of North London and worth a visit.

For the Fitzrovia Chapel, Pearson was forced to work in miniature on a cramped site at the north-western corner of the main hospital

building. Limitations of space don't appear to have dampened his enthusiasm for the ornate, however: although the exterior is plain red brick and dressed Portland stone, he seems to have managed to squeeze a whole cathedral's worth of gold and marble into the interior.

This took time – the mosaic ceiling was still being worked on in 1936 for the lying-in-state of Rudyard Kipling – but eventually, Pearson's "expensive" design was finished, just in time for the Second World War and the Blitz, during which the hospital was bombed.

The chapel has been fully restored as part of the conditions of sale of the hospital site to the current developers, and is open to the public one day a week. It also hosts events: check the website for details.

Gothic Revivalist

Pearson was a prominent Gothic Revivalist. This style of architecture, which originated in the UK, sought to recreate medieval Gothic architecture. Pugin's Palace of Westminster is the best-known example in London, but the capital is full of it. Strawberry Hill House in Richmond is the earliest example of the style in the UK – frankly, it's bananas and well worth a trip. Tower Bridge and St Pancras station are good examples of how the Victorians sought to romanticise the most functional of buildings, using the style. Bear in mind that these two were built at around the same time as the Eiffel Tower and the Brooklyn Bridge, both of which still feel modern by comparison.

FITZROY HOUSE

A literary landmark (of sorts)

37 Fitzroy Street, W1T 6DX
0207 255 2422
www.fitzroyhouse.org
Daily by appointment 11am-5pm
To book a tour, email info@fitzroyhouse.org
Admission free
Warren Street or Great Portland Street tube

This Georgian town house, just round the corner from the serenity and splendour of the Adam brothers' Fitzroy Square, was not only the home of Nobel Literature laureate George Bernard Shaw and of Robert Tressell, author of the working-class classic *The Ragged Trousered Philanthropists*, but also, from early 1957, of L. Ron Hubbard, holder of the Guinness Book of World Records title for Most Published Author (1,084 publications). Possibly better known as the originator of Dianetics and founder of the Church of Scientology, Hubbard was based here for several years before moving to Saint Hill Manor, an 18th-century country house in Sussex, bought in 1952 from the Maharajah of Jaipur.

The five-storey house has been fully renovated and restored. Scientology is still at the heart of the building – it serves as a meeting place and education centre for the Church – and there are numerous Hubbard-related displays, including a pictorial history of his life. In fairness to the man, it was an extremely eventful one – he apparently travelled in the Far East at an early age, was an accomplished sailor, could fly a glider, dabbled in gold prospecting and joined The Explorers Club in 1940. Many of Hubbard's claims about his life are disputed; however, he was certainly a well-known and prolific writer for pulp-fiction magazines during the 1930s. The covers of these, as well as posters for some of the cliffhanger movie serials he was involved with, including the mind-bending *The Secret of Treasure Island*, are some of the highlights of the tour. Hubbard's ground-floor offices have also been carefully restored and include archaic office equipment such as an early fax machine that wrote with a hot needle, an allegedly silent typewriter and some unwieldy-looking recording devices.

Given the Church's reputation for high levels of persuasiveness, the tour touches on this side of the building lightly. Of course, there is some discussion of the man and his work – this is a Scientology Centre, after all – but talk stays away from the wilder shores of the Church. Other things to keep an eye out for are Hubbard's photographs of London in the 1950s.

Fitzroy Square, at the top of the street, deserves to be better known, but it's at the wrong end of Tottenham Court Road. Virginia Woolf and George Bernard Shaw lived here; Francisco de Miranda, the Venezuelan revolutionary, lived on nearby Grafton Way and has a statue just off the square; and French literary giants Arthur Rimbaud and Paul Verlaine lived round the corner.

THE GRANT MUSEUM OF ZOOLOGY

Dodo bones and jellied eels

Rockefeller Building, University College London, 21 University Street, WC1E 6DE
0203 1082052
www.ucl.ac.uk/museums/zoology
Mon-Sat 1-5pm
Admission free. Children under 11 must be accompanied by an adult
Euston Square or Warren Street tube

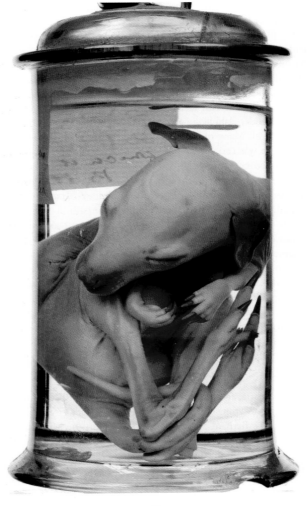

One of the oldest – and oddest – natural history museums in Britain, this peculiar collection is buried in the labyrinthine campus of University College London. Navigate a course through the parked bicycles and security gates, and you find yourself in a bizarre shrine to animal anatomy. The cluttered gallery is like a cross between the Victorian attic of a compulsive collector and the studio of Damien Hirst. Musty cases are stuffed full of monkey skeletons, pickled toads, jars of worms, and giant elephant skulls.

The collection contains around 62,000 specimens, covering the whole animal kingdom. Some of the exhibits are truly terrifying, such as the curling skeleton of a 250-kilo anaconda, or the bisected head of a wallaby preserved in formaldehyde. Others, like the elephant heart or the hellbender – a bloated amphibian with sagging flesh – are simply gruesome. There are obscure species, like the three-toothed puffer fish, and extinct ones, like the quagga, a type of zebra. There is even a box of dodo bones. A cast of the oldest known bird, the archaeopteryx, provides evidence that birds evolved from dinosaurs. One of the weirdest exhibits is a glass jar stuffed with 18 preserved moles, which even has its own Twitter account (https://twitter.com/GlassJarofMoles).

The museum was founded in 1827 by Robert Grant, a pioneer of the theory of evolution and the first Professor of Zoology and Comparative Anatomy in England. When Grant set up his department at the newly founded University of London (later University College London), he realised that he had no teaching materials. So he set about amassing these specimens, which are still used by biology students, schools, and artists. Although Grant was paid a pittance, he taught at UCL from 1828 until his death in 1874.

Robert Edmond Grant was a Scottish zoologist and radical. While teaching at Edinburgh University in 1826, he met the young Charles Darwin, who was a squeamish and reluctant student of medicine at the time. Grant befriended Darwin and became his mentor, until the two fell out some years later. By a strange twist of fate, Darwin lived in a house on this site, at 12 Upper Gower Street, between 1839 and 1842.

NEARBY

Warren Street maze   ⑪

While you're waiting for the tube at Warren Street, look out for the red and black maze on the platform. A visual pun on the name of the station, the maze was designed by Alan Fletcher, a god among graphic designers. Since the average interval between trains is three minutes, Fletcher mischievously created a puzzle that would take longer to solve.

MIN'S PENIS

Saucy antiquities

The Petrie Museum, University College London, Malet Place, WC1E 6BT
0207 679 2884
www.ucl.ac.uk/museums/petrie
Tues-Sat 1-5pm
Admission free
Euston Square, Goodge Street or Warren Street tube, Euston tube/rail

Beneath the scholarly air that hangs over this collection of Egyptian and Sudanese antiquities lurk some very saucy artefacts. Set up in 1892 as a teaching resource for University College's Egyptian Archaeology and Philology department, the Petrie Museum is named after the department's first professor, William Flanders Petrie. A serial excavator, Petrie himself unearthed many of the 80,000 objects, dating from pre-history through Pharaonic, Roman, and Coptic Egypt, up to the Islamic period.

Perhaps the most striking exhibit is the marble bas relief of the Egyptian god Min. Invariably portrayed with a huge, erect penis, Min was the god of fertility and sexuality. At the beginning of the harvest, his image was taken out into the fields, where naked men would climb a huge pole in his honour. Apparently, Min used long-leaf lettuce to

stimulate his sex drive. However, the results may have been negligible: lettuce was considered an aphrodisiac by the ancient Egyptians because it was tall, straight and secreted milky juices when squeezed.

Costume plays a key part in the collection – look for the world's oldest dress, worn by a dancer around 2500 BC. Besides extraordinary hieroglyphs and papyri, the plethora of everyday objects includes a 3000-year-old rat trap. There are also strangely affecting Roman funerary masks; since most Egyptian art is nearly abstract, these portraits breathe life into a culture that often feels impassive or monumental.

Although it houses one of the most important Egyptology collections in the world, the Petrie does not punch at the same weight as the Egyptian collection of the British Museum. However, this is to its advantage. The Petrie feels less dependent on plunder than the British Museum, and the collection is more thoughtfully assembled. Access to the Petrie is also easier. The Egyptian funerary rooms at the British Museum, where the most deliciously gruesome stuff is displayed, are usually packed with coach parties; even the vigorous use of knee and elbow is no guarantee of a clear view.

THE AUTO-ICON OF JEREMY BENTHAM

Mummified philosopher

South Cloisters, University College London, Gower Street, WC1E 6BT
0207 679 2825
www.ucl.ac.uk/Bentham-Project/who/autoicon
Bentham is usually woken up at 8am and put to sleep at 6pm, Mon-Fri. Out of hours viewings can be arranged
Admission free
Euston Square, Warren Street or Goodge Street tube

Sitting serenely in a wooden cabinet on a landing of University College London (UCL) is the preserved skeleton of Jeremy Bentham (1748-1832), a radical philosopher and reformer. As stipulated in his will, Bentham has been seated here in the same thoughtful pose, 'wearing his usual clothes and sitting on his favourite chair,' since 1850.

Bentham called this perverse monument to himself an Auto-Icon ('man in his own image'), whereby a man's actual corpse replaced the traditional memorial statue. In fact, the body beneath his fine clothes is made of nothing but straw. At a time when only the corpses of hanged criminals were available for medical research, Bentham left his organs 'to illustrate a series of lectures, to which scientific and literary men are to be invited,' and then be dissected by students of anatomy.

The only part of his body that Bentham did not bequeath to science was his head, which was to be preserved by a Maori practice of desiccation and placed on his Auto-Icon. For ten years before his death, Bentham allegedly carried the glass eyes that were to adorn it in his pocket. Unfortunately, the mummified head deteriorated rapidly, so it was replaced with a less grotesque wax likeness.

For several years, the real head lay between Bentham's legs. However, in 1975, a group of students from King's College 'kidnapped' the head and demanded a ransom of £100 to be paid to the homeless charity Shelter. UCL negotiated the ransom down to £10 and the head was returned to its rightful owner. The head has since been safely stowed in the college vaults; permission to view it is granted 'only in exceptional circumstances.'

Although Bentham was almost 80 when UCL was founded in 1826, as the first English university to welcome all students, regardless of race, creed or political belief, it embodied Bentham's conviction that education should be available to all. Marx may have called him 'genius by way of bourgeois stupidity,' but Bentham was a visionary who also believed in universal suffrage, the legalisation of homosexuality, and utilitarianism, a doctrine that aims to promote the greatest happiness of the greatest number.

According to one apocryphal tale, the Auto-Icon attends meetings of the College Council. Its presence is recorded in the minutes with the words 'Jeremy Bentham - present but not voting.' In 2013, the Auto-Icon was indeed wheeled into the last council meeting attended by the provost, Sir Malcom Grant, before he retired.

Visitors' reactions to the mummified philosopher are captured by a webcam mounted above his head. The 'Panopticam' – a tongue-in-cheek reference to Bentham's sinister Panopticon, a circular prison that allowed for the constant surveillance of all inmates – takes a photo every five seconds. An ironic commentary on the desire for self-preservation, or a post-modern critique of the surveillance state?

INSTITUTE OF MAKING

Please do touch

Malet Place, University College London, WC1E 7JE
0207 679 3248
www.instituteofmaking.org.uk
Sign up to the mailing list to find out about masterclasses, open days and the annual Festival of Stuff. You can also visit the Materials Library by appointment
Admission free, but some events must be booked in advance
Euston Square, Russell Square or Warren Street tube

'You never know what you're going to learn in here,' says Zoe Laughlin, the charismatic co-founder and co-director of the Institute of Making. Located in what was a 'rat-infested dump' at University College London (UCL), this isn't your average science lab. For a start, it's multidisciplinary – a bright space, fizzing with creative energy, where engineers and artists, architects and physicists can explore the interface between science, art, craft and design. Membership is open to all staff and students at UCL, but the public can also have a go at regular symposia, open days and masterclasses in delightfully obscure subjects such as flint napping, glass blowing or felt making.

The Institute grew out of the Materials Library, an ongoing archive of over 2,000 extraordinary materials displayed in vast glass cabinets and wooden drawers. Visitors are encouraged to 'fiddle with things'. You can try on a pair of lead-lined gloves used for handling radioactive waste; slice through ice using a wafer of aluminium nitride; or hold the world's lightest solid – a translucent blob of Aerogel (designed by NASA to catch stardust), which consists of 99.8% air. Blast a twist of wire with a blowtorch and it miraculously morphs into a paper clip – it's made of shape-memory alloy, an ingenious material used mainly for keyhole surgery, which returns to its original shape when heated.

One of the oddest objects is self-healing concrete, containing dormant bacteria and starch: when the concrete cracks and water seeps in, the bacteria wake up, snack on the starch and excrete calcite, which closes the crack. The bacteria can survive for 50 years. (If you want to explore the collection in more depth, download the excellent @Materials Library app.)

These and more familiar materials are explored in the MakeSpace, a workshop where prototype heart valves, laser-engraved chopsticks, made-to-measure bicycle helmets and a 3D printer that uses clay have all been created. The Institute also holds the Guinness World Record for the largest laser cutter, using the canary yellow, 10-ton gantry crane that dominates the space.

A cross between a learning resource, research laboratory, studio and playground, the Institute of Making is a celebration of stuff. From the wonder of science to the alchemy of the everyday, it's enlightening, inspiring and good, old-fashioned fun.

MAGIC CIRCLE MUSEUM

Abracadabra

12 Stephenson Way, NW1 2HD
0207 387 2222
http://themagiccircle.co.uk/public-events
The museum can only be accessed when you attend a magic show or open day.
Check website for details on public events and admission
Euston tube/rail, Euston Square tube

F irst of all, get one thing straight – the only way you're getting into this museum is if you buy a ticket for one of the Magic Circle's public events, most of which are magic shows in the upstairs theatre. Don't turn up at HQ, knock on the door and expect to be welcomed – it drives the magicians crazy and they'll probably saw you in half. Anyway, the shows feature some of the best magicians in Britain and are well worth the entrance fee.

Once you've found the place, down a back street in Euston with only the sign of the Circle as a guide, check out the floating spiral stairs that run through the building – apparently very popular with staircase enthusiasts. There is barely an empty space on any of the walls; the Magic Circle's members have been collecting tools of the trade since its foundation in 1905 as an organisation to promote the art of magic and protect its secrets. The magicians take their motto, *Indocilis Privata Loqui* (not apt to disclose secrets) seriously.

There are hundreds of vintage posters, but the real glory is the collection of magic props and memorabilia. The Devant Room, named after the first president of the Circle, contains TV legend Tommy Cooper's famous fez. John Nevil Maskelyne, the second president, was a hugely successful magician and also found time to invent the pay toilet lock, source of the expression "to spend a penny". Naturally, one of these locks is on display. You can also admire the original working model of Robert Harbin's Zig Zag Girl illusion, which "chops" a lady into three parts – supposedly the most stolen trick ever.

The museum proper is in the basement and is stuffed with goodies. These include the original Marauder's Map from the Harry Potter films, designed by Magic Circle members; a magical money printer; the shoes Dynamo wore to walk across the Thames (without a bridge); and an original Sooty puppet. The robes of the unfortunate Chung Ling Soo are also on display – this was the stage name of William Robinson, who died onstage at the Wood Green Empire in 1918 after his famous bullet catch trick went wrong.

If you want to duck buying a ticket, you could try joining the Magic Circle. It's not easy, but you do get access to its top-secret inner sanctum and vast library of over 20,000 books on magic. Prince Charles is a member – the props from the cup and ball trick he performed at his audition are on display in the museum – but apparently he doesn't get down there as much as he should.

BLEIGIESSEN

A fortune-telling sculpture

Gibbs Building, Wellcome Trust, 215 Euston Road, NW1 2BE
0207 611 8888
www.wellcome.ac.uk
Tours of Bleigiessen take place at 2pm on the last Friday of every month. Email
Elayne Hodgson (e.hodgson@wellcome.ac.uk) to book a place. Group tours can
be arranged on request
Admission free
Euston Square tube, Euston tube/rail

When the Wellcome Trust, the UK's largest medical research charity, redesigned its headquarters on Euston Road, several art works were commissioned to embellish its new premises. The Trust chose Thomas Heatherwick to design the centrepiece: an installation for the ten-storey atrium of the Gibbs Building. The designer faced a serious challenge: while the sculpture had to fill the 30-metre vertical space, its components also had to fit through a regular-sized door. Heatherwick resolved to design something that could fit through a letterbox instead.

Inspired by the pool of water at the bottom of the atrium, Heatherwick based his design on flowing liquid. By pouring molten metal into cold water, he created over 400 prototypes before a five-centimetre shape was selected as the outline for the sculpture. This form was laser-scanned and replicated using 150,000 glass spheres, produced in a Polish spectacle lens factory. Reflective film was sandwiched inside the beads to create a rainbow effect. All the spheres were numbered and assembled on site – a painstaking process, which involved threading the beads onto almost 1 million metres of steel wire, rolled onto a giant drum then stretched between frames. A team of 18 people worked for five months, day and night, to complete the sculpture, which weighs in at 14 tons. The result is like a glowing cloud of particles suspended in mid-air. Shapes fade in and out of focus depending on how the light strikes.

Heatherwick's German grandmother christened the work *Bleigiessen*, or 'lead guessing.' This New Year's Eve ritual is still practiced in Eastern Europe: molten lead is poured into cold water, and the resulting shapes are interpreted to predict a person's fortune for the coming year.

The best way to see this monumental work is to take the monthly guided tour. Visitors are whisked to the top of the building in a glass lift. Alternatively, you can get a reasonably good view of the sculpture from Gower Street. It looks best at night when the empty building is illuminated and the baubles shimmer behind the glass walls.

Fake trees

The Wellcome Trust contains another secret: half the ficus trees in the soaring atrium are fake. The original trees planted here did not thrive, so their trunks and principal branches were kiln dried and covered with silk leaves.

THE COADE STONE CARYATIDS

Maidens without midriffs

St Pancras Church, Euston Road, NW1 2BA
www.stpancraschurch.org
Mon-Thurs 8am-6pm, Sun 7.30-11.30am, 5.30-7pm
Admission free
Euston or King's Cross tube/rail

When it was built in 1819 for a whopping £89,296, St Pancras Church was the most expensive house of worship since the reconstruction of St Paul's Cathedral. Modelled on the Erechtheum of the Acropolis, the church's exterior has lost much of its lustre thanks to the traffic hurtling down Euston Road, one of London's least lovely thoroughfares. But the striking façade of caryatids that prop up the porch still turns heads.

On closer inspection, these maidens are stumpier than their Greek counterparts (one of whom is on display in the British Museum, courtesy of Lord Elgin). Sculptor Charles Rossi (1762-1839) spent almost three years crafting the caryatids out of Coade stone, an artificial material much favoured for the neoclassical monuments so popular in the 18th and early 19th centuries. The figures were built up in sections around cast-iron columns. But when Rossi transported them from his studio to the church, he discovered to his horror that the statues were too tall. Under the gaze of a bemused crowd of onlookers, Rossi took drastic action: he cut out their midriffs. Thankfully, their draped Grecian gowns help to conceal their stunted torsos.

The church hosts free recitals every Thursday afternoon, and exhibitions and concerts in the Crypt Gallery (cryptgallery.org). 557 people lay buried in these underground vaults, which were used as an air raid shelter during WWII.

What is coade stone?

Founded by Mrs Eleanor Coade in 1769, Coade's Artificial Stone Manufactory dominated London's trade in statues, busts, tombstones, architectural and garden ornaments for almost 65 years. Cheap, easy to mould and weather-resistant, Coade stone was made to a secret formula. According to an anonymous account from 1806: 'It is possessed of the peculiar property of resisting frost, and consequently it retains its sharpness in which it excels every species of stone, and even equals marble'. This quality is evident in the many Coade stone monuments scattered around London, notably Captain Bligh's tomb in St Mary's Lambeth (see p. 249), Nelson's pediment at the Royal Naval College Chapel in Greenwich, and the 13-ton lion on Westminster Bridge, one of a pair of that once crowned the Red Lion brewery on the South Bank. The other lion guards the All-England Rugby Club at Twickenham, near the Rowland Hill Memorial Gate. Despite this success, the company went bankrupt not long after Eleanor Coade's death in 1796 at the grand old age of 88. She is buried in Bunhill Fields.

THE FOUNDLING MUSEUM

Children lost and found

40 Brunswick Square, WC1N 1AZ
0207 841 3600
www.foundlingmuseum.org.uk
Tues-Sat 10am-5pm; Sun 11am-5pm. Closed Monday
Check website for admission prices
Russell Square tube, King's Cross or Euston tube /rail

There is a lingering idea among tourists that London is a place of Victorian propriety, full of well-mannered, uptight ladies and gentlemen. Apart from a very brief 19th-century flirtation with moral rectitude, the character of the city has always been base; drunkenness for its own sake is still very much a London pastime, as is fighting. This wildness and cruelty was at its apogee in the 18th century, when a man could be hanged for stealing spoons.

One by-product of a society like this was hordes of unwanted children. Up to a thousand babies a year were abandoned in the streets of London in the early 18th century. Fortunately, in 1739, after 17 years of tireless fundraising, the philanthropist Thomas Coram founded a 'Hospital for the Maintenance and Education of Exposed and Deserted Children', which cared for more than 27,000 children at a site on Lamb's Conduit Fields, before relocating to the countryside in 1953. The remarkable Foundling Museum tells the story of those children.

Thanks to William Hogarth, one of the original governors of the hospital, the museum also houses an impressive art collection, displayed in interiors restored to their original 18th-century condition. Hogarth's own art is often hard-bitten and deeply cynical – his famous etching of Gin Lane is full of disgust at how the people who abandoned these children lived. But there must have been a well of compassion in him: Hogarth persuaded leading artists like Gainsborough and Reynolds to donate works to the hospital, and in doing so created the country's first public exhibition space. This eventually led to the formation of the Royal Academy of Arts in 1768. In keeping with its founding principles, most of The Foundling Museum's workshops and concerts are aimed at children.

The peaceful café is run by The People's Supermarket, a not-for-profit grocery store on Lamb's Conduit Street, run by local volunteers.

Handel & Hendrix

The German composer George Friedrich Handel was also a one-time governor of the hospital, which explains why the museum holds a collection of Handel material. Annual performances of his *Messiah* provided a source of revenue for the hospital. Today, you can catch live music by Handel and his contemporaries every Thursday at Handel & Hendrix (handelhendrix.org), the composer's former home at 25 Brook Street, Mayfair. Rock star Jimi Hendrix lived next door at 23 Brook Street in 1968-9. Now open to the public, Hendrix's third-floor flat has a few psychedelic flourishes, but presents a surprisingly domesticated picture.

THE HORSE HOSPITAL

Salon of the avant garde

Colonnade, WC1N
0207 833 3644
www.thehorsehospital.com
Exhibitions generally open Mon-Sat 12-6pm; for special events check website
Admission varies
Russell Square tube

Buried away down a cobbled mews off tourist-trodden Russell Square, the Horse Hospital really was a sanctuary for sick horses back in its Victorian heyday. These days, it's a haven for avant-garde artists and disciples of all things underground. From the blood red hall, a steep ramp with wooden slats originally intended to stop the horses slipping (beware – it's lethal in heels) leads down to a slightly spooky and faintly musty salon with a few battered seats. Mismatched cobblestones echo underfoot. Other original features, including tethering rings, cast iron pillars, and barred windows, have a whiff of S&M about them.

This is the self-styled Chamber of Pop Culture, where an audience of eccentrics enjoy the most eclectic line-up of art events in London, from cult films to performance poets, clairvoyant workshops and queer porn. Anything goes – as long as it's defiantly anti-establishment. The small bar at the back is one of those rare places in London where you can easily slip into conversation with strangers. This sense of community, along with the spirit of experimentation, is like a throwback to the Arts Labs of the '60s.

Often dubbed 'an alternative ICA', the Horse Hospital was founded in 1993 by stylist and costume designer Richard Burton, one of the pioneers of punk fashion along with Vivienne Westwood and Malcolm McLaren, whose original boutique, World's End, was designed by Burton. The Horse Hospital opened with a splash 13 years later with the first retrospective of Westwood's punk designs. It's run on a shoestring by a staff of two: Burton and programmer Tai Shani. Long may they continue to celebrate culture that champions 'the outsider, the unfashionable and the other.'

Contemporary Wardrobe Collection

The upper floor of the Horse Hospital is home to the Contemporary Wardrobe Collection, set up by Burton in 1978 to supply vintage clothes and accessories to the film, TV and fashion industries. His collection now exceeds 15,000 garments dating back to 1945. There's a rare selection by seminal British designers from the 1960s, such as Ossie Clark, Biba, and Seditionaries. As well as providing costumes for films like *Quadrophenia* and *Sid & Nancy*, pieces have been modelled by over 400 pop stars, from the late, great David Bowie to Kanye West. Visits are by appointment only. Twice a year, items are sold off to raise funds for The Horse Hospital. Check www.contemporarywardrobe.com for details.

JAPANESE ROOF GARDEN

⑳

Forgive and forget

Brunei Gallery, School of Oriental and African Studies
10 Thornhaugh Street, WC1H 0XG
0207 898 4023/4026
www.soas.ac.uk/visitors/roofgarden
Tues-Sat 10.30am-5pm. Late night Thurs, open until 8pm
Admission free
Russell Square tube

Completed in 1937, Senate House – the University of London's Art Deco HQ – was the centrepiece of a grand new campus that would, in the words of Vice-Chancellor William Beveridge, be 'an academic island in swirling tides of traffic, a world of learning in a world of affairs'. By 1939, Europe was at war and the students and professors had been replaced by spies and spin doctors employed at the Ministry of Information – the government's censorship and propaganda machine, which inspired the Ministry of Truth in George Orwell's *Nineteen Eighty-Four*.

If you want to spy on the university administrators and librarians who work in Senate House, there's a secret garden with a great vantage point over the angular 19-storey tower. Hidden on the roof of the School of Oriental and African Studies' Brunei Gallery – a cool, calm space devoted to art from Asia, Africa and the Middle East – is a formal Japanese garden. There's not much greenery: apart from a dreamy row of benches shaded by wisteria (heavenly in spring) and a few symmetrically planted squares of lemon thyme, it's mostly artfully placed pebbles, immaculately raked gravel and slabs of grey rock. The effect, though austere, is deeply soothing.

Look out for the granite water feature engraved with the Japanese symbol for forgiveness. There's a raised 'stage' at one end for occasional concerts, performances, and tea and flower ceremonies.

The Brunei Gallery always had a roof garden; the original one featured a series of pools, which sprang a leak and had to be drained. So it was eventually replaced with this low-maintenance design.

Most of the time, especially on Saturdays, the garden is deserted. So you can just sit quietly and let the swirl of the surrounding city drift away…

Ismaili Centre Roof Garden

London's most spectacular roof garden is on top of the Ismaili Centre, a cubist monolith that seems to shun visitors. Screened from the traffic roaring down Cromwell Road, this elegant garden is as reclusive as the Ismailis' spiritual and political leader, the Aga Khan. The geometric design alludes to the Qu'ranic garden of paradise, with a central fountain connected to four granite pools that symbolise the celestial rivers flowing with water, honey, milk and wine. Sadly, it's only open on Open Garden Squares Weekend (opensquares.org).

NEW LONDON ARCHITECTURE ㉑

A glimpse into London's future

The Building Centre, 26 Store Street, WC1 E 7BT
0207 6364044
www.newlondonarchitecture.org
Mon-Fri 9am-6pm, Sat 10am-5pm
Admission free
Goodge Street or Russell Square tube

In the ground floor galleries at New London Architecture (NLA), a think thank dedicated to the capital's built environment, is a monumental 1:2000 scale model of central London. 12.5 metres long and featuring some 170,000 buildings, it covers more than 85 square kilometres, from King's Cross in the north to Peckham in the south, and the Royal Docks in the east to Old Oak Common in the west. Through interactive projections and illuminations, historic events, such as the Great Fire of London, and new developments, such as Crossrail, can be digitally animated across the surface of the model. Using touch-screens, visitors can call up key facts about the future projects and landmarks that will shape the capital. With 263 skyscrapers in the pipeline, the model offers an unnerving glimpse into the future, as the land grab by property developers and overseas investors continues to swallow whole chunks of London.

Billing itself as 'a vital addition to the public debate about the future of London', the NLA hosts talks about the opportunities and challenges for urban regeneration, from waste management to affordable housing. Architectural walking tours of 8 central London neighbourhoods – taking place on the second Saturday and last Wednesday of each month – reveal how the capital's streetscapes are changing. There's an excellent architectural bookshop and reference library, as well as a cute little café populated by bespectacled architects clad in standard issue monochrome.

The City Centre

NLA also run The City Centre (www.thecitycentre.london), dedicated to the urban environment of the Square Mile. No other district better encapsulates the awkward friction between conservation and innovation, between London's rich architectural heritage and the radical interventions of 21st-century real estate developers. On display is a 1:1500 scale model of the City of London, which lights up to reveal all the buildings that currently have planning permission – another ominous portent of the capital's ever-changing skyline.

JOHN SNOW'S CHOLERA PUMP

Drink beer, not water

Broadwick Street, W1F 9QJ
Oxford Circus or Piccadilly Circus tube

Soho has always had its insalubrious side. As Judith Summers writes in *A History of London's Most Colourful Neighborhood*: 'By the middle of the 19th century, Soho had become an unsanitary place of cow-sheds, animal droppings, slaughterhouses, grease-boiling dens and primitive, decaying sewers. And underneath the floorboards of the overcrowded cellars lurked something even worse – a fetid sea of cesspits as old as the houses, and many of which had never been drained. It was only a matter of time before this hidden festering time-bomb exploded. It finally did so in the summer of 1854.'

In September 1854 alone, 500 Soho residents died of cholera. Dr John Snow, an anaesthetist and epidemiologist who lived on Soho Square, concluded that the polluted water pump on Broad Street (as it was called then) had caused the epidemic. Initially, the establishment scoffed at Snow's theory. The Reverend Henry Whitehead, vicar of St Luke's church on nearby Berwick Street, claimed the deceased were the victims of divine intervention. But soon after Snow forcibly removed the handle of the water pump, the outbreak ended.

In his research into the causes of the disease, Dr Snow had to look no further than the Broad Street brewery. One of the perks of employees was an allowance of free beer, so they all abstained from drinking water. None of the 70 workers caught cholera.

For years, a replica water pump stood on the corner of Broadwick and Poland Street. It was removed in 2015 to accommodate the construction of an office block. Westminster Council has pledged to return the pump to its original location, outside the John Snow, a cosy old boozer pub on the corner of Broadwick and Lexington Street. A pink granite kerbstone outside the pub marks the spot where the original pump stood.

Ironically, Snow himself was teetotal. Aged 23, he gave an impassioned speech railing against 'drunkenness in all its hideousness' and 'the physical evils sustained to your health by using intoxicating liquors even in the greatest moderation.' Something to ponder as you settle into the John Snow's snug.

John Snow was already famous for an earlier discovery in 1853: chloroform. Queen Victoria used this primitive anaesthetic to overcome the agonies of labour during the birth of her son, Prince Leopold (see p. 24). But Snow's medical research and abstemious lifestyle did not help his own health; he died of a stroke in 1858, aged 45.

K2 TELEPHONE BOXES

The smallest listed buildings in London

Burlington House, Piccadilly, W1S 3ET
Daily 10am-6pm, except Fri 10am-10pm
Green Park or Piccadilly Circus tube

A British design classic, the tomato red telephone box has been rendered obsolete by the mobile phone. Upstaged by uninspired British Telecom booths in the 1980s and '90s, the few original kiosks that survive are plastered with explicit adverts for buxom call girls or used by lager louts to relieve themselves. Some phone boxes have even been converted into miniature salad bars or 'work stations'.

Just inside the gates of the Royal Academy, on either side of the arched entrance, two of the first kiosks designed by Sir Giles Gilbert Scott in 1926 remain intact, though sadly neglected. They are the smallest listed buildings in London. In 1924, the General Post Office launched a competition to design a new telephone kiosk to replace the first 1921 model. All the prototypes were put into public service around London, but Scott's winning design is the only one that survived.

Known as K2 (Kiosk 2), Scott's cast-iron booths had a domed roof with tiny holes to provide ventilation. At first, they were widely reviled; people particularly objected to their bright red colour. In fact, Scott had specified a silver exterior and blue interior for the K2, but the Post office plumped for vermillion. Instantly recognisable, the red phone box is now an icon of 20th-century Britain.

After three more modifications by Scott, in 1936 the improved K6 was launched to commemorate King George V's Silver Jubilee. Some 60,000 booths were installed nationwide. However, vandalism and high maintenance costs led to their gradual withdrawal and substitution with utilitarian modern booths. There was even a scheme to convert the old kiosks into mobile phone masts. After a conservation campaign in the 1990s, some of the old telephone boxes have been renovated and re-installed. The rest have been sold off for scrap or as souvenirs.

> Sir Giles Gilbert Scott (1880-1960) was the architect of many other London icons, including Waterloo Bridge, Battersea Power Station and Bankside Power Station (now Tate Modern).

NEARBY
The Fortnum and Mason clock   (24)
181 Piccadilly, W1A 1ER

Above the entrance to London's finest food emporium (and inventor of the Scotch egg) is a clock flanked by two miniature sentry boxes. Every 15 minutes, an 18th-century jingle tinkles on the clock's 18 bells. On the hour, four-foot replicas of the original Mr Fortnum and Mr Mason pop out and bow to each other as the clock chimes. According to the store's website, 'Messrs F&M themselves appear to check that standards are being upkept.'

THE LONDON LIBRARY

A literary institution

14 St James's Square, SW1Y 4LG
0207 766 4700
www.londonlibrary.co.uk
Mon-Wed 9.30am-8pm, Thurs-Sat 9.30am-5.30pm. Closed Sun
Day, weekly or annual membership fees apply. Day and weekly membership
must be booked in advance. Occasional public tours for non-members can be
booked online
Green Park or Piccadilly Circus tube

The London Library was founded by the curmudgeonly author and historian Thomas Carlyle in 1841. Carlyle's desperate – and fruitless – quest for a 'silent study' (he loathed the British Library, then housed in the British Museum, because it was full of 'snorers, snufflers, wheezers, [and] spitters') inspired him to create what has become the world's largest independent lending library.

Seventeen miles of books are beautifully arranged in two town houses on one of the most exclusive – and gorgeous – squares in London. The deceptively narrow entrance leads into a warren of floor-upon-floor of row-upon-row of bookshelves, which is delightfully disorienting.

With its cracked leather armchairs and aged portraits, the interior has retained all its original charm, as well as a quirky Edwardian cataloguing system. Books are stored alphabetically by subject matter; so you might stumble upon a book on bullfighting while looking for a treatise on celibacy.

When the Library opened in 1841, the collection consisted of 3,000 books. Today, it houses over one million books and periodicals, dating from 1500. One room contains a full run of the *Times* newspaper from 1820 until 2000.

All but the most fragile editions can be browsed on open-access shelves, taken home, or dispatched to members anywhere in Europe so, like Carlyle, you can peruse them in private. Better still, there is no due date: you can hold onto a book for two months, unless another reader requests it. As author John Mcnally eloquently puts it: 'It is the stuff of fiction, the gentleperson's Google.'

To accommodate about 8,000 new titles a year, the library has embarked on an ambitious expansion programme. In 2004, it purchased an adjoining building, which houses a new art room and refurbished reading rooms. There will eventually be three more floors of books and a rooftop reading room. By the time the work is complete, every book in the library will have been moved. But it will be worth it. As former President T.S. Eliot said in 1952: 'I am convinced that if this library disappeared, it would be a disaster to the world of letters, and would leave a vacancy that no other form of library could fill.'

Many illustrious writers have used the reading rooms as their study, including Charles Dickens, Charles Darwin, Arthur Conan Doyle, Henry James, and Tom Stoppard. Membership is open to anyone who can afford it, and library rules are set by the readers.

PICKERING PLACE

Last bastion of the Republic of Texas

Behind 7 St James's Street, SW1A 1EA
Green Park tube

Pay close attention when looking for this tiny courtyard tucked away behind swanky St James's Street. If the gate is closed, the only indication you are at Pickering Place is the number 3 on it. The narrow, arched alleyway leading to the courtyard retains its 18th-century timber wainscoting. A relatively unspoilt Georgian cul-de-sac still lit by original gaslights, Pickering Place is named after William Pickering, the founder of a coffee business in the premises now occupied by the famous wine merchants Berry Bros. & Rudd.

Graham Greene, who lived in a flat in Pickering Place, housed his fictional character Colonel Daintry from *The Human Factor* in a two-roomed flat looking out over the paved courtyard with its sundial. In real life, Pickering Place was the base of the diplomatic office of the independent Republic of Texas, before it joined the United States in 1845.

In the 18th century, Pickering Place was notorious for its gambling dens. Its seclusion also made it a favourite spot for duels, although the limited space suggests that fooling around with any kind of weapon – let alone pistols – would have been instantly fatal. It is claimed that the last duel in England was fought here, although an episode with pistols between two Frenchmen at Windsor in 1852 is the more likely contender. Beau Brummel, a notorious dandy and friend of King George IV, is also said to have fought here. But it is hard to imagine the man who invented the cravat, took five hours to dress, and recommended that boots be polished with champagne, having anything to do with bloodshed. Indeed, Brummel embarked upon a military career as a young man, but promptly resigned his commission when he learned that his regiment was to be sent to Manchester.

NEARBY

A secret cellar (27)

Located at 3 St James's Street since 1698, Berry Bros. & Rudd is Britain's oldest wine merchant. The shop has the quality of a (very expensive) museum. Its underground cellars, previously part of Henry VIII's royal residence and later a hideout for the exiled Napoleon III (the famous Napoleon's nephew) have been converted into private dining rooms. However, a secret tunnel, now blocked by wine bottles, leads to St James's Palace. It was allegedly used by philandering royals to pay clandestine visits to the ladies of the night who hung out at the shop in the 18th century. Or perhaps they just wanted a nightcap.

QUEEN ALEXANDRA MEMORIAL

Tribute to a cuckquean

Marlborough Road, SW1A 1BG
Green Park tube

Tucked away on Marlborough Gate, beside St James's Palace, is this dreamy (but not necessarily in a pleasant way) Art Nouveau memorial to Queen Alexandra, long-suffering wife of King Edward VII. The memorial is set into the garden wall of Marlborough House, once Queen Alexandra's London home. Cast in bronze and finished in blackened enamel, the statue has a ghostly, neo-gothic appearance. The Queen is seated behind allegorical figures representing faith, hope and charity.

Commissioned in 1926, the memorial was sculpted by Alfred Gilbert, who created the famous statue of Eros on Piccadilly Circus. The Alexandra Memorial was a great boon to Alfred Gilbert, exiled in Belgium at the time, after declaring bankruptcy. The terms of the commission, which included a permanent residence in Kensington Palace, relieved Gilbert of his financial worries. The day after King George V unveiled the memorial on 8 June 1932, Gilbert was knighted. He was subsequently given to swanning around St James's wearing a giant fedora hat.

Gilbert also created a spectacular memorial to Edward and Alexandra's son, Albert Victor, in Windsor Castle. A very odd character, Victor was implicated in a gay brothel scandal and subsequently earmarked as a suspect for the Ripper murders by the lurid conspiracy theorists that case has attracted.

Edward VII, a spectacularly rotten husband

An active commissioner of good deeds, Queen Alexandra was a universally loved member of the royal family. However, Edward VII was a spectacularly rotten husband. Although doubtless colourful and famously charming, he was noted throughout Europe for his gluttony and kept a string of very public mistresses, including the actress Lily Langtry, Jennie Jerome (mother of Winston Churchill) and Alice Keppel, great-grandmother of Prince Charles's second wife, Camilla Parker Bowles. Edward was twice a witness in court – unheard of for a royal. He appeared in a divorce case where he perjured himself about an affair with a young woman. He also testified in a case concerning a friend accused of cheating at baccarat, an illegal card game that Edward played heavily. Edward spent years waiting to become King, which may explain his excesses. On the other hand, he was unusually tolerant for his time and deplored the casual racism that characterised the British Empire.

GIRO'S GRAVE

Epitaph to an ambassador's pooch

Next to 9 Carlton House Terrace, SW1Y 5AG
Piccadilly Circus or Charing Cross tube

Between St James's Park and Piccadilly Circus, Waterloo Place was designed by the 19th-century architect John Nash as an overblown testament to the splendour of the British Empire. Countless statues of heroic commanders and louche aristocrats vie to outdo each other in size and stature. Buried among these grand memorials, a tiny tombstone lies at the foot of an enormous tree between the Duke of York Steps and an underground garage. Shielded by what appears to be a miniature kennel, the German epitaph on the gravestone reads: 'Giro, ein treuer Begleiter! London, im Februar 1934, Hoesch'. This 'true companion', Giro, was the beloved dog of the German Ambassador, Leopold von Hoesch, who served in London from 1932 to 1936. Now fenced off by railings, his grave lies on a patch of land that was once the garden of the ambassador's residence at 9 Carlton House Terrace.

The hapless Giro met his maker after colliding with an electricity cable while scampering about in what is now the Institute of Contemporary Arts. Apocryphal reports suggest that Giro received a full Nazi burial, though this seems highly unlikely since Hoesch was openly opposed to the rise of the Third Reich. The strain proved too much for Hoesch, who died of a stroke in 1936. The ambassador was granted a state funeral. But the Nazis had the last laugh: his coffin was swaddled in a giant swastika and embassy staff gave the Nazi salute as the funeral cortège marched by.

The marble staircase of Mussolini

After Hoesch's replacement – and Hitler's close associate – Joachim von Ribbentrop moved into Carlton House Terrace, the Führer's favourite architect, Albert Speer, was dispatched to London to give the embassy a flashy revamp. The British government did not deport Hitler's diplomats until 1939, when the building was taken over by the Foreign Office and stripped of its Nazi trappings – although a staircase of Italian marble, donated by Mussolini, is apparently still intact.

NEARBY

The Duke of Wellington's mounting steps ㉛

The British Empire may be defunct, but gentlemen's clubs still reign supreme in this upper crust corner of London. Both the Athenaeum Club and the Institute of Directors preside over Waterloo Place, their lavish interiors off limits to the hoi polloi. Outside each is a pair of kerb stones, bearing a rusty plaque: 'This horseblock was erected by desire of the Duke of Wellington 1830'. They allowed the Duke to mount and dismount from his horse with ease while visiting the Athenaeum. Whether the shorter members of the club were also permitted to take advantage of the Duke's steps is unknown.

THE JEAN COCTEAU MURALS AT NOTRE DAME DE FRANCE

Cocteau does Soho

5 Leicester Place, WC2H 7BX
0207 437 9363
www.ndfchurch.org/en/
Daily 9am-9pm
Admission free
Leicester Square tube

The French have been in London for a very long time. The first great influx was that of the Huguenots in 1675, who built fortunes in the textile industry in the East End. Notre Dame de France is the most recent incarnation of a Catholic church that has been rebuilt several times since it was founded in 1865 to take care of the 'lower-class French' of London. Soho was, until relatively recently, a French enclave; this is one of the ghosts of that time. The original church was designed by Louis Auguste Boileau as a rotunda made entirely out of iron, and not surprisingly was quite a local talking point. This was bombed out in 1940, and the current church was inaugurated in 1955 after two years of construction.

The building itself is fairly unremarkable, although circular churches in Britain are rare. The glory of the church is the artwork within it, above all the murals by legendary French filmmaker, artist, and designer Jean Cocteau, which fill one side chapel. Cocteau came to London to paint the murals in November 1959. Such was his fame that a screen was erected to keep the public and press at bay while he painted the murals in just nine days. Depicting themes from the Crucifixion and the Assumption of Mary, the work is vigorous, sexy and full of life in a manner quite unlike British religious art. Oddities include a black sun, and the fact that the viewer can only see the feet of Christ, as muscular soldiers in tiny skirts play dice for his robe at the base of the Cross. Cocteau included a self-portrait in the mural. Apparently, he was transported while painting it, talking to the figures as he worked.

In 2003, rendering work led to the rediscovery of a mosaic of the nativity, outlined in brilliant enamel by Boris Anrep, a Russian artist best known for his mosaics in Westminster Cathedral and the National Gallery (see p. 68). Cocteau had deliberately covered up Anrep's work, which infuriated the latter. In 2012, an unknown vandal added his own cryptic signature (T_A*) to one of the paintings, and drew a circle around Cocteau's sun. The restored murals are now displayed behind glass panels.

Unlike so many other churches in London, Notre Dame, which also operates a refugee centre, is very much alive. Other notable features in the church are the tapestry above the altar by Robert De Caunac, depicting Mary as the new Eve, and a vast statue of the Virgin of Mercy by Georges Saupique, who made the sculptures of the Palais du Trocadéro in Paris. Light a candle, as Cocteau did every morning before he set to work, then plunge into the fleshpots of Soho and Leicester Square.

BORIS ANREP'S MOSAICS

Art underfoot

National Gallery, Trafalgar Square, WC2N 5DN
0207 747 2885
www.nationalgallery.org.uk/paintings/history/sculptures-and-mosaics
Daily 10am-6pm, Fri 10am-9pm
Admission free
Charing Cross or Leicester Square tube

The throng of visitors who traipse through the grand foyer of the National Gallery each day barely spare a glance for the intricate mosaics that decorate the three vestibules and halfway landing. Created between 1928 and 1952 by Russian artist Boris Anrep (1885-1969), the mosaics were sponsored by Samuel Courtauld and other private patrons. Although Anrep used Byzantine techniques and colours, the four mosaics are a celebration of everyday life, peppered with famous personalities and inside jokes.

Anrep liked the idea of visitors walking on his works of art, so it could be viewed from different angles and approached with less reverence than a framed, hanging painting. This irreverent attitude is plain in Anrep's choice of subject matter. In *The Awakening of the Muses*, he casts his contemporaries from the Bloomsbury group as modern heroes: Virginia Woolf as Clio, muse of history, and art critic Clive Bell as a strangely sober Bacchus. There's even a cameo from Greta Garbo as Melpomene, muse of tragedy. Only Calliope, muse of poetry, is an unknown sitter – perhaps one of Anrep's secret crushes.

The Modern Virtues continues the theme of 'eminent people in fantastic situations'. Defiance is embodied by Winston Churchill on the white cliffs of Dover, fending off a fearsome beast shaped like a swastika. Look out for Margot Fonteyn as Delectation, Bertrand Russell as Lucidity, and Loretta Young as Compromise. In *Leisure*, TS Eliot contemplates Einstein's formula, while a naked girl frolics in Loch Ness with the fabled monster. One of Anrep's biggest patrons, Maud Russell, represents Folly – a strange gesture of gratitude! But Anrep also shows a healthy degree of self-mockery: *Here I Lie* depicts his own tomb, complete with a self-portrait.

The Labours of Life features – as far as we know – ordinary working folk: a Covent Garden porter, a woman washing a pig, a coal miner. *The Pleasures of Life* are summed up by a Christmas pudding, mud pies, cricket, football and less traditional pursuits such as Profane Love – a man with two lovers.

The mosaics were not laid in situ. Cartoons were traced onto backing paper and laid in reverse, then glued into place and polished. Anrep's glorious, mischievous work was inspired by the pavement chalk artists whose successors are still at work on Trafalgar Square today.

Anrep also created the mosaic floors in the Blake Room at Tate Britain, the altar mosaic at Notre Dame De France (see p. 66) and several religious mosaics in Westminster Cathedral.

Ghost Stations on the Underground

Mystery lurks in the London Underground – and not just the Robot Yeti that terrified a generation of children on the 1970s TV show, *Doctor Who*. There are 267 Tube stations in operation. However, several stations do not appear on any maps: 21 have been taken off-line since 1900. Most of them were closed when London Transport was created in 1933, merging several independent transit operators who had built stations very close to each other to compete for passengers.

Some are a real loss for commuters – British Museum, Aldwych (see also p. 141) and Lord's were all deemed economically unviable. Others were just badly designed, such as King William Street, the northbound terminus of the City & South London railway – the world's first electric underground railway. The station was opened by the Prince of Wales (later Edward VII), but the inaugural train broke down on its return journey. A commemorative plaque marks the site of the old station near the Monument. Brompton Road was so rarely used that train drivers didn't bother to stop there during rush hour. The cry 'Passing Brompton Road' became the title of a 1928 stage play.

Most of these ghost stations have been abandoned or walled up. Some were used as air raid shelters during the Second World War. Down Street was the underground operation centre for Churchill, before he moved to the Cabinet War Rooms in Whitehall. Churchill's bath is still down there. The brick and concrete drum above the old entrance to the Northern Line branch of Stockwell station was the entrance to the bomb shelters, now used for document and film storage. The drum is covered in a mural depicting French Resistance heroine Violette Szabo, who lived nearby.

Visiting these ghost stations is largely impossible. However, keen eyes will see remains of platforms as they pass through deserted stations. Bull and Bush – a station that never actually opened – can be glimpsed between Hampstead and Golders Green on the Northern Line. Wood Lane is visible when travelling east between White City and Shepherd's Bush. The white walls of British Museum station can be seen through the right-hand windows of the Central Line train between Holborn and Tottenham Court Road. This station was the setting for *Death Line*, a 1970s horror movie in which trapped construction workers morph into commuter-eating zombies.

Above ground, look out for the ox-blood tiles that line the former entrances to Down Street and South Kentish Town station on Kentish Town Road, now a shop. The station was closed during a power cut – and never opened again. However, a passenger once alighted at the closed station by mistake – the inspiration for John Betjeman's short story, 'South Kentish Town'.

See underground-history.co.uk and abandonedstations.org.uk for more tales of the hidden Underground.

MONSTERS OF TRAFALGAR SQUARE

Less than perfect lions

Trafalgar Square, WC2N 5DN
Charing Cross tube

Everyone knows the four bronze lions at the base of Nelson's Column in Trafalgar Square, but fewer people know the story behind them. The column itself was completed in 1843, but William Railton's design included four lions to set it off. However, lack of funds and arguments over the sculptor delayed the commission of the brass beasts until 1858. The Board of Works in charge of the whole monument chose Sir Edwin Landseer.

This was a controversial choice. On the one hand, Landseer was Queen Victoria's favourite painter, who taught both Victoria and Albert to etch and had an unrivalled reputation as an animal painter; on the other, he had never sculpted anything. The project, already running late, was further delayed by Landseer's health problems. Four years later, Landseer was still drafting sketches. He asked to be supplied with copies of casts of a real lion made by the Art Academy in Turin – these were eventually sent to London. He also spent hours studying his subjects at London Zoo. Finally, he asked the zoo for a dead lion as a studio model – but had to wait two years for one to die. Unfortunately, the lion started to rot before Landseer finished the work, so he had to improvise, using a domestic cat as a model for the paws and (supposedly) a dog for the tongue. These hybrid monsters were finally installed in 1868.

Charles I and the years in hiding

The equestrian statue of Charles I, stranded in traffic south of Nelson's Column and staring down at the site of his beheading on Whitehall, disappeared during the English Civil War. After the Roundheads beat the Royalists, the statue was sold to a metalsmith called John Rivet, who was told to melt it down. Instead, Rivet shrewdly hid it, allegedly in the vaults of St Paul's Church in Covent Garden. Rivet then made a pretty penny selling cutlery and trinkets that he claimed were made from fragments of the statue. After the Restoration, he sold it back to the Crown.

NEARBY

St Olav's statue

(35)

Above 21-24 Cockspur Street, now a Thai restaurant, stands a gilt statue of St Olav. This is a legacy of the building's original use as the Norwegian Chamber of Commerce, built around 1890. Olav, decked out in helmet, cloak and sword, was an odd choice as a figurehead for Norway's business in London: pre-sainthood, he was a fairly brutal Viking king who sacked London and led a raid up the river to pull down London Bridge. This is thought to be the origin of the nursery rhyme 'London Bridge is Falling Down'.

BRITAIN'S SMALLEST POLICE STATION

A peeping pillar

Trafalgar Square, WC2N 5DP
Charing Cross or Leicester Square tube

On the south-east corner of Trafalgar Square, surely London's biggest tourist trap, is Britain's smallest police station. The hordes of tourists posing before Nelson's Column and clambering on Sir Edwin Landseer's bronze lions are oblivious to this one-man sentry box fashioned from a hollowed-out granite lamp post. Allegedly, the secret police box was installed by Scotland Yard in 1926 so that the cops could keep an eye on the demonstrators and agitators who routinely gathered in Trafalgar Square (still London's most popular protest site). With its narrow slits for windows and claustrophobic proportions, this human CCTV camera must have been even more unpleasant during a riot. It was equipped with a telephone with a direct line to Canon Row Police Station in case things got out of hand.

Originally installed in 1826, the ornamental light on the top is probably not from Nelson's HMS Victory, as some guides would have you believe. However, it did flash whenever the police officer trapped inside picked up the telephone, alerting any fellow officers in the vicinity to come to his rescue.

Today, the lookout post is used to store street cleaning equipment. The only clue that it has links to the police is a faded list of by-laws hanging outside. For the record, offences in Trafalgar Square include feeding birds, camping, parking a caravan, public speaking, playing music, washing or drying clothes, exercising, bathing, boating or canoeing in the fountains, flying a kite, or using any 'foot-propelled device' – unless you have written permission from the Mayor.

NEARBY

Imperial standards (37)

At the foot of the steps below the National Gallery, well worn by the boots of weary sightseers, a series of small brass plaques mark the standard imperial measures of an inch, a foot, two feet and a yard. Replicas of the standards of measurements at the Royal Observatory in Greenwich (see p. 290), they were installed by the Board of Trade in 1876.

The centre of London (38)

A plaque on the pavement at the north end of Whitehall marks the official centre of London – the spot from which all mileage distances in Britain are measured. When Queen Eleanor of Castile died in 1290, Edward I erected a cross at each of the twelve stops on her funeral procession from Lincoln to Westminster Abbey. All distances from the capital are still measured from the queen's resting place. Although Eleanor's cross has been replaced by a statue of King Charles I, a replica stands outside Charing Cross station.

THE BRITISH OPTICAL ASSOCIATION MUSEUM

Eyeballs galore

42 Craven Street, WC2N 5NG
0207 766 4353
www.college-optometrists.org/museum
By appointment only, Mon-Fri 9.30am-5pm
Admission free; charge applies for a tour of the meeting rooms
Charing Cross or Embankment tube

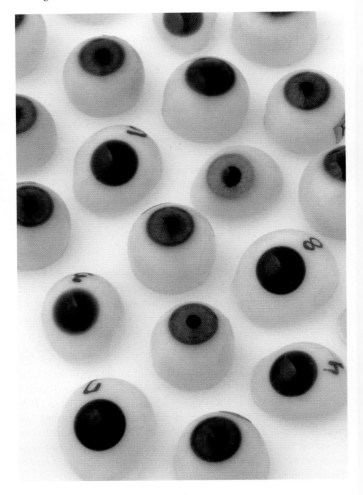

In the basement of a fine Georgian terrace a stone's throw from Trafalgar Square, this obscure but delightful museum contains thousands of eye-catching objects relating to the history of optometry. Founded in 1901, the collection includes over 3,000 pairs of eyeglasses. There are pince-nez, lorgnettes, magnifiers, quizzing glasses, goggles and monocles, opera glasses with secret snuff compartments, 'jealousy glasses' with lenses concealed in the sides, rose-tinted sunglasses, wig spectacles that slid into your hairpiece, and all manner of fancy spectacle receptacles.

There are celebrity specs, including Dr Johnson, Ronnie Corbett and Dr Crippen, and Leonardo de Caprio's contact lenses. Some models – like the windscreen wiper glasses with battery attached and a spring-loaded contraption to catapult contact lenses into the eyeball – did not take off.

Curator Neil Handley gives every visitor a personal guided tour, pointing out rare items such as an ancient Egyptian amulet of the eye of Horus, ensuring the dead could see in the afterlife, and a 16th-century statue of Saint Odilia, bearing two eyeballs on a bible. The optometric instruments are historical eye-openers, such as a Victorian self-testing machine with a religious text, designed to improve users' morals as well as their vision. Visitors can test their eyesight in a 1930s optician's chair with a built-in refraction unit, try on different frames, or explore foreign cities through an early View-Master. A drawer full of artificial, diseased, deformed and injured eyes, dating from 1880, is definitely not for the squeamish.

For a fee, you can also view the portraits of bespectacled sitters and optically-themed prints and satirical drawings in the meeting rooms on the first floor.

NEARBY
Benjamin Franklin's house
36 Craven Street WC2N 5NF
0207 925 1405
www.benjaminfranklinhouse.org

He may be famous as one of the founding fathers of the United States, but in 1790, the year of his death, Benjamin Franklin also invented bifocal spectacles. Franklin's only surviving home, a few doors down from the Optical Association Museum, is now a museum, where actors in period costumes carry on for visitors. During the restoration, a stockpile of cut and trepanned bones was unearthed in the basement – the remnants of an anatomy school run by Franklin's friend, William Hewson. Franklin probably attended Hewson's public dissections of human bodies.

SHERLOCK HOLMES ROOM

41

Dining next to the detectives

The Sherlock Holmes, 10 Northumberland Street, WC2N 5DB
0207 930 2644
www.sherlockholmes-stjames.co.uk
Sun-Thurs 8am-11pm, Fri-Sat 8am-12pm
Admission free
Charing Cross or Embankment tube

221b Baker Street is by far the best-known fictional address in London. However, as conceived by Arthur Conan Doyle, the rooms where Sherlock Holmes and Dr John Watson lived never actually existed – at the time the stories were written, house numbers on the street only went as high as 85 before Baker Street became York Place. In the 1930s, Baker Street was extended. The Abbey National Building Society moved into 219–229 Baker Street, and a full-time secretary was employed to answer mail addressed to the great detective.

In 1951, as part of the Festival of Britain, the building society staged an exhibition at its offices, re-creating the sitting room of 221b according to the plans of theatre designer Michael Weight. The exhibition was so successful that it was relocated to New York in 1952. In 1957, it was moved again: brewing giants Whitbread refurbished a small hotel they owned called the Northumberland Arms, and reopened it as the Sherlock Holmes.

The pub is full of Holmesiana, but the *pièce de résistance* is the Sherlock Holmes Room, reconstructed in a closed-off corner of the restaurant on the first floor. It's a little bit odd – you stare through the glass while oblivious diners eat away – but the attention to detail is worth it. There are clues from stories including *The Red-Headed League* and *The Adventure of the Dancing Men*. As well as vials of borax, and Holmes's violin and famous deerstalker, there's a wax dummy of the detective with a bullet wound in his forehead, a reference to *The Adventure of the Empty House*. Of course, the real Holmes survived 'to devote his life to examining those interesting little problems which the complex life of London so plentifully presents'.

The Festival of Britain

This national exhibition was held in 1951 to engender a sense of recovery and hope after the Second World War. London was the centre of the festival, which must have been a tricky proposition – rationing was in place until 1954 and large parts of the city were still bombsites. Most of the exhibition was temporary. The South Bank Exhibition was demolished (with the exception of the Royal Festival Hall, still going strong). The Festival Pleasure Gardens in Battersea Park have also survived – well worth a visit for their 1950s feel.

YORK HOUSE WATERGATE

42

Remains of a riverside pleasure palace

Embankment Gardens, WC2N 6DU
Embankment or Charing Cross tube

The enclosure of the Thames within the Embankment in the second half of the 19th century is generally held to be a miracle of Victorian engineering, giving London a state-of-the-art water and sewage system and creating 52 acres of new land for building. However, it dramatically changed the city's relationship to the river; nowhere is this more visible than this watergate in Embankment Gardens.

At first sight, the baroque archway looks like a folly – a gate to nowhere marooned in a small park. In fact, it was once the river entrance to York House, one of a line of mansions that originally stood along the route from the commercial City of London to the royal court at Westminster. The river now lies about 100 metres from the bottom step of the watergate, giving an idea of how far into the city the tidal Thames previously extended. If you stand on the opposite embankment at high tide, especially near Blackfriars Bridge on the South Bank, the height of the water and its closeness to the lip of the wall both underline the river's power.

The watergate itself was probably created by Inigo Jones in 1626, as an extension to the palace built by the first Duke of Buckingham in 1620. When in London, the Duke usually resided at Wallingford House in Whitehall, but threw lavish parties at York House. The design looks florid in comparison to its surroundings, and still bears the Buckingham family coat of arms. Alongside Banqueting House and the Temple Bar Arch next to St Paul's, it is one of the few surviving reminders in London of the Italianate tastes of King Charles I. The second Duke of Buckingham was the King's favourite, and one of London's wealthiest landowners. Like the King, the Duke was an art lover. The 1635 inventory of his collection shows 22 paintings and 59 pieces of Roman sculpture in the great chamber alone. Gentileschi and Rubens both lodged at the house during their visits to London.

George Villiers, Duke of Buckingham's cryptic namesake

On the wall of York Place, next to the McDonalds on the Strand, is a grimy little plaque commemorating the street's original name, Of Alley. The second Duke of Buckingham sold York House to developers in 1672, but made it a condition of the sale that his name and title should be commemorated by George Street, Villiers Street, Duke Street, Of Alley, and Buckingham Street (thus spelling out George Villiers, Duke of Buckingham). The streets are still there, though Of Alley was renamed York Place and George Street is now York Buildings.

FREEMASONS' HALL

43

Yes, the Freemasons' Hall is open to the public

60 Great Queen Street, Holborn, WC2B 5AZ
020 7831 9811
Mon–Sat 10am–5pm
Closed Bank Holiday weekends, Christmas and New Year
No booking required for the museum or library, but book online for tour to include the Grand Temple: https://museumfreemasonry.org.uk/tours - tours begin at 11am, 12pm, 2pm, 3pm and 4pm
Admission free
Holborn tube

© UGLE

Time was when everyone thought there was nothing more secretive than a Freemason. But since the 1980s, the holiest of holies, the Freemasons' Hall near Covent Garden, has been open to the public, with a dedicated museum, an exhibition space in its library, and free hour-long tours of the building including the Grand Temple.

Opened in 1933 when freemasonry was flourishing, the hall is an art deco beast of a building that dominates the street. It is often used as a film location and has doubled as Saddam Hussein's palace. There is something melancholic about the place; membership numbers are in decline, which undoubtedly lies behind the decision to modernise and open up. The museum does a good job of explaining the history of freemasonry in the UK, and how the medieval stonemasons' guilds, with their secret words and symbols, were adapted to become the guiding model for the organisation.

Highlights include a display of Masonic regalia, including ornate aprons and gauntlet cuffs, items belonging to famous Freemasons including King Edward VII and Winston Churchill, and best of all, the colossal Grand Master's Throne. Built in 1791, its first occupant was the Prince Regent, later George IV. George was notoriously fat – in his later years, he had to sleep sitting up in order to breathe – and the chair looks as if it was designed with his elephantine backside in mind.

The glory of the hall, however, is the Grand Temple. Enter it through bronze doors that each weigh over a ton, and gaze up at its 18-metre mosaic ceiling. The grand days of the brotherhood may be behind them, but they're still well housed.

© UGLE

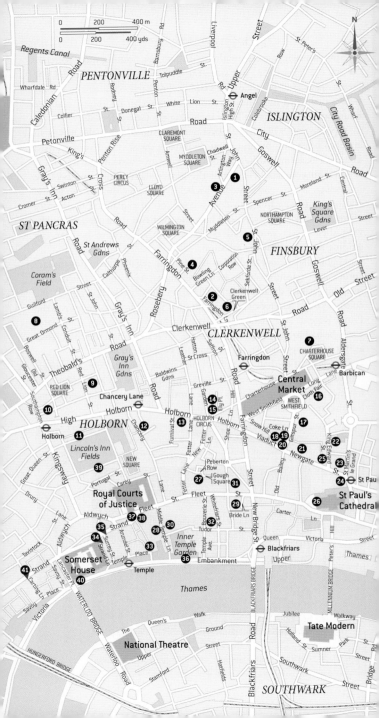

Temple to Angel

108 ROSEBERY AVENUE

Window into an artist's world

108 Rosebery Avenue, Islington EC1R 4TL
www.whitechapelgallery.org/first-thursdays/galleries/108-rosebery-ave/
Open 24 hours
Admission free
Angel tube. Bus 9, 38 and 341

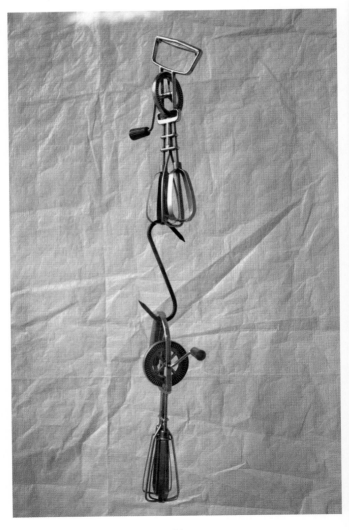

With retail rents going crazy in London, it might seem strange to see a vacant shop on Islington's affluent Rosebery Avenue. But number 108 is no ordinary shop window. Artist Maggie Ellenby has used it as an installation space for over 100 different pieces since 1993. The way the work is framed by the window and the speed of change suggest a slow slide show. The format often changes – some are assemblages, some are large prints, neon or text works.

Recent works include the 'Animale' series of prints that often come in pairs, for example conger eels or snails. *Ceratodon purpureus*, a large text work, is taken from the name of one of three species of moss found on the bumper of the artist's car.

The simplicity is deliberate. The installations are designed to be seen by viewers in transit whose eyes can flick over the image and retain it as they pass, either on foot or, fleetingly, from the bus. The works are unlabelled, adding to their mystery. Light, another recurring feature, creates a startling effect if you are driving by after dark – in fact, some pieces can only be seen at night. You might spot a backlit climber scaling the window pane, or an illuminated 'Speed Kills, Jesus Saves.' And whenever Ellenby is contemplating her next project, she puts up a 'Pause' sign.

THE CLERK'S WELL

Medieval water source

14–16 Farringdon Lane, EC1R 3AU
Call Islington Local History Centre on 0207 5277988 to arrange a visit
Farringdon tube

Londons first suburb, medieval Clerkenwell was a leafy neighbourhood north of the City walls, peppered with farms, spas, and 'excellent springs, the water of which is sweet, clear and salubrious,' according to William Fitzstephen, who compiled the first topographical history of London in the 12th century.

The area takes its name from the Clerk's Well, or *Fons Clericorum*, which has remarkably survived from the Middle Ages to this day. Although the well is now locked inside the basement of the Well Court office building, with limited public access, you can peer through the glass walls and read about the history of the well and the surrounding area.

The well was originally located in the boundary wall of St Mary's, an Augustinian nunnery founded in 1140. It was nicknamed the 'Clerks' Well' because parish clerks performed Mystery Plays based on biblical themes close to this spot, one of the cultural highlights of the medieval calendar. After the dissolution of the nunnery during the Reformation, the boundary wall was destroyed and the well was covered over by new buildings. In 1800, a pump was placed at street level to facilitate public use, but it was closed in 1857 because of pollution. The well was rediscovered by accident in 1924 during building work in Farringdon Lane.

NEARBY
Sadler's Wells
Rosebery Avenue, EC1R 4TN; www.sadlerswells.com

Now a world famous dance theatre, Sadler's Wells has housed performances ever since Dick Sadler opened his 'musick house' here in the 1680s. When an ancient well was discovered in the grounds, the enterprising Mr Sadler was quick to promote the water's medicinal properties. Although the spa fell out of fashion, the theatre is still known as Sadler's Wells.

Finsbury Health Centre ④
17 Pine Street, EC1R 0L

Designed by Berthold Lubetkin in 1936-8, this modernist landmark behind Exmouth Market is still used as a medical centre. With its glass walls, red and blue interior, and colourful murals exhorting locals to enjoy 'fresh air night and day,' the building embodied Lubetkin's belief in modern architecture as a tool for social progress. Finsbury was one of London's poorest boroughs and this health centre was the *pièce de resistance* of its socialist health and housing policy. As Lubetkin famously commented, 'Nothing is too good for ordinary people.' Besides doctors' surgeries, the clinic contained a delousing station, a TB clinic, and a solarium – symbols of how times have changed.

JOE ORTON'S LIBRARY BOOKS

Vandalised volumes

Islington Local History Centre, Finsbury Library, 245 St. John Street, EC1V 4NB
0207 527 7988
archiveshub.ac.uk/data/gb1032-s/ort
By appointment Mon-Fri 9.30am-1pm and 2-5pm, and every second Saturday
of the month. Late opening until 8pm every Thurs
Admission free
Angel tube, Farringdon tube /rail

'Libraries might as well not exist; they've got endless shelves for rubbish and hardly any space for good books,' Joe Orton bemoaned in 1967. Orton, a playwright and provocateur, achieved notoriety in the 1960s for his black comedies, and even more so for his premature death at the age of 34 – bludgeoned to death by his jealous boyfriend Kenneth Halliwell, who then committed suicide. Halliwell and Orton had been lovers since they met at drama school.

They shared a cramped bedsit at 25 Noel Road in Islington, which they decorated with images torn out of local library books. In addition to stealing volumes that took their fancy, the pair developed a taste for defacing books, by altering their covers and writing new, crude blurbs in their dust jackets.

Orton enjoyed loitering in his local library, watching the bemused or outraged reactions of readers to his handiwork. Islington Library was not amused. Extra staff failed to nail the culprits. It was Sydney Porrett, a clerk at Islington Council, who caught them out. He sent a letter to Halliwell asking him to remove an illegally parked car. The typed reply matched typeface irregularities in the defaced books. On 28 April 1962, police raided Orton and Halliwell's flat and retrieved 72 stolen books, which they had used to 'wallpaper' their flat. They were sentenced to six months in prison and fined £262. Later, Orton claimed this unreasonably harsh sentence was 'because we were queers.'

Today, the 44 vandalised volumes are the pride of Islington's Local History Centre. Colour copies are kept in two ordinary-looking photo albums, which you would expect to contain wedding or family photos. Instead there are curious collages of subversive images. John Betjeman is replaced by an elderly man in his underpants, covered in tattoos. *The Collected Plays of Emlyn Williams* is covered with crude slogans like 'Knickers MUST FALL' and 'OLIVIA PRUDE FUCKED BY MONTY.'

Queen's Favourite shows two half-naked men wrestling. The yellow rose on the cover of Collins *Guide to Roses* has a gorilla face. The pair had a penchant for reworking Shakespeare covers with rather elegant collages. Other books received less reverential treatment: the blurb of *Clouds of Witness* has been re-imagined as a tale of a child-molesting policewoman, which concludes: 'Have a good shit while you're reading!' If you want to see the originals, you must apply in writing, although a few of them are on permanent display in the Islington Museum downstairs.

MARX MEMORIAL LIBRARY ⑥

Lenin's London office

37a Clerkenwell Green, EC1R 0DU
0207 253 1485
www.marxlibrary.org.uk
Mon-Thurs 12-4pm. Guided tours every Tuesday and Thursday at 1pm
Admission free
Farringdon tube

The bright red door is the only clue to what lies inside this Georgian townhouse that sits inconspicuously beside the snazzy jewellery and architecture studios of Clerkenwell Green. A brass plaque by the doorbell proclaims that this is the Marx Memorial Library, home to over 150,000 volumes of leftist literature.

From the Peasants' Revolt in 1381 to the Poll Tax demonstrations of the 1980s, this quaint corner of London has long been a breeding ground for rebels, rioters, and political refugees. Among them was Vladimir Ilyich Ulyanov who in 1902-3 shared space in this building with Harry Quelch, editor of the left-wing *Twentieth Century Press*. Lenin's poky office is intact, with its blue cupboards, leather-bound socialist tracts, a Braille edition of the Communist Manifesto, and countless busts of the man himself donated by admirers. This is where Lenin edited issues 22-38 of his Russian newspaper *Iskra (The Spark)*, printed on extra thin paper so it was easier to smuggle into Tsarist Russia.

Built in 1737 as a charitable school for Welsh boys, the building acquired its first radical residents when the London Patriotic Society arrived in 1872. The Marx Memorial Library and Workers' School was established 1933, on the 50th anniversary of Marx's death, as an angry response to the public burning of books in Nazi Germany. In 1935, Viscount Jack Hastings, an aristocratic Communist and pupil of the Mexican radical artist Diego Riviera, painted a giant mural grandly titled '*Worker of the Future Clearing Away the Chaos of Capitalism*'; the figures of Marx, Engels, and Lenin loom larger than life behind the reception desk. Downstairs, the archive of the International Brigade has pride of place in a meeting room decked with revolutionary posters. The library's red shelves and blue linoleum floors are scuffed, old-fashioned, slightly down at heel – exactly as they should be. In keeping with its socialist principles, membership costs just £20 a year (£10 for concessions).

In 1986, some 14th-century tunnels were discovered in the basement, which can be viewed on Open House weekend.

Marx in London

Karl Marx wrote much of *Das Kapital* seated in Chair G7 at the British Museum Reading Room. In 1850-55, Marx lived in a squalid apartment above what is now the Quo Vadis restaurant in Soho. But the restaurant's original owner, Peppino Leoni, was loath to have a blue plaque commemorating a communist outside his fancy establishment at 28 Dean Street.

CHARTERHOUSE

Cloistered home for retired gentlemen

Charterhouse Square, EC1M 6AN
0207 251 5002
www.thecharterhouse.org
Guided tours take place on Tues, Wed, Thurs and every other Sat
Admission charges apply. Pre-booking essential; check availability at
www.thecharterhouse.org/tours/
Barbican tube, Farringdon tube/rail

Wandering beneath the plane trees of Charterhouse Square, it's hard to believe this was once a plague pit, where 50,000 victims of the Black Death were buried in the 14th century. A Carthusian monastery was founded here in 1371, but the monks' cloistered existence was brutally interrupted by the Reformation: the Prior was hung, drawn, and quartered, with one of his arms being nailed to the gate.

After the monastery was shut down in 1537, it became a playground for the aristocracy. Lord North turned it into a sumptuous mansion, where he treated Queen Elizabeth I to such extravagant hospitality that he went broke and fled to the country. Charterhouse (the name is an anglicised corruption of Carthusian) was eventually purchased by Sir Thomas Sutton, a philanthropist, who endowed a school for 40 poor boys and an almshouse for 80 male pensioners ('gentlemen by descent and in poverty, soldiers that have borne arms by sea or land, merchants decayed by piracy or shipwreck, or servants in household to the King or Queen's Majesty').

The only surviving Tudor town house in London, Charterhouse is still home to around 40 'retired gentlemen'. The criteria for entry are less rigorous these days – even Catholics are acceptable – but there's still a strict pecking order among residents, not unlike the eponymous boarding school, which moved to Surrey in 1872. Three times a week, year round, one of the 'Brothers' guides visitors around the cobbled compound they call home. The oldest resident is 102.

Behind the 15th-century gateway, there's no trace of the place's sinister past and little evidence of modernity – although visitors are required to watch a dated 15-minute video seated on antique leather chairs. Despite damage during the Blitz, the buildings are marvellously preserved, with quaint names like Master's Court, Preacher's Court, and Washhouse Court.

Tables are laid for afternoon tea in the Great Hall, where 80 knights were once dubbed by King James I, overlooked by portraits of dashing aristocrats with Bee Gees hairdos.

Charterhouse makes a handsome income by renting flats and offices in a separate building. But the waiting list for the affordable accommodation is very long indeed.

The chapel is open to the public on Sundays – if you can get past the guard at the front gate. Look out for Sutton's tomb and the carved dog heads that decorate the pews. 'They've optimistically provided a font for baptisms,' laughs our guide, Peter. 'Presumably it's for grandchildren!'

THE LULLABY FACTORY

Industrial soothing and sleep system

Great Ormond Street Hospital, Great Ormond Street, WC1N 3JH
Daily 9am-5pm
Russell Square tube

The Lullaby Factory is hard to explain. There's an awkward space between two buildings at Great Ormond Street, London's world-renowned children's hospital. One of the buildings is due to be pulled down in 2028. Into this gap, architects Studio Weave have installed the Lullaby Factory, a flourish of pipes, horns and petals that climbs like a berserk plant up the side of the 1930s Southwood Building. These pipes echo the structure of the hospital, but in fact, this is a beautiful machine that broadcasts calming and soothing lullabies for the hospital's young patients. Put your ear to the huge drooping pods at ground level and you hear the music created by sound artist Jessica Curry, or tune into it via a special radio station.

The design incorporates old taps and gauges reclaimed from a hospital boiler house that was being decommissioned. As a result, the visual tone is like something from a Heath Robinson drawing – copper piping, repurposed gramophone horns and musical instruments all feature in the Factory. The only regret is that there isn't more of it. It would be great to see it crawling all over the building and into the next street. To reach the Lullaby Factory, go through the main entrance and look for

the Lagoon café, then through sliding doors onto a wooden deck, which also contains London's only marimba/bench hybrid.

The hospital specialises in heart treatment for children, and developed the first children's heart and lung bypass machine in 1962. It also devised an improved shunt valve for children with water on the brain with the help of children's author Roald Dahl. His Big Friendly Giant would have thoroughly approved of the hospital's lullaby delivery system.

A replica skeleton of Joseph Merrick, the Elephant Man

Snooping round London hospitals for a bit of sightseeing might seem ghoulish, but there's all sorts of places worth seeking out. Check out the Royal London Hospital Museum (Free entry – open Tues–Fri 10am–12.30pm and 1pm–4pm, closed Christmas, New Year, Easter and public holidays) in the former crypt of St Philip's Church. This little museum houses a replica skeleton of Joseph Merrick, the Elephant Man (the original is now too delicate), who lived and died in the hospital, as well a display of gruesome medical instruments and material relating to the local Jack the Ripper murders.

NOVELTY AUTOMATION

Is it Art?

1a Princeton Street, WC1R 4AX
www.novelty-automation.com
Wed-Sat 11am-6pm; late opening Thurs 12am-8pm. Open every day 11am-6pm during half term and school holidays
Admission free. Machines cost £1-£2 to play
Holborn tube

Billing itself as 'a mad arcade of satirical slot machines', Tim Hunkin's Novelty Automation is work of eccentric genius. A flashing neon arrow directs you to a mock Tudor house on a Holborn back street. Inside is a collection of coin-operated automata that poke fun at British politics and mores.

Like *Private Eye* in 3D, it's a celebration of the absurd. You can settle a lamb's fate (pet or meat?); test your nerve by sticking your hand inside the cage of a panting, red-eyed Rottweiler that drools saliva; submit to a groping from the auto-frisker; take a three-minute micro-break on a magic carpet (no risk of deep-vein thrombosis!); have your foot examined by a creepy chiropodist (be warned: wear socks!); or hone your money-laundering skills (a great British success story!). An 'instant weight loss' machine dispenses a single piece of popcorn that magically makes you shrink.

Hunkin also takes a satirical swipe at the pretentious elitism of the art world. Pop the contents of your pockets into a slot and a dummy that looks uncannily like (former Tate director) Nicholas Serota will decide: 'Is it Art?' Serota's verdict on my son's lollipop? He shakes his head with an almost imperceptible flash of his forked tongue.

Hunkin, a trained engineer who moonlights as a cartoonist, illustrator, set designer and documentary filmmaker, spends four to nine months building each machine by hand. A winning combination of low and high tech, his automata are a refreshing antidote to the virtual age of the 'i-Zombie'.

'I'm lucky to have lived through the transition from analogue to digital. The potential for adding bits of digital wizardry to old-fashioned electromechanical stuff is vast unexplored territory,' says Hunkin. 'By showing it's still possible to make interesting stuff by hand, I hope some kids may be encouraged to try making their own stuff – engineering has such a disastrously boring image in the UK.'

Ultimately, Hunkin's aim is simple: to make people laugh. Judging by the irrepressible shrieks, giggles, chuckles and cackles that ripple through the arcade, he has accomplished his mission.

A stopped clock

The arcade is located in Tudor House, an early 17th-century building that was originally a tavern. Barrels of beer were delivered by a stream that ran past the back door. A few blocks away is another old boozer, The Dolphin Tavern, where the clock is permanently stopped at 10:40 – the time a Zeppelin bomb struck in 1915.

KINGSWAY TRAM SUBWAY

Tracks from the past

Southampton Row, WC2
Holborn Tube

If you are brave enough to dodge the traffic roaring down Kingsway, in the middle of Southampton Row, just beyond Holborn tube station, is a ramp leading to a disused tunnel. This is one of the last vestiges of London's tram network, which criss-crossed the city until the early 1950s.

The gates to the tunnel are now permanently locked, but if you peek through the railings you can see the old tram tracks running along the cobblestones. Between the tracks, you can just make out the underground electricity cable that powered the trams along this route from Angel to Aldwych. It took just ten minutes to make the journey from Islington to Waterloo Bridge – an enviable record by today's standards. Built in 1906, the two-way tunnel originally passed though a subterranean station at Holborn, and then down the length of Kingsway to another tram stop at Aldwych, before surfacing by Waterloo Bridge. The subway was part of a grand urban regeneration scheme, intended to clean up the slums to the east of the Strand and to create a commercial hub on Kingsway, London's widest boulevard at the time. Named in honour of King Edward VII, Kingsway embodied the modern face of London. In the early 1930s, the tunnel was extended to accommodate the new double-decker trams, which proved to be a huge hit with the public. But the advent of the automobile soon put paid to the popularity of the tram. In the early 1950s, the tram network was dismantled. The last tram clattered through Kingsway on 5 July 1952.

In 1964, part of the tunnel was converted into the Strand underpass to ease traffic congestion. The rest of the tunnel was used as a flood control centre in the 1970s, but this was closed down in 1984 when the Thames Barrier opened (see p. 298). The derelict Kingsway subway is now used to store old street signs and traffic cones. Although attempts to convert it into a film studio were rejected on safety grounds, the tunnel has featured in several movies, including *Bhowani Junction* (1955) and *The Avengers* (1998). It was put to most imaginative use in 2004 by a group of art students from Central St Martin's, who staged an exhibition called 'Thought-Crime,' inspired by George Orwell's *1984*, in this spooky subterranean setting. London's authorities periodically announce plans to reinstate a tram network in the capital, but so far only the remote corners of South London have it. Whether the trams come back into town and the Kingsway subway will be revived remains to be seen.

CANDLELIT TOURS
OF SIR JOHN SOANE'S MUSEUM

Crepuscular sepulchres

12-13 Lincoln's Inn Fields, WC2
0207 405 2107; www.soane.org
Tues-Sat 10am-5pm (last entry at 4.30pm). Candlelit tours 6-9pm on the first Tuesday of every month. The first 200 visitors in the queue at 5.30pm are guaranteed entry. After that, it's one-in-one-out until last entry at 8.30pm
Admission free
Holborn or Temple tube

A bricklayer's son, Sir John Soane (1753-1837) rose to become one of the foremost architects of his day. He designed Dulwich Picture Gallery and the Bank of England, though many of his designs remained unbuilt – a great pity as they were often wildly eccentric, such as a proposed piazza across the Thames, supported by hundreds of columns, which would have blocked most river traffic.

Soane's own home grew exponentially with his growing collection of antiquities, art, architectural drawings and models. From 1792 to 1824, Soane demolished and rebuilt three houses overlooking Lincoln's Inn Fields to accommodate this extraordinary hoard.

The collection reflects a magpie mentality, but the overall effect is intensely personal and visually rich. There are sarcophagi and stained glass, watches and clocks, a stockpile of gems, bust-filled alcoves, sky-lit statues, and secret panels that are ceremoniously flung open by witty, white-gloved guides to reveal masterpieces by Canaletto, Turner, and Hogarth.

After the death of his wife, Soane lived alone amidst his collection, constantly adding to and rearranging it. Partly to spite his son, George, a penniless author, Soane negotiated an Act of Parliament in 1833 to bequeath the house and its contents to the nation – a museum to which 'amateurs and students in Painting, Sculpture and Architecture' should have free access, with the proviso that it should remain intact and unchanged.

Over the years, incremental changes did happen: Soane's private apartments were turned into offices, some rooms were sealed, and artifacts stowed away in a futile attempt to make the space less cluttered. Now, after a seven-year restoration, Nos. 12 and 13 have finally been returned to their original splendour, the interiors bathed in an amber glow, which the architect dubbed 'a light subdued, but not exhausted'.

Soane was fascinated with the manipulation of light and shade to create 'those fanciful effects that constitute the poetry of architecture', using coloured and stained glass, mirrors and domes, to create different moods. On the first Tuesday of every month, from 6-9pm, visitors can experience this strange and surprising trove as its owner would have done after dark – by candlelight. The over-populated collection retreats into shadow, creating a fantastically gothic atmosphere. You'll have to queue to get a look in, but it's totally worth the wait.

LONDON SILVER VAULTS

Subterranean shrine to silverware

Chancery Lane, WC2A 1QS
0207 242 3844
www.thesilvervaults.com
Mon-Fri 9am-5.30pm, Sat 9am-1pm
Admission free
Chancery Lane tube

Containing the world's largest retail collection of antique silver, London's silver vaults are located two floors underground, below a non-descript office block. It's an improbable setting for a glittering arcade of 25 shops, their dazzling wares crammed into converted safety deposit boxes. Originally known as the Chancery Lane Safe Deposit, this subterranean store house opened in 1876 as a place where wealthy Londoners could safeguard their valuables. Impressed by the tight security, the silver dealers and jewellers of nearby Hatton garden, the centre of London's diamond trade, began using the strong rooms to stash their precious goods overnight. Before long, it evolved into a kind of discount outlet, where bargain hunters could buy direct from dealers at wholesale prices. Today, it's more like a museum than a shopping mall. The shops still have the original walls reinforced with steel. Dealers trade in all manner of silverware from candlesticks to cutlery, pepper pots to place-card holders, watches to wine goblets. Many a royal banquet has been served on a silver service purchased from these vaults. Don't worry about buying a fake. According to a 14th-century law, all silver items over 7.78 g must be hallmarked before sale to verify their purity. In those days, forgers were hanged; today, they face a spell in jail. Although the building upstairs was bombed during World War II, there was no damage below ground. The original front door also remains intact; almost a metre thick, it's a heavy-duty deterrent for thieves. So far, no heist has even been attempted.

NEARBY

Free lectures at Gresham College ⑬

Barnard's Inn Hall, Holborn EC1
0207 831 0575
www.gresham.ac.uk

Founded in 1597, Gresham College moved to these Tudor premises, featured in Dickens' *Great Expectations*, in 1991. Tucked away behind the Inns of Court, it provides free public lectures. The original professorships were Commerce, Astronomy, Divinity, Geometry, Law, Music, Physic, and Rhetoric, but the college has added a wider range of subjects since 1597. Topics range from extra-terrestrial intelligence to maritime architecture. There are occasional free chamber music recitals in a medieval hall overlooking a secret courtyard.

THE RELIC OF ST ETHELDREDA ⑭

Withered hands and sore throats

St Etheldreda's Church, 14 Ely Place, EC1N 6RY
0207 405 1061
www.stetheldreda.com
Mon-Fri 7.45am-7pm
Admission free
Chancery Lane or Farringdon tube

'To the public it is one of those unsatisfactory streets which lead nowhere; to the inhabitants it is quiet and pleasant; to the student of old London it is possessed of all the charms which can be given by five centuries of change and the long residence of the great and noble.' Thus wrote George Walter Thornbury of Ely Place in 1878.

Today, Ely Place remains a fascinating little cul-de-sac, guarded by a formidable gate and miniature lodge for the beadles who once patrolled the street. Every hour, beadles in top hats and greatcoats would cry out the time and a weather report to the fortunate inhabitants of the grand Georgian townhouses.

Tucked between them is St Etheldreda's, one of only two extant buildings in London built in the reign of Edward I. Built in 1250, this is the last vestige of the palace of the Bishops of Ely, whose 58 acres of orchards, vineyards and lawns stretched down to the Thames. Administered by the See of Ely, 100 miles away in Cambridgeshire, the estate was beyond the jurisdiction of the City of London – and thus much favoured by criminals on the run.

Inside the small, gothic, and rather gloomy church, among the martyrs of the Reformation, is a creepy relic of its patron, St Etheldreda. A fragment of her uncorrupted pale white hand, donated to the church in the 19th century, is kept in a jewel casket to the right of the high altar. Removed in Norman times, her hand was hidden during the persecution of Catholics on the Duke of Norfolk's estate.

The tasty strawberries from St Etheldreda's garden are mentioned in Shakespeare's *Richard III*.

The blessing of sore throats

As well as patron saint of chastity (she died a virgin, despite being married twice), Etheldreda is believed to cure sore throats. She died of the plague in 679, blaming the tumour on her neck on her sinful fondness for fancy necklaces. In February, on the day of St Blaise (apparently, he was sainted for saving a child from choking to death on a fishbone), people with throat and neck infections flock to St Etheldreda to be anointed with two lit candles that are tied together.

Henry VIII and his first wife Catherine of Aragon binged at a five-day feast in the crypt of St Etheldreda in 1531.

THE CHERRY TREE
AT THE MITRE TAVERN

Quaint vestige of an Elizabethan feud

Ye Olde Mitre, Ely Court (between Hatton Garden and Ely Place), EC1N 6SJ
Mon-Fri 11am-11pm
Chancery Lane or Farringdon tube

Just off Hatton Garden, London's jewellery district, is Ely Court, where Ye Olde Mitre is hidden. The pub's largely intact 18th-century interior is split into three small rooms downstairs, one of which, known as Ye Closet, is large enough to hold a table surrounded by benches and nothing more. Best of all, there is no piped music or fruit machines, a far rarer thing in London pubs than might be imagined.

Inside a glass case in the front bar is the preserved remains of a cherry tree trunk – the land on which the pub was built was originally part of the garden of Ely Palace, property of the Bishop of Eely (see p. 107). In 1576, Elizabeth I's favourite, Christopher Hatton, finagled his way into possession of the site, with the connivance of the queen and against the wishes of the bishop. The cherry tree marked the dividing line where, like two teenagers sharing a bedroom, the two men split the garden. Legend has it that the queen danced the maypole around the tree, but this smells of Merrie England wishful thinking.

Other notable pub interiors nearby include the Jerusalem Tavern on Britton Street, a former watchmaker's shop dating from 1720 that looks like a Georgian coffee house, and The Black Friar on Queen Victoria Street. The latter's marble and copper interior is decorated with bas-reliefs of jolly monks, and there's a barrel-vaulted snug lined with mottoes such as 'Finery is Foolery' and 'Wisdom is Rare', presumably there for the pleasure of more lugubrious drinkers.

London's worst statues

Ely Place faces Holborn Viaduct, a Victorian bridge whose parapets are adorned with statues representing Commerce, Agriculture, Science and Fine Arts. At the north-west corner, above the steps down to Farringdon Street, is one of London's least flattering statues of public figures: Sir William Walworth, killer of Wat Tyler, depicted with teeny-weeny legs.

Competition in the ugly statue stakes includes the British Library's bust of Anne Frank, rendered rather like an arthritic gnome; the library, to its credit, has hidden it in a dark corner near the cloakroom.

A recent addition to this ignominious list is Paul Day's *The Meeting Place* at St Pancras station, one of London's most beautiful public spaces. Featuring two reunited lovers embracing, this 30-foot bronze looks like an aesthetic hybrid of Stalin and Barbara Cartland.

SECRETS OF ST BARTHOLOMEW'S THE GREATER

Bad puns, briny floods

West Smithfield, EC1A 9DS
0207 600 0440
www.greatstbarts.com
14 Feb-10 Nov, Mon-Fri 8.30am-5pm; 11 Nov-13 Feb, Mon-Fri 8.30am-4pm;
Sat (all year) 10.30am-4pm; Sun (all year) 8.30am-8pm
Check website for admission details
Barbican Farringdon or St Paul's tube

Very little of early medieval London remains intact today, because Londoners, like the unwise little pig, built houses of wood, and the city burned down in 1077, 1087, 1132, 1136, 1203, 1212, 1220 and 1227. Almost anything left intact from these was destroyed in the Great Fire of 1666. This church is a rare survivor, despite having suffered from Zeppelin bombing in World War I and the Blitz in World War II. It was also occupied by squatters in the 18th century. The Lady Chapel was used as a commercial property; Benjamin Franklin served a year there as a journeyman printer.

Inside, the crossing and choir are mostly Norman, with round arching and massive decorated pillars; these muffle sound and light, creating a grey, crepuscular atmosphere. Notable features include the tomb of Rahere, founder of the church. Opposite this is an oriel window into an oratory, or semi-private chapel, for a wealthy Prior named Bolton. The window is decorated with Bolton's rebus, a visual pun depicting the symbol of a barrel pierced by an arrow (a bolt plus a tun, meaning barrel). There's also the bust of Edward Cooke made of 'weeping marble'. This used to cry if the weather was wet enough; nowadays, unfortunately, central heating has dried out the stone. The inscription beneath the statue still exhorts visitors to 'unsluice your briny floods'.

Bart's remains connected to the hospital across the street that was founded at the same time. Within the hospital is a smaller church, called (naturally) Bartholomew the Lesser. The hospital also has a small museum open Tuesday to Friday, 10am-4pm (call in advance 0203 465 5798), whose crowning glory is an unusual pair of large murals by William Hogarth depicting the Good Samaritan and the Christ at the pool of Bethesda. Hogarth allegedly painted them for free in order to prevent an Italian getting his hands on the job.

The church has historic links with the 'Worshipful Companies' of London. These include traditional professions such as The Haberdashers' Company, The Butchers' Company and The Fletchers' Company (a guild for arrow makers), as well as as modern ones like the Information Technologists' Company, the Tax Advisors' Company, and the Guild of Public Relations Practitioners.

BARTS PATHOLOGY MUSEUM

A potted history of pathology

3rd floor, Robin Brook Centre, St Bartholomew's Hospital, West Smithfield, EC1A 7BE
0207 882 8766
www.qmul.ac.uk/bartspathology
Open for bookable events and occasional open days. Check website for details
Admission varies
Barbican, Farringdon or St Paul's tube; Farringdon rail

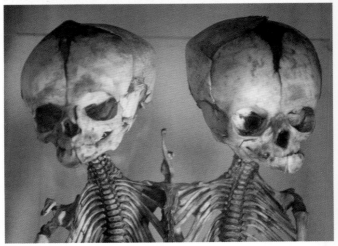

It might be distracting to sit your exams in a cavernous, glass-roofed hall lined with jars of pickled body parts, but that's what students have to contend with at the London School of Medicine and Dentistry (part of Queen Mary University of London). The exam hall doubles as a gruesome pathology showroom inside St Bartholomew's, London's oldest hospital.

The study of anatomy and pathology has changed dramatically since this Victorian museum was purpose-built in 1879. Around 5,000 diseased specimens in various shades of putrid yellow, gangrenous green and bilious orange are neatly arranged on three open-plan floors linked by a spiral staircase. Only the ground floor is open to the public, with the upper galleries reserved for teaching, cataloguing and conservation.

Carla Valentine, a sassy mortician who looks like a 1950s pin-up, worked as an autopsy assistant before landing her 'dream job' as the museum's technical curator. Prior to her appointment, the museum was in a desperate state of disrepair. The roof was leaking – and some of the potted organs were too. All the pieces downstairs are over 100 years old; those upstairs are 'fresher'. Some of Valentine's favourites include the deformed liver of a 'tight-lacer' (corset-wearer), the misshapen bandaged foot of a Chinese woman and the skull of John Bellingham, who was hanged and anatomised in 1812 after he assassinated the Prime Minister, Spencer Perceval. (The surgeons were thrilled to note that Bellingham's heart continued to move for almost four hours after his death.) Prior to the Anatomy Act of 1832, there were only two ways in which medical schools could acquire cadavers: prisoners sentenced to death and dissection, or corpses purchased from body snatchers popularly known as 'resurrection men'.

The museum's limited funding doesn't stretch to a public viewing licence, so Valentine has introduced a brilliant series of talks and workshops inspired by the collection. There are taxidermy classes, lectures on funerary cannibalism and the history of syphilis, and festivals dedicated to bodily decay and broken hearts. A glass of wine and the chance to make new friends among severed hands and trepanned skulls. What's not to like?

St Bartholomew's Hospital Museum

Located in the hospital's north wing, this museum traces the evolution of medical care since Barts was founded in 1123. It contains some fine paintings, gruesome surgical tools and a tribute to Arthur Conan Doyle, who wrote some of his Sherlock Holmes stories while studying medicine here. A commemorative plaque quotes Holmes' quip upon first meeting Watson in a chemistry lab at Barts: 'You have been in Afghanistan, I perceive.' (Open Tues-Fri 10am-4pm.)

THE EXECUTIONER'S BELL OF ST SEPULCHRE-WITHOUT-NEWGATE

For whom the death bell tolls

Holborn Viaduct, EC1A 2DQ
11am-3pm, although occasionally closed for concerts
Admission free
St Paul's or Chancery Lane tube, Farringdon tube or rail, City Thameslink rail

St Sepulchre Church is one of the 'cockney bells' of London. It's immortalized in the nursery rhyme 'Oranges and Lemons' as the 'bells of Old Bailey', the nickname for the Central Criminal Court across the road. The latter was formerly the site of the infamous Newgate prison (see p. 120), thankfully demolished in 1902. This rather plain church was rebuilt after the Great Fire, but subsequently butchered by the Victorians. The odd name refers to the church's position outside London Wall, specifically at Newgate, which was the north-western entrance to the City.

The area between the prison and church became London's execution ground when the gallows was moved from Tyburn in 1783. Eighteenth-century London law was bloodthirsty. Over 350 crimes were punishable by death, but by 1861 only treason, piracy, mutiny and murder were capital offences. Public executions were still hugely popular events – in 1840, Charles Dickens witnessed one along with 40,000 other spectators, including William Thackeray – but in 1868, the gallows was moved inside the prison.

The tenor bell at St Sepulchre-without-Newgate was rung for an impending execution. The hand-held 'execution bell,' still in the church, was also rung between the 17th and 19th centuries. A clerk would pace outside the cells of the condemned, ringing the bell and reciting the following 'wholesome advice' three times:

Prepare you, for tomorrow you will die.
Watch all, and pray, the hour is drawing near
That you before th' Almighty must appear.
Examine well yourselves, in time repent,
That you may not t' eternal flames be sent;
And when St Sepulchre's bell tomorrow tolls,
The Lord have mercy on your souls!

A pious, or possibly ghoulish, merchant named Robert Dove gave £40 to the parish in 1604 to ensure that this gruesome ritual was performed in perpetuity.

Bouquets at the Old Bailey

Trials at the Old Bailey are open to the public, but you cannot reserve a seat. Queuing for the public gallery starts at about 9.30am. A list of trials is published outside the main gate; Court One is generally where the most notorious trials are set. One tradition that has survived since the Old Bailey was located in the grounds of Newgate prison is that the judges carry a bunch of flowers at the start of each session, a practice initiated as a feeble attempt to mask the noxious stench from the cells.

THE GOLDEN BOY OF PYE CORNER

Glutton who got the rap for the Great Fire ⑲

Cock Lane and Giltspur Street, EC1A 9DD
St Paul's tube, Farringdon tube or rail

This Boy is
in Memmory Put up
for the late FIRE of
LONDON
Occasion'd by the

High above the corner of Cock Lane and Giltspur Street is a gilded statue of a fat little boy that marks the limits of the Great Fire of London.

The Golden Boy was erected to put an end to the conflicting theories surrounding the cause of the Great Fire. At first, the Fire was blamed on a deranged French silversmith called Robert Hubert after he made a confession. He was promptly executed, but it was later discovered that he had arrived in the country two days after the fire started. William Lilly, a famous astrologer who predicted a fire the year before, almost went to the scaffold with the unfortunate Hubert, but talked his way out of it in front of a special committee at the House of Commons.

The Catholics were the next to get the rap. Eventually, the City Elders decided to blame the fire on the sin of gluttony. To make their point, they inscribed the pudgy effigy thus: 'The Boy at Pye Corner was erected to commemorate the staying of the Great Fire which beginning at Pudding Lane was ascribed to the sin of gluttony when not attributed to the Papists as on the Monument, and the Boy was made prodigiously fat to enforce the moral.'

The site of the Golden Boy used to be home to The Fortunes of War, a pub favoured by 'resurrection men' who sold corpses to the anatomists at St Bartholomew's hospital over the road. The corpses – fresh from the road, the river, or occasionally the grave – were exhibited in an upstairs room by the landlord, labelled with the finder's name.

The only public statue of Henry VIII in London

Further down the street, another prodigiously fat boy is immortalised in stone. Henry VIII, at his most whale-like, glowers above the Henry Gate entrance to St Bartholomew's Hospital. Topped with a strange little crown and wearing a codpiece that draws the eye, this is the only public statue of Henry VIII in London.

LONDON'S FIRST DRINKING FOUNTAIN

Replace the cup

Corner of Giltspur Street and Holborn Viaduct, EC1A 2DQ
St Paul's tube, Farringdon tube/rail, City Thameslink rail

As well as an execution site for heretics and dissidents, Smithfield meat market was once a slaughterhouse. The anxious herds awaiting the butcher's blade were at least granted a drink of water at the cattle trough on West Smithfield. The trough bears the logo of the Metropolitan Drinking Fountain and Cattle Trough Association, 'the only agency for providing free supplies of water for man and beast in the streets of London', according to early advertisements. The association was established in 1859 by Samuel Gurney, an MP alarmed by the insalubrious quality of London's drinking water after Dr John Snow (see p. 52) had identified it as the source of a cholera outbreak. Down the road from Smithfield, on the corner of Giltspur Street and Holborn Viaduct, is London's first drinking fountain. It's an inconspicuous red granite memorial to Gurney's philanthropy, set into the railings of St Sepulchre Church. The church was keen to be seen as a patron of the poor – and to provide an antidote to beer.

Huge crowds gathered for the fountain's inauguration on 21 April 1859. Mrs Wilson, daughter of the Archbishop of Canterbury, was the first to taste the water from a silver cup. The filtered water came from the New River (see p. 326). The inscription urges thirsty passers-by to 'REPLACE THE CUP'. Today, in less trusting times, the two original (somewhat mildewed) metal mugs are fastened to the railings with chains. By 1870, the Drinking Fountain Association had installed 140 fountains in London. Many of them have also survived.

The Geffrye Museum (see p. 157) contains an impression of the original fountain, which was more elaborate, painted by W.A. Atkinson in 1860.

Miniature bluecoats

On the corner of Hatton Garden and St Cross Street, embedded into the façade of an office building, stand the twee statuettes of a boy holding a cap and Bible and a girl who seems to be clutching a shopping list. These figurines, which are found across London, signal that this was once a charitable "blewcoat" school for underprivileged girls and boys. In Tudor and Stuart times, blue clothes were the mark of the lower classes as blue was the cheapest dye available. This school, dating from 1690, was probably designed by Christopher Wren. The 18th-century figurines were stowed away in Berkshire for safekeeping during the Blitz – a wise move, as the building was damaged by bombs.

NEWGATE CELLS

Not your average cellar

Beneath the Viaduct Tavern, 126 Newgate Street, EC1A 7AA
www.viaducttavern.co.uk
Mon-Fri 8.30am-11.30pm
Admission free
St Paul's tube, City Thameslink rail

Eighteenth- and nineteenth-century London was obsessed with imprisonment and punishment. Capital crimes included impersonating an Egyptian (a gypsy), stealing an heiress, or poaching a rabbit, and as a result punishment centres flourished. Tate Britain is built on the site of Millbank prison, which was eventually closed because inmates tiresomely kept dying.

Little remains of the infamous Newgate prison, the city's main jail for almost five centuries. Originally located by a medieval gate in the Roman London Wall, it was extended over the years, and remained in use between 1188 and 1902, with its last incarnation built in an *'architecture terrible'* style intended to discourage law-breaking. The Central Criminal Courts now stand on the site. However, if you go into the Viaduct Tavern and ask nicely when it's not too busy, the staff will show you cells that survived the prison's closure.

The underground cells still look like the real deal. Although the pub owners have hung prints in the passage down to the cells, there is no suggestion of a tourist recreation. One of the cells is popular with ghost hunters, but you don't need to be psychic to sniff out the misery. The cells are genuinely horrible: cold, damp and dark. Up to twenty criminals – usually debtors – were crammed into each one. There was no toilet; one jailer described the stench as being bad enough to choke a horse. The only daylight came from a tube leading to street level, used by relatives or sympathetic passers-by to drop down scraps of food. Because prisons were privately run, prisoners had to pay for the privilege of being locked up – or starve to death.

Wealthy prisoners could opt for private cells, complete with regular visits from prostitutes. Even more grisly is the old cell for the condemned across the road at the Old Bailey. This was larger than normal cells, as those waiting to be hanged received more visitors. The corridor leading from the cell to the scaffold is increasingly narrow, making it harder for the condemned to turn and run. A sinister example of form and function in architecture.

In contrast, the Viaduct Tavern itself is a beautiful Victorian pub, with a wrought copper ceiling and a triptych of oils representing the four statues of Commerce, Agriculture, Science and Fine Arts on nearby Holborn Viaduct. The floor above allegedly housed an opium den in the 19th century.

THE MEMORIAL TO HEROIC SELF-SACRIFICE

Epitaphs for everyday heroes

Postman's Park, King Edward Street, EC1A 4AS
www.postmanspark.org.uk
Open during daylight hours
St Paul's or Barbican tube

Thrillingly gruesome or horribly sad (or just plain horrible) depending on your point of view, these memorials line one side of Postman's Park, named after the General Post Office on its southern boundary. Set up by G.F. Watts and unveiled in 1900 for Queen Victoria's Jubilee, they memorialise fatal acts of heroism by ordinary Londoners.

The descriptions of these acts are full-blooded, with lots of children, burning, drowning, and train accidents. The earliest death commemorated was pantomime artiste Sarah Smith, who 'died of terrible injuries received when attempting in her inflammable dress to extinguish the flames which had enveloped her companion' in 1863. Eight-year-old Henry Bristow is the youngest, who 'saved his little sister's life by tearing off her flaming clothes but caught fire himself and died of burns and shock'. John Cranmer Cambridge 'was drowned near Ostend whilst saving the life of a stranger and a foreigner', presumably the same person.

The thought, or hope, of heroism like this is pleasing. The ceramics of the memorial are a homely counterpoint to the marble statues of war heroes in the capital.

The glazed tiles, bearing decorative motifs reminiscent of William Morris, were made at the famous Doulton factory, still in operation today.

Watts hoped to see similar memorials erected in every town in England. Ever the optimist, he left lots of space on the walls of the park so people could continue to put up tablets. He died in 1904, passing the running of the memorial over to his wife Alice. By the time she died, only 53 of the planned 120 tiles were completed. However, in 2009, the first new tile in 78 years was unveiled: 'Leigh Pitt, Reprographic Operator, Aged 30, saved a drowning boy from the canal at Thamesmead, but sadly was unable to save himself'.

England's Michelangelo

Watts, a noted Victorian painter dubbed 'England's Michelangelo,' was outspokenly socialist. He declared in a letter to the *Times* of London that 'the national prosperity of a Nation is not an abiding possession, the deeds of its people are.' This progressive ideology was the inspiration for his memorial.

POLICE CALL BOX

23

Kiosks for coppers

St Martin Le Grand, EC1A 4EU
St Paul's tube

The BBC's perennially popular hero, Doctor Who, journeys through space and time in his TARDIS, a time machine that looks like a blue telephone box. The TARDIS has now entered British parlance as a synonym for something that appears deceptively small, but contains hidden depths. A few of these mysterious blue boxes have survived on the streets of London, like this disused signal post outside Postman's Park (see p. 74).

Before the advent of the walkie-talkie and the mobile phone, British 'bobbies' on the beat relied on these police boxes to report crimes, request back-up, or even to lock up a suspect until a patrol car arrived. If the blue light on the roof was flashing, passing officers would pop in to call the nearest station then hotfoot it to the crime scene. The phones also served as emergency hotlines for the public.

The first wooden police boxes appeared in Britain in 1888. They cost a trifling £13 to build and were equipped with a desk, log book, first aid kit, fire extinguisher and electric heater. No doubt they also contained a kettle in case coppers wanted a cuppa. In 1929, Gilbert Mackenzie Trench devised a sturdier concrete design. With sirens replacing the flashing lights, they doubled as air raid warning signals during World War II. By 1953, there were 685 police boxes in London; but technology soon rendered them obsolete and in 1969 the Home Secretary ordered their removal.

Very few police posts have survived in London, most of them in the City. You can locate them on Victoria Embankment (opposite Middle Temple Lane), at the corner of Queen Victoria and Friday Street, on Walbrook (opposite Bucklersbury), in Guildhall Yard, outside St Botolph Church in Aldgate, outside Liverpool Street station, and on Aldersgate Street near Little Britain. Look out for other survivors on Piccadilly Circus and outside the US Embassy on Grosvenor Square. Ironically, the latter is not locked and is still in working order, despite the heavy 24-hour police presence.

In 1996, a brand new police box appeared on Earl's Court Road, outside the tube station. In keeping with the Metropolitan Police's obsession with surveillance, it was fitted with a CCTV camera, allegedly to scare off prank callers. Plans to distribute similar boxes throughout London were abandoned. Perhaps it was no coincidence that this box materialised soon after the BBC attempted to copyright the TARDIS for merchandising purposes.

24

THE BREAD BASKET BOY

An enigmatic statue

Panyer Alley, EC1M 8AD
St Paul's tube

Smokers huddled outside Café Nero and commuters dashing in and out of St Paul's tube station are oblivious to the naked boy perched on a bread basket who watches over them, proffering what appears to be a bunch of grapes. Beneath this little stone relief is a weathered inscription: 'When ye have sought the citty round yet still this is the highest ground. August the 27, 1688.' This couplet does not make much sense in reference to its current location, a decidedly flat passage running between the tube station and St Paul's churchyard; however, the statue originally stood in Paternoster Row. When the building on which he sat was demolished in 1892, the boy was moved to Farrows Bank on Cheapside as its mascot. The baker boy's luck must have run out, because the bank folded in 1930.

In 1964, the statue was moved to this innocuous alley, which was once the centre of London's baking business. Panyer Alley was named after the boys who sold their wares from baskets, or panniers, after a law was passed in the 14th century forbidding the sale of bread in bakers' houses; it could only be sold in the king's markets. Bakers bypassed the law by selling loaves in baskets on the streets. As commuters rush past, croissants in hand, they should spare a thought for the bread peddlers of bygone years.

NEARBY

Christchurch Greyfriars Garden (25)

Newgate Street & King Edward Street, EC1A 7BA

A stone's throw from St Paul's cathedral, this peculiar little rose garden is contained within the bombed-out walls of a derelict church. This was the site of a Franciscan monastery in the Middle Ages, whose monks were so devout that folk believed that anyone buried in their grey robes would go straight to heaven. Perhaps that is why four queens chose to be buried in the church, before it burned down in the Great Fire. Christopher Wren soon set to work on a new church, which was completed in 1704. But German bombs destroyed Wren's handiwork in 1940, leaving only the west tower standing. This small rose garden matches the floor plan of Wren's church. On either side of the central aisle are hedges and flowerbeds where the pews once stood; the ten wooden towers covered with climbing roses and clematis represent the pillars which held up the roof.

The garden is said to be haunted by the ghost of Queen Isabella, the ruthless French princess who allegedly murdered her bisexual husband, King Edward II, by sticking a red hot poker up his bum. Avoid visiting after dark.

ST PAUL'S TRIFORIUM

Backstage at the cathedral

St Paul's Cathedral, Ludgate Hill, EC4
0207 246 8357
www.stpauls.co.uk
Mon, Tues 11.30am and 2pm, Fri 2pm
Other times by prior arrangement; booking essential
Check website for admission details
St Paul's tube

St Paul's is hardly a London secret; however, the triforium of the cathedral is relatively unknown to the public, and with a little planning can be toured. A triforium is usually a gallery of arches between the inner and outer wall of a church, standing high above the nave. This wall space can be huge, and in effect is a secret passage running the length of a wall.

The triforia (one on each side) in St Paul's are wide and full of surprises. The effect is like being backstage in a theatre. Furnishings and props from the cathedral are stored there, including two old pulpits, one a Victorian monster of coloured marble that looks as if it was looted from an Italian church. They are linked by a passageway across the western entrance to the cathedral, with a full view down the length of the nave.

There's also a row of electric trumpets, installed for royal visits. However, they apparently sound like the opening of the gates of hell, so when the Queen visits, a more discreet fanfare of live trumpeters herald her arrival from the balcony.

The glory of the triforium lies in two rooms on either side of the church. One is the library, a bibliophile's fantasy – wood-lined, comfortable, quiet, and heavily decorated by master woodcarver Grinling Gibbons in the 18th century. The other is the Trophy Room: Nelson's prizes were displayed here after his death. Now, it houses an extraordinary collection relating to the cathedral's construction, including Wren's Great Model, an earlier design based on a Greek cross with an extra dome.

Other treasures are plentiful: parts of the old cathedral that was destroyed by fire in 1666, and a bust of Dean Inge, nicknamed 'The Gloomy Dean' and apparently given to reading detective novels during service. The geometric staircase inside the great clock tower that leads up to the triforium is also astonishing. Each step is supported only by its predecessor and a four-inch join with the wall, which accounts for its nickname, the Flying Staircase.

Influenced by the Baroque, Wren's original plan for St Paul's was far more European. However, it looked a little too papal to London's puritanical Church Commissioners, and Wren was forced to redraw the cathedral along more conventional lines. Several drafts and models line the Trophy Room, including the 'Pineapple', which would have given London a very early version of the Swiss Re building, better known as Norman Foster's 'gherkin'.

DR JOHNSON'S HOUSE

Home to a harmless drudge

17 Gough Square, EC4A 3DE
0207 353 3745
www.drjohnsonshouse.org
Oct-April Mon-Sat 11am-5pm, May-Sept Mon-Sat 11am-5.30pm
Closed on Sundays and Bank Holidays
Check website for admission prices
Blackfriars, Temple, Holborn or Chancery Lane tube. City Thameslink,
Blackfriars or Farringdon rail

Londons loves Dr Johnson, who confirmed the superiority of the place: 'You find no man, at all intellectual, who is willing to leave London. No, Sir, when a man is tired of London, he is tired of life; for there is in London all that life can afford'.

However, like most people living here, 'Dictionary' Johnson wasn't a native, but from the Midlands city of Lichfield. He arrived in London in 1737 aged 28, after a disastrous career as a schoolteacher. He scraped a living for the next thirty years writing biographies, poetry, essays, pamphlets and parliamentary reports, and most famously his dictionary, which he compiled in the garret of this house in Gough Square. It took him nearly nine years to complete all 42,773 entries, with the help of five or six assistants. Perhaps it took so long because Johnson, who defined a lexicographer as 'a harmless drudge', rarely got out of bed before noon.

The house, where Johnson lived between 1748 and 1759, is a little hard to find among the surrounding maze of courtyards and passages. It is one of the few remnants of Georgian London left in the City. Built in 1700, it fell into disarray and was used variously as a hotel, a print shop, and a storehouse, until it was eventually acquired in 1911 by MP Cecil Harmsworth, who restored and opened it to the public. The lovely, delicate interior is characteristic of the era, with panelled rooms and a collection of period furniture, prints and portraits. The Curator's House next door is allegedly the smallest residential building in the Square Mile.

Dr Johnson was famously fond of cats. There is a statue of Hodge, his black cat, in the square outside the house, perched on a dictionary beside a couple of empty oyster shells. Johnson would go out personally to buy oysters for his favourite feline, rather than risk his servants resenting the cat if they were dispatched to fetch his supper.

John Wilkes, rake and radical

Johnson didn't choose this house by accident. It lies close to Fetter Lane and Fleet Street, historically London's hotbed of journalism. On Fetter Lane, look out for the flattering statue of Johnson's contemporary John Wilkes, an incendiary radical, journalist and politician who was famously hideous but also had a rake's reputation (he claimed it 'took him only half an hour to talk away his face'). Wilkes' writing made him many enemies in the monarchy and government, yet thanks to popular support he was largely able to resist imprisonment.

FOUNTAIN COURT

Literary oasis in a legal maze

Middle Temple, EC4Y 9AT
Chancery Lane or Temple tube

The cooling waters of Fountain Court are a perfect place to rest after exploring the City. This hidden square is in the Middle Temple, part of the labyrinthine legal district known as the Inns of Court, which were set up on the remains of properties belonging to the Knights Templar in the 14th century. Middle Temple (and the neighbouring Inner Temple) is one of the few remaining liberties, historically not governed by the City of London Corporation and outside the ecclesiastical jurisdiction of the Bishop of London – the City of London Police have policed the Temples since 1857 by consent rather than by imposition.

There has been a small fountain here for around three hundred years. Once surrounded by railings, the fountain now stands free. A single jet of water rises some ten feet, dropping into a basin full of goldfish. The courtyard's name may also derive from one Sir Edward de la Fontaigne, who owned a house in the Temple.

Literary landmark

Fountain Court turns up regularly in connection with literary London. Charles Dickens uses it in *Martin Chuzzlewit* as the meeting-place between Ruth Pinch and her lover. Irish playwright Oliver Goldsmith lived close by, at No. 2 Garden Court, in a house that has long since disappeared. And Paul Verlaine stayed here while he was giving lectures in England after his release from prison in Belgium.

NEARBY

St Brides' Church ㉙

St Brides' Church has historically served as the journalists' church, thanks to its proximity to Fleet Street. Its multi-tiered steeple is also said to be the inspiration for the modern wedding cake, after a local cake-maker, Thomas Rich, created a replica in icing. Literary parishioners of St Brides include John Milton, Dr Johnson and Samuel Pepys, London's most famous diarist.

Middle Temple Hall ㉚

The large gothic building at the edge of Fountain Court is Middle Temple Hall, where Shakespeare's acting troupe, the Chamberlain's Men, gave the first recorded performance of *Twelfth Night* in 1602, with Shakespeare himself in the cast. Finished in 1573, and with a spectacular hammer beam ceiling, its remains almost unchanged having survived the Great Fire and both World Wars. Tours of the hall are available, but for a minimum of ten people – call or check website to arrange (www.middletemple.org.uk, 0207 427 4820).

THE CHARNEL HOUSE
AT ST BRIDE'S

Down among the dead men

Fleet Street, EC4Y 8AU
www.stbrides.com
Mon–Fri 8am–6pm, Sat 10am–3.30pm, Sun 10am–6.30pm
Guided tours (the only way to view the Charnel House) are on Tuesdays at
2.15pm (with a fee)
Admission free
Blackfriars tube

St Bride's, at the bottom of Fleet Street, has a number of claims to fame. Widely known as the Journalists' Church, its tiered spire was also the prototype for the modern wedding cake: local baker Thomas Rich made a pile of money with the design from his nearby bakery on Ludgate Hill.

The current church, reckoned to be the eighth version, is a Wren design that was bombed out in the Blitz, and then rebuilt using clear glass and less furniture. This means the interior is lighter and airier than most Wren churches in the capital.

When Wren rebuilt using the footprint of the previous church, he raised the floor level and added a crypt where the wealthier parishioners could be buried. This is now a museum, mostly of the history of the church and its links with Fleet Street. There is some medieval stained glass, an iron coffin designed to deter grave robbers, and allegedly you

can hear the buried river Fleet flowing nearby, but if you take the guided tour you get to see the spooky stuff.

St Bride's still has its charnel house. These were repositories of old bones from the churchyard that were tidied away in preparation for the Resurrection. Almost all of the bones in the house are skulls and long bones, so presumably God will fill in the gaps when the trumpets sound and the dead rise. They were moved to make room for fresh burials; unless you were wealthy enough to pay for burial in the church, you'd eventually end up here. It was possible to hurry the process – Samuel Pepys paid to have bones moved from the churchyard so his brother could be buried somewhere nice. The practice only stopped with the arrival of coffin burials, which drastically slowed decomposition and led to rapid overcrowding; before this, everyone was buried in a shroud and returned to the earth at speed. The church has a bone collection from the crypt burials, all in individual cardboard boxes with disconcerting labels like "skull", "mandible", "hair".

The church is also well known for its music and has an excellent choir and organist.

They would build a pub for themselves

Right next to the churchyard is a pub called the Old Bell Tavern, which from Fleet Street doesn't look that special, but in fact, has a lovely old interior from the same era as the church. Apparently, whenever workmen started on a Wren church, they would build a pub for themselves before anything else. Admirable stuff.

MAGPIE ALLEY CRYPT

Relics of a medieval monastery

Between Bouverie Street and Whitefriars Street, EC4Y 8JJ
Blackfriars tube

Back in the 13th century, the Carmelite order of the White Friars – so called because they wore white cloaks over their drab brown habits on special occasions – owned a swathe of land that contained cloisters, a church, and cemetery and stretched all the way from Fleet Street to the Thames. All that remains is this crumbling crypt from the late 14th century, now trapped behind glass and hemmed in by the dark granite fortress of a modern office building.

Whitefriars Monastery was one of the few buildings that survived the 1381 Peasants Revolt unscathed. However, Henry VIII pulled the plug on the priory in the mid-16th century and appropriated most of the monks' property for his doctor, William Butte. The great hall was converted into the Whitefriars Playhouse, a theatre for child actors, and the crypt was used as a coal cellar. The area soon degenerated into a seedy slum, nicknamed 'Alsatia' after Alsace, the territory disputed by France and Germany. Outlaws on the run sought refuge in the monastic crypt, exploiting the legal immunity once enjoyed by the friars.

The crypt lay buried for centuries until it was unearthed in 1895, but it was not restored until the 1920s when the *News of the World* moved in. The *Daily News*, *Punch*, *News Chronicle*, *Daily Mirror*, and the *Sun* all once had their offices in Bouverie Street. Just as little trace of the publishing industry remains, there is no sign to alert visitors to the crypt's existence. Walk down Bouverie Street and turn into Magpie Alley (where the monks' dormitories once stood). At the end of the alley is a courtyard; go down two flights of stairs on the left to the basement where you will find the crypt. A fake lantern burns in the doorway day and night.

Magpie Alley murals

Printed onto the white tiles of Magpie Alley, a series of black and white photographs, illustrations, and captions tell the potted history of Fleet Street's publishers. From Wynkyn de Worde's first primitive printing press, set up around 1500, to the grubby tabloid newsrooms of the 1960s, Fleet Street was synonymous with the newspaper industry until the acrimonious exodus to Wapping in 1986. Beaming paper boys on bicycles, bearing posters of the day's headlines – 'Burglars with dynamite in Holborn!' – seem far more sophisticated than the hawkers thrusting free trash at today's harried commuters.

TWO TEMPLE PLACE

Astor's inner sanctum

Two Temple Place, WC2R 3BD
0207 836 3715
www.twotempleplace.org
Annual exhibition runs Jan-April. Group tours are available during the exhibition
and on specified dates throughout the year. To book a tour, contact Alex Edwards on
0207 240 6044 or email Alexandra@bulldogtrust.org. Annual Friends membership
includes a tour of the building and a private view of the exhibition
Admission free
Temple tube

This mansion overlooking Victoria Embankment only recently opened to the public on a regular basis. Next to Middle Temple, you could easily mistake it for an extension of the Inns of Court. Though undeniably impressive, the crenellated Portland stone façade looks almost plain compared to the elaborate craftsmanship inside. A clue to the original owner sails above the roof: a golden weathervane of the *Santa Maria*, the ship on which Columbus set sail to 'discover' America.

Completed in 1895, this was the estate office of William Waldorf Astor, one of the world's richest men. When Astor quit New York for London, he wanted an HQ that reflected his status, ancestry and personal passions. He persuaded John Loughborough Pearson to take on the project, with the promise of 'a free hand to erect a perfect building irrespective of cost'. Pearson blew £250,000 (equivalent to £10 million today) of Astor's fortune. It was money well spent.

The front door is lit by two bronze lamps, draped with cherubs chatting on the telephone and waving light bulbs, an allusion to the new-fangled apparatus inside. A hybrid of Tudor, Gothic Revivalist and Renaissance styles, the interior works surprisingly well. From the floor inlaid with coloured marble and precious stones to the stained glass skylight, the Staircase Hall takes your breath away. The mahogany balustrade is punctuated by statues of Astor's literary heroes, the Three Musketeers. On the landing, ten ebony columns support carved scenes from Shakespeare and American classics like *The Scarlet Letter* and *The Last of the Mohicans*.

Astor's oak-panelled library is fitted with secret cupboards and a hidden door so that he could surprise visitors in the meeting room. 'Ornamental' is an understatement. There's a medieval hammer-beam ceiling, twin inglenooks decorated with stained-glass landscapes, and a gilded frieze of 50 of Astor's favourite real and fictional characters, from Machiavelli to Martin Luther.

Like Scrooge McDuck, Astor kept bags of gold sovereigns in three different strongrooms. After his wife died, Astor slept in a four-poster bed next to the safe. Though intensely private and pernickety, Astor was desperate to infiltrate the British aristocracy. He donated vast sums to charity and the Conservative Party. His generosity paid off: two years before he died, he became Lord Astor.

Now owned by The Bulldog Trust, an incubator for charities, Two Temple Place hosts excellent winter exhibitions drawn from the collections of regional British galleries and museums.

ROMAN BATH

Not Roman. Not a Bath

5 Strand Lane, WC2R 1AP
Temple tube

Strand Lane allegedly follows a stream that once ran from Drury Lane to the Thames. Today, it is a dingy cul-de-sac littered with rubbish bins, wedged among the grand old buildings of Victoria embankment and the inevitable construction sites of 21st-century London. Ignore the nastiness of the alley; half way up, you will find a street sign confirming that this is, indeed, Strand Lane. At the end, on your right, behind a dirty window is a sunken brick tank that 19th-century Londoners desperately wanted to believe was a Roman bath. However, it now seems likely that it is the remains of a cistern that fed a spectacular fountain in the neighbouring gardens of Somerset House, which was refurbished and extended for James I's queen, Anne of Denmark, in the early 17th century.

Flick on the light switch (and hope that it's working) and peer through the window. You can't see much: the remains of an old plunge pool in a vaulted room, although it's possible to visit on Open House Days, and the National Trust is seeking to widen access beyond this.

The myth of the Roman Bath is pervasive. In 1854, author Charles Knight wrote of an 'old Roman spring bath' and suggested its healing waters came from the Holy Well of St Clement. In the late 19th century, its proprietor boasted that it 'is known to be the most pure and healthy bath in London, ensuring every comfort and convenience to those availing themselves of this luxury.' At the time, a spring fed the bath with ten tons of fresh water a day. Charles Dickens subjected David Copperfield to several icy plunges here.

NEARBY

An abandoned Underground station ㉟

Closed since 1994, the ox-blood red brick façade of Aldwych Underground still stands on the corner of the Strand and Surrey Street. During the Second World War, the station was used as an air-raid shelter, while the Elgin Marbles and other treasures from the British Museum were stashed away in its tunnels. Today, the abandoned station is often featured in film shoots, from *Patriot Games* to *V for Vendetta*. One platform allegedly serves as a rifle range for the King's College shooting club. Access to the public is denied, but visits can sometimes be arranged through the London Transport Museum (www.ltmuseum.co.uk).

Camel benches ㊱

Along Victoria embankment are benches with front row views of the River Thames that are worth a closer look: each end is decorated with a sculpted camel, complete with a golden tassel around its neck. The decoration probably refers to the short-lived Imperial Camel Corps, formed in 1916 to serve in the Middle East.

TWININGS TEA MUSEUM

Teapots and tips

216 Strand, WC2R 1AP
0207 353 3511
www.twinings.com
Mon-Fri 9.30am-7pm, Sat 10am-5pm, Sun 10.30am-16.30pm
Admission free
Temple tube

Drinking tea may be as quintessentially British as sinking pints on a Friday night, but the tradition of taking tea originated in China back in 2737 BC. This heritage is hinted at in the exotic façade of Twinings tea shop on the Strand, with the figures of two Chinamen draped over the doorway.

Thomas Twining bought Tom's Coffee House in 1706 on a site behind the existing shop. Ironically, tea was first introduced to London society at the city's disreputable coffee houses. Competition between the coffee houses was fierce, with fresh ideas needed to keep the business alive. The difference at Tom's was tea, although Twinings still stocks coffee among the packets of Earl Grey and English Breakfast. With success came expansion. By 1717, Thomas had acquired three adjacent houses and converted them into the shop that stands on the Strand today.

Thankfully, prices have dropped since the early 18th century, when tea cost the equivalent of £160 for 100g. At the back of this fragrant little shop, fetchingly decorated with portraits of the Twinings dynasty through the ages, is a small museum. The collection includes a copy of Queen Victoria's Royal Warrant from 1837 (Twinings has supplied every successive British monarch since), antique tea caddies, invoices and advertisements. The most remarkable exhibit is a plain wooden box bearing the initials T.I.P. – short for "To Insure Promptness". Patrons of coffee-houses would drop a few pennies into these boxes to encourage swifter service – the origins of the modern-day "tip".

> If you'd like to go deeper into tea, Twinings opened a Loose Tea Bar at their flagship store in 2013. It offers a variety of masterclasses and tasting sessions that include the etiquette of taking tea in the UK. Call the store to book.

NEARBY
Lloyds Bank Law Courts Branch (38)

In 1825, the Twining family branched out into banking. Twinings Bank merged with Lloyds Bank in 1892; their joint venture at 215 Strand (now Lloyds Bank, Law Courts Branch) is surely the most flamboyant bank in London. The ceramic beehive above the intricate wrought-iron entrance is the first clue that this is no ordinary depository. The foyer is clad in a kaleidoscope of green, white and gold Doulton tiles, punctuated with fluted columns, gilded fish and gleaming marble basins. Built in 1883, this was originally The Royal Courts of Justice Restaurant; the gaudy décor must have made diners vaguely nauseous, as the restaurant closed shortly afterwards.

HUNTERIAN MUSEUM

Frankenstein's torture chamber

Royal College of Surgeons, 35-43 Lincoln's Inn Fields, WC2A 3PE
0207 405 3474
www.rcseng.ac.uk/museums
Tues-Sat 10am-5pm
Admission free
Holborn tube

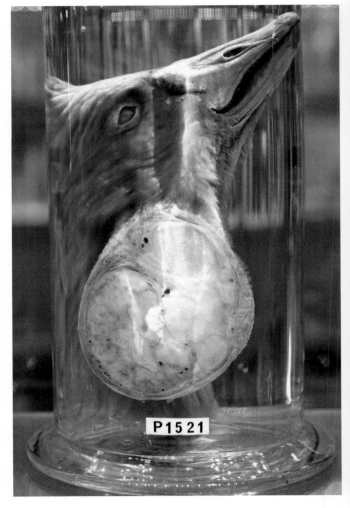

Originally part of the medieval guild of Barber-Surgeons, the Royal College of Surgeons houses two museums: the Wellcome Museum (only open to medical practitioners and students), and the Hunterian, based on the eminent 18th-century surgeon John Hunter's gruesome collection of comparative anatomy and pathology specimens.

Hunter started out as an assistant in the anatomy school of his elder brother, William. A fast learner with a knack for the dissection of the dead, John Hunter developed new treatments for common ailments such as gunshot wounds and venereal disease. An avid collector, he moved to a large house in Leicester Square in 1783, where he organised his collection into a museum. (There is still a statue of him in the square). A notorious curmudgeon, Hunter became the leading teacher of surgery of his time. Success did not mellow him: he died in 1793 after suffering a fit during an argument.

His collection was then bought by the government in 1799, and became part of the Museum of the Royal College of Surgeons when it opened in 1813. By the end of the 19th century, the museum comprised some 65,000 specimens covering anatomy and pathology, zoology, palaeontology, archaeology and anthropology. Today, the museum contains skeletons, bones, skulls and teeth; alarming wax teaching models; historic surgical and dental instruments; paintings, drawings, and sculpture. Rows of random 'things' in glass jars lend the place the atmosphere of a Frankenstein movie.

The skeleton of a 7'7" giant

In the 18th century, surgeons were widely regarded as butchers and the museum still has one foot in the seamier past of the anatomy trade. One of the centrepieces of Hunter's collection is the skeleton of Charles O'Brien, an Irish giant who stood at 7'7" and caused a sensation at fairs and fetes nationwide. When O'Brien fell ill in 1782, Hunter haunted his sickbed. Knowing his body would be a great prize for the anatomist, O'Brien gave strict instructions that his corpse should be sealed in a lead coffin and paid some fishermen to bury him at sea. Hunter was not to be thwarted. After O'Brien's death, he paid the fishermen £500 for the corpse, which was then boiled in a copper vat so that only the bones remained. They are on display in the museum.

THE DEAD HOUSE

The riddle of the tombstones

Strand, WC2R 1L
0207 845 4600
www.somersethouse.org.uk
The Old Palaces Tour (includes access to Strand Lane Baths) takes place every
Tuesday at 12.45pm and 2.15pm. Historical Highlights of Somerset House Tour
takes place every Thursday at 1.15pm and 2.45pm and every Saturday
at 12.15pm, 1.15pm, 2.15pm and 3.15pm. Tickets are available, on the day
only, from the Information Desk in the Seamen's Waiting Hall
Admission free
Temple, Covent Garden or Embankment tube

With its skating rink in winter and jet fountains in summer, the magnificent courtyard of Somerset House throngs with visitors all year round. It's hard to believe it was closed to the public until 2000 and used as a car park for tax inspectors from the Inland Revenue (who still rent offices here). Besides the elegant Courtauld Institute galleries and Spring restaurant, this former palace contains layers of history that are revealed on fortnightly tours of Somerset House's Hidden Spaces.

Little remains of the original Somerset House, built in 1547 by Edward Seymour, Duke of Somerset and self-proclaimed protector of his nephew Edward VI, the under-age heir to Henry VIII. 'Uncle Eddy's big job gave him a big head, so now he needed a big house,' our American guide informed us. Seymour's ambition led to a sticky end. After his execution in 1552, Somerset House was used by a succession of queens as a venue for glitzy pageants until George III commissioned William Chambers to raze the riverside plot and put up a Palladian office block for government offices and learned societies. Above the arched entrance, Chambers built statues representing the four continents – the fifth had yet to be 'discovered' by the British.

The first tenant was the Navy Board, which stayed for 90 years, leaving a rich collection of nautical art and architectural flourishes such as Nelson's staircase, a cantilevered design that resembles the prow of a ship. Before Joseph Bazalgette built the Thames embankment (see p. 80), naval officers could access their HQ through an archway on the river and moor in what is now the courtyard. One of their gold and scarlet barges is parked in the basement.

Walking along the light well that surrounds Somerset House like a moat, you can see why it's popular for Jack the Ripper shoots. Spookiest of all is the Dead House, a damp, disused vault where five tombstones are inlaid in the walls. One of the deceased appears to be a Portuguese surgeon; another commemorates Father Hyacinth 'who died 1691½' (presumably this refers to the date, not his age). How and why they ended up there is a mystery. The theory goes that these were Roman Catholics employed by Queen Henrietta Maria, French wife of Charles I. She commissioned Inigo Jones to build her a Catholic chapel on this site in 1630 – the only one in England at the time. The queen also created a small Catholic cemetery in the grounds of Somerset House, where members of her household could be buried. These five tombs are, apparently, all that remain.

PATENT SEWER VENTILATING LAMP

The odyssey of 'Iron Lily'

Carting Lane, WC2R 0ET
Charing Cross, Embankment, or Temple tube

Now powered by conventional household gas, the ornate lamp post opposite the stage door of the Savoy Theatre was originally designed to burn methane waste from the sewage system. The Patent Sewer Ventilating lamp was invented by J.E. Webb, who realised that 'firedamp' from London's new-fangled sewage system could be recycled as a cheap source of energy and blended with the mains gas. Equipped with a hollow post to allow waste gas from the sewers running beneath the Thames Embankment to shoot up to the flame, the sewage lamp thus fulfilled two important functions: illuminating this scruffy back alley and burning off unpleasant smells for residents at the nearby Savoy Hotel. Little did these glamorous guests realise their effluents were being used to cast light on Carting Lane (otherwise known as Farting Lane).

Webb patented his sewage lamp in 1895, and sold around 2,500 of them worldwide, but their success was limited by the risk of stinky leaks and dangerous explosions from the highly combustible gasses. In 1950, a careless lorry driver backed into the light, thus destroying one of the last vestiges of Victorian ingenuity. 'Iron Lily' was restored and operates as the standard gas lamp that you see today.

London records

London's first gaslit street: Pall Mall (1807)
London's longest road: Western Avenue (11.3 miles)
London's smallest square: Pickering Place (see p. 58)
London's longest bridge: Waterloo (381 metres)
London's narrowest street: Brydges Place (15 inches wide)

The wrong-way street

Savoy Lane, a tiny street running from the Strand to the entrance of the Savoy Hotel, is the only street in Britain where traffic drives on the right. A law was introduced in 1902 so that carriages and cabs dropping people off at the Savoy Theatre next door would not block the hotel's entrance. This quirk dates back to the time when hansom cabs delivered guests to the hotel, but is just as useful today when most of the moneyed guests arrive in stretch limousines or black cabs, which are too big to turn around in such tight space. Drivers have to perform a U-turn to exit the street, staying on the right-hand side.

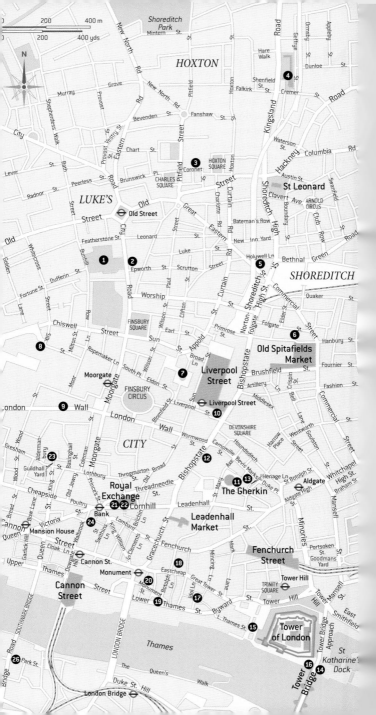

Tower Bridge to Shoreditch

BUNHILL FIELDS

Deliverance for dissenters

38 City Rd, EC1Y 2BG
0208 4723584
Oct-March Mon-Fri 7.30am–4pm, Sat-Sun 9.30am-4pm,
April-Sept Mon-Fri 7.30am-7pm, Sat-Sun 9.30am-4pm
Admission free
Old Street tube/rail

Bunhill Fields is the site of a small graveyard to the north of the old City Wall. Bunhill supposedly derives from Bone Hill: around the year 1549, the charnel house (or bone deposit) of St Paul's was cleared for new burials, and over a thousand cartloads of bones were dumped here, on what was damp, marshy ground – enough to provide foundations for three new windmills.

In 1665, the City of London Corporation decided to use the land as a burial ground for those who could not be buried in conventional churchyards, primarily plague victims. Enclosing walls for the cemetery were built, but it seems to have never been consecrated and as a result became popular with Nonconformist Protestants who practiced outside the orthodoxy of the Church of England.

Catholic and Jewish Londoners who could afford the fees were also buried there. The list of burials in this small yard reads like a who's who of dissenters in London intellectual life – the visionary poet and painter William Blake, *Robinson Crusoe* author Daniel Defoe, anti-slavery philanthropist Thomas Fowell Buxton, and poet and hymn-writer Isaac Watts are the most noted examples. The London poet Robert Southey called it the 'Campo Santo of the Dissenters.'

The Fields were filled with 120,000 graves before being closed in 1853. Most of the graves are fenced off, but an on-site curator will happily escort you around any of them.

Abney Park Cemetery

In 1840, Nonconformist burials were moved to Abney Park in Stoke Newington, another graveyard well worth a visit – one of the original seven cemeteries circling London that include Nunhead and Kensal Green (see p. 380 and 200). The entrance to Abney Park is built in the Egyptian Revival style – a conscious decision, as it was the first cemetery in Europe explicitly designated as nondenominational, or with 'no invidious dividing lines,' according to the group of Nonconformists led by George Collison who founded it. The most famous internees are Catherine and William Booth, founders of the Salvation Army, but large numbers of abolitionists and 19th-century missionaries are typical residents. The overgrown park is full of mature woods now. It also contains one of the two UXBs (unexploded bombs) known in Stoke Newington, so don't go digging no holes!

JOHN WESLEY'S HOUSE

The Venerable Crapper

49 City Road, EC1Y 1AU
0207 253 2262
www.wesleyschapel.org.uk
Mon-Sat 10am-4pm, Sunday (for those attending morning worship) 12.30pm-1.45pm, Closed every Thursday between 12.45pm and 1.30pm (for service)
Admission free, donations welcome
Old Street or Moorgate tube

The world is my parish' pronounces the statue of John Wesley, founder of Methodism, in the courtyard of Wesley Chapel, a welcome refuge from the thrum of City Road. During his 88 years, Wesley lived up to his word, travelling a quarter of a million miles on horseback to deliver some 40,000 sermons.

From 1779 until his death in 1791, Wesley spent his winters in the compact Georgian townhouse beside the chapel. Though simple to the point of severity by today's standards, Wesley's three-storey home was fitted with all mod cons – wallpaper, built-in cupboards, and a fireplace in every room. New-fangled furniture included a 'cock fighting chair', to be straddled like a modern massage chair, with an adjustable easel for reading and writing. The bureau has secret compartments where Wesley hid correspondence from his jealous wife, Mary Vazielle.

Wesley was fond of his Chamber Horse, precursor of the exercise bike, a tall wooden chair with a springy seat that simulates riding a horse. Apparently, 'the vigorous bouncing would stimulate the liver'. Another example of Wesley's fascination with 'Primitive Physick' is the Electrical Machine, which administered electric shocks to cure depression, migraine, and all manner of ailments. Wesley did not try this out himself until he had experimented with his flock for a good three years.

Downstairs are a few of Wesley's personal possessions including a pair of 'straights', buckled shoes that could be worn on either foot, and his 'laptop' – a wooden writing case with quills and ink, which he would balance on his saddle, composing sermons as he trotted through the countryside.

In Wesley's day, the house had no running water. His chamber pot was concealed in a wooden box in his bedroom. But in 1899, Methodist ministers installed a fine set of gentlemen's toilets to serve the congregation at the chapel, which are miraculously intact. With their red-mottled marble urinals and a dressing room with frosted-glass partitions, these public conveniences must have been the height of Victorian hygiene. The mahogany cubicles contain original Thomas Crapper toilets, their rims imprinted with 'The Venerable' in red letters. The porcelain handle on the chain instructs users to: 'Pull and let go'.

A Museum of Methodism

In the crypt of John Wesley's Chapel next door is a small Museum of Methodism, which tells the history of this faction of the Anglican church, aimed at social outcasts and taught mainly by itinerant preachers.

CIRCUS SPACE

Electric acrobats

Coronet Street, N1 6HD
0207 613 4141
www.nationalcircus.org.uk
Open for classes and performances only
Admission varies
Old Street tube

Unbeknown to the poseurs pressed into Hoxton Square's style bars and galleries, a block away a bunch of less self-conscious Londoners tumble around in a huge, red brick building. In a former power station, the Circus Space, which offers the only university degree in circus skills in Britain (a Circus Arts BTEC, Foundation and BA Hons Degrees and Postgraduate Certificate, no less), is where aspiring acrobats and trapeze artists from all over Europe hone their skills. But plucky amateurs can also sign up for evening and weekend classes in tight-wire walking, trampoline, stilt-walking or trapeze.

The building had been derelict since the 1950s until a troupe of circus performers took it over as a rehearsal space in 1994. Thanks to a £1.2 million redevelopment, students now rehearse in post-industrial style in the vast, vaulted Chamber and Combustion Chamber.

Also worth a look out for are the student shows, usually held at the beginning of summer. Check the website early for availability.

NEARBY
The Geffrye Museum   ④
136 Kingsland Road, E2 8EA; www.geffrye-museum.org.uk

Due to reopen in Spring 2020 (check website for details), the Geffrye Museum is dedicated to the British living room. Housed in a row of 18th-century Grade I-listed almshouses that formerly belonged to the Ironmongers' Company, the museum contains a variety of recreated domestic spaces, from the oak panelled austerity of the Tudors to the flamboyance of the Victorians. Period music and other audio snippets help bring these stage sets to life. The remodelling is set to open up new spaces for exhibition, as well as increasing the size of the garden, adding a new cafe and allowing the Museum to offer more events.

VILLAGE UNDERGROUND ⑤

Mind the gap

54 Holywell Lane EC2A 3PQ
0207 422 7505
www.villageunderground.co.uk
Open occasionally for special events
Admission varies
Old Street tube

Avoid the Tube at all costs? Some Londoners pay good money to spend eight hours a day in a tube carriage. Mainly designers, architects, and film-makers, they share four Jubilee line carriages salvaged from the scrap heap and recycled as affordable offices for creative start-ups. 'I needed a studio space but couldn't afford one, so I figured I'd build my own,' shrugs furniture designer Auro Foxcroft, who spent four years realising his ambition. After persuading London Undergound to sell him four obsolete carriages for £500 each, Foxcroft spent two years searching for somewhere to park them. Eventually, the local council granted permission for the carriages to be hoisted onto a viaduct in Shoreditch, as long as Foxcroft renovated the derelict warehouse below it. Now this cavernous space – all brick vaults and skylights – has evolved into Village Underground, a non-profit space set up for everything from concerts and club nights to exhibitions, theatre, live art and other performances.

The four tube carriages are accessed via a vertiginous spiral staircase on the side of the building. The offices are private, but if you ask nicely, someone will show you around. They might even grill you a hot dog on the 'roof garden,' high above the traffic roaring down Great Eastern Street.

Foxcroft and architect Nicholas Laurent remodelled the carriages using eco-friendly features like biodegradable paint, reclaimed materials, and solar panels. They spent months dismantling the 'mad amount' of electronic wiring hidden under the seats. Otherwise, all the original fittings from 1983 are intact, including retro handles and 'No Smoking' signs. And the doors still open at the press of a button. Like all tube trains, they are a magnet for graffiti artists; one carriage is covered in around 50 layers of paint.

Village Undergound has opened a second outpost in Lisbon. Social entrepreneurship is harder to sustain in London, with property prices at a premium.

Walthamstow Pumphouse Museum

At Great Ormond Street children's hospital, a defunct tube carriage has been converted into a radio station for young patients. At Walthamstow Pumphouse Museum (www.e17pumphouse. org.uk), you can have dinner in a vintage Victoria line carriage, occasionally transformed into an 'underground' supper club by Basement Galley (www.basementgalley.com). The industrial pumps, steam engines, and Victorian fire-fighting equipment will excite small boys and engineering geeks.

DENNIS SEVERS' HOUSE

Still life

18 Folgate Street, E1 6BX
0207 247 4013
www.dennissevershouse.co.uk
12pm-2pm every Monday, 12pm-4pm every Sunday, 'Silent nights' 5pm-9pm
on Monday, Wednesday and Friday
Check website for admission details
Liverpool Street tube/rail

One house stands out among the spruce Georgian terraces of Folgate Street. With its flaming lantern and cutout silhouettes framed by crimson shutters, number 18 seems strangely detached from the commercial throb of nearby Bishopsgate, where City traders scurry about their business. When Dennis Severs, a Canadian artist, bought this ten-room house in the late 1970s, Spitalfields was a slum. He filled his dilapidated home with chipped antiques and anonymous portraits picked up from flea markets, determined to recreate an authentic 18th-century household. Armed with a candle and bedpan, Severs slept in every room, soaking up the energy and imagining the lives of its previous inhabitants. Gradually, these imaginary companions took shape as the Jervis family, Huguenot silk-weavers whose make-believe lives became an elaborate 'still life drama' for visitors to explore.

Although Severs died in 1999, visitors can still immerse themselves in his decaying fantasy world. Each room is designed to evoke a moment in time as experienced by successive generations of the Jervises from 1724 to 1914. The experience is an assault on the senses where every object is apparently charged with hidden meaning – not just a visual overload, but also the smells of ginger biscuits and mulled wine, the sounds of horse hooves, church bells, and whispered snatches of conversation. The effect is deliberately theatrical as you follow a trail of clues that suggest the ghostly presence of the Jervis clan – a half-eaten boiled egg and soldiers, a black cat asleep on an unmade bed, and what appears to be a chamber pot full of pee.

There is social commentary, too. In the gloomy servants' quarters, soiled white undergarments are strung between cobwebs, a blackened pot of mouldy cabbage sits beside a filthy hearth, and gunshots sound a death knell. It all conjures up a deeply bleak existence.

Sadly, the compelling atmosphere is punctured by patronising notes telling patrons to shut up and use their imagination. For example: 'A visit requires the same style of concentration as does an Old Masters exhibition, and a most absurd but commonly made error is to assume that it might be either amusing or appropriate for children.'

A young man still lives in the attic. Well, someone has to feed the cat and canaries.

BROADGATE ICE SKATING RINK ⑦

Skating with stockbrokers

Exchange Square, Broadgate Circus, EC2A 2BQ
0845 653 1424
www.broadgate.co.uk/ice-rink-london
Nov-Feb 10am-10pm
Check website for admission details
Liverpool Street tube / rail

Despite its location in the beating heart of investment banking, this is probably London's cheapest outdoor ice skating rink. Hemmed in by office blocks, the rink itself is not very big – around 22 square metres – and has less of the gimmickry or festive pageantry of its Christmas counterparts at Somerset House or Kew Gardens. Ringed by limestone steps and benches, it looks like a movie set dropped into the City. On weekdays, the ice rink tends to be empty except for a handful of teenage truants skidding around to an incongruous '80s soundtrack. Apart from the investment bankers who stare longingly at the skaters from their glass towers, few people seem to know it is here.

Broadgate Circus livens up considerably on Tuesday evenings, however, when broomball matches are held from 7-9pm. A kind of postmodern spin on ice hockey, substituting brooms for sticks and sneakers for skates, this six-a-side sport is strictly for rubber-jointed adrenaline junkies. Big in Canada for over a century, broomball probably originated in Iceland, where a bloodthirsty sport known as knattleikr has been played since the 10th century. Apparently, casualties were commonplace, and games involving whole villages could last two weeks.

The rest of the year, Broadgate Circus ice rink is converted into an outdoor performance and exhibition space.

The Cornhill devils

According to an inscription in the churchyard, St Peter upon Cornhill, on the corner of Cornhill and Gracechurch Streets, is the earliest Christian site in Britain, founded in 187. However, the church is most famous for the three devilish gargoyles perched on the Victorian office block next door. During its construction, the architect attempted to steal a foot-wide strip of church land; but the eagle-eyed vicar kicked up such a stink that the architect had to redraw the plans. In a fit of pique, he set these gruesome devils on the roof, which continue to curse the congregation as they enter. One spits, another sticks its fingers up like a rebellious teenager, while the devil closest to the street apparently bears a striking resemblance to the bothersome reverend. The devils are visible silhouetted against the sky if you stand on the north side of the building.

BARBICAN CONSERVATORY

Urban hothouse

Barbican Centre, Silk Street, EC2Y 8DS
Sundays & Bank Holidays 12-5pm (occasionally booked for private functions;
call 0207 638 4141 to check)
Admission free
Barbican tube

This tropical garden is hidden in London's brutalist landmark. As you approach the Barbican from Silk Street, a greenhouse comes into view. The lushness of the conservatory – which contains over 2,000 species of trees and plants, as well as tropical finches, quails, and exotic fish – is thrown into vibrant contrast by the surrounding glass, steel and raw concrete.

The main difficulty in visiting this garden in the sky is its limited opening times. When it was inaugurated in 1982, the conservatory was permanently open to everyone; but feeble public response saw the Corporation of the City of London whittle away visiting hours. It is now mainly used for private parties, but there are regular tours and you can even have afternoon tea in the conservatory on occasional Sundays (though you have to book in advance). Many of the ingredients, including lavender, dill, avocado and turmeric, are grown on the spot or on the surrounding estate. The conservatory itself is wrapped around the fly tower (from where scenery is lowered onto the stage below) of the Barbican's main theatre.

Low visitor response has bedevilled the Barbican since it opened. It forms part of the Barbican Estate, a hermetically sealed island within the city. Navigating the estate and the Centre is often bewildering, as the seemingly endless walkways and blank concrete walls can disorient newcomers. Even the entrances to the performance spaces are low key, certainly in comparison to traditional theatres like the Haymarket or Drury Lane.

The Barbican Estate has enjoyed a renaissance in recent years. Originally constructed for workers in the Corporation, the retro design, central location and cohesive urban system of the estate meant that when London flooded with money in the 1980s, flats were snapped up by City workers. A fashion for modernism means that London's original distaste for the estate has turned around, and it is now listed. If you can't get into the conservatory, take one of the excellent architecture tours (www.barbican.org.uk).

LONDON WALL

A Roman hunk

Tower Hill, EC3N 4DJ
Open during daylight hours
Admission free
Tower Hill or Moorgate tube

Like most great European cities, London is a palimpsest of generations of building. What we mostly see today is a very strongly built Victorian city, on top of dainty Georgian foundations that retain the medieval street pattern that was laid over the original Roman plan.

Ghosts of the Roman past litter the city, but require a certain amount of seeking out. The Temple of Mithras on Walbrook Street is one example. Battle Bridge in King's Cross is another – reputedly the site of the final battle between the Romans and Boudicca, who is buried, legend has it, under Platform 9 at King's Cross station.

However, the largest remains are those of the defensive wall built by the Romans after Boudicca sacked the city in 60 AD (the only time the city has been utterly wiped out), which remained largely intact for the next 1,000 years. London Wall is mostly built from stone shipped up the River Thames from Maidstone in Kent. Originally enclosing an area of about 1.3 km², in comparison to the monstrous 1,579 km² that Greater London has become, the wall stretched from Blackfriars in the west, via Ludgate, Moorgate and Aldgate to the Tower of London in the east.

London Wall must have been an astonishing edifice in Roman times. It stood about five metres high, with a two-metre-deep ditch in front of it, and was lined with a number of bastions. The best preserved of these is in the Barbican estate, next to the church of St Giles-without-Cripplegate – a fragment of old London entirely surrounded by an extremely modern landscape.

What remains of London Wall today is largely the core, as much of its facing and cut stone was carted off for other building after the Romans left Britain. The biggest intact section lines the street now known, imaginatively, as London Wall. Other chunks stand at Tower Hill and within the Museum of London, but a careful walk of the streets that would have formed the wall often turns up other bits and pieces.

The oddest location for a fragment of Roman London is on display in the basement of Nicholson and Griffins (www.nicholsonandgriffin.com), a hairdresser in Leadenhall Market. This is the base of an arch in what was the city's basilica, or civic centre. At over 150 metres, it was the same length as St Paul's, and the largest building north of the Alps in 150 AD. This suggests that London was not a colonial backwater of the Roman Empire.

THE MASONIC TEMPLE AT ANDAZ HOTEL

Occult lodgings

40 Liverpool Street, EC2M 7QN
0207 961 1234
londonliverpoolstreet.andaz.hyatt.com
By appointment or for special events
Admission varies
Liverpool Street tube/rail

With its distinctive red brick façade, the former Great Eastern Hotel is an impressive Victorian landmark beside Liverpool Street station. Built for the Great Eastern Railway Company, the hotel was designed by Charles and Edward Barry, whose father (another Charles Barry) built the Houses of Parliament.

When it opened in 1884, the Great Eastern Hotel had its own tracks into the station for the delivery of provisions, including sea water for the hotel's salt-water baths. Despite this swanky heritage, the hotel gradually fell into disrepair until restaurateur Terence Conran snapped it up in the late 1990s and embarked on an extravagant makeover.

During the renovation, concealed behind a false wall, the builders were surprised to discover a wood-panelled antechamber leading to an intact Masonic temple. Decked in twelve types of Italian marble, with a blue and gold ceiling decorated with the signs of the zodiac and a mahogany throne at either end, this Gothic showstopper was built in 1912 for £50,000, the equivalent of around £4 million today. The Freemasons, who helped to build the Great Eastern Hotel, held clandestine meetings here for decades.

A second temple, decorated with Egyptian motifs with seating around a chequerboard floor, was discovered in the basement. Evidently not intimidated by the occult, Conran converted it into a gym.

Now owned by the Hyatt hotel group, the building has been rebranded as the Andaz. To avoid tampering with the original architectural fittings, the Andaz is fitted with vacuum drainage like that used on planes. So when you flush the toilet, the waste is sucked upwards and disposed of through the hotel roof.

NEARBY
Roman girl's grave ⑪

During construction of Norman Foster's Swiss Re building (better known as the 'gherkin'), builders stumbled on an extraordinary discovery: the grave of a teenage girl who died between AD 350-400. An inscription in the low, slate bench running around the back of the building marks the spot where she was given a Roman reburial. The epitaph – in Latin and English – reads: 'To the spirits of the dead the unknown young girl from Roman London lies buried here.'

THE TENT

Peace camp

St Ethelburga's Centre for Reconciliation and Peace, 78 Bishopsgate, EC2N 4AG
0207 496 1610
www.stethelburgas.org
Wed 11am-3pm. Visits at other times by prior arrangement
Admission free
Liverpool Street or Bank tube

I t's easy to walk past St Ethelburga's without noticing it. The slender church sits quietly amid the hubbub of Bishopsgate, with its high-rise offices and harried bankers. When it was founded around 1400, St Ethelburga's was the largest building on Bishopsgate: today, it's the smallest.

Behind the medieval façade is a surprisingly modern interior, empty apart from a simple wooden altar and a handful of artworks. Though it survived the Great Fire and the Blitz, the church collapsed after an IRA bomb blast nearby in 1993. Fragments of the original features were salvaged to create this new space. Though consecrated, it's no longer technically a church; there's no parish and no priest. It's now a Centre for Reconciliation and Peace, focusing on the role of faith in war and conflict resolution.

The derelict land behind the church has been transformed into a peace garden (also accessible via an alleyway off Bishopsgate). With its intricate mosaic tiling and tinkling fountain, it's like stepping into a Moroccan riad. The centrepiece is The Tent, a 16-sided structure with walls of woven goats' hair, modelled on traditional Bedouin tents. Tents are also associated with the nomadic origins of Judaism, Christianity and Islam – just the thing for a sacred space dedicated to inter-faith dialogue. Take off your shoes and step into a serene cocoon, carpeted with rugs woven in conflict regions and lined with low benches. The seven stained-glass windows contain messages of peace written in Chinese, Sanskrit, Arabic, Japanese, Hebrew, English and Inuit. Even the occasional siren cannot shatter the peace.

The Tent hosts devotional gatherings, meditation, storytelling and recitals. In the main building, you might stumble upon a Tibetan sand mandala, and Afro-Cuban concert or a discussion on civil disobedience. The unifying philosophy underlying all these events is that peace begins within.

St Ethelburga's has a long tradition as a progressive church. William Bedwell, rector from 1601 to 1632, was an Arabic scholar. In 1861, rector John Rodwell published the first reliable English translation of the Qur'an (still in print). And in the 1930s and 1940s, this was one of the few churches in London where divorced people could remarry.

BEVIS MARKS SYNAGOGUE

⑬

The oldest synagogue in England

2 Henage Lane, EC3A 5DQ
0207 626 1274
www.sephardi.org.uk/bevis-marks/
Mon, Wed, Thurs 10.30am-2pm, Tues, Fri 10.30am-1pm,
Sun 10.30am-12.30pm
Tours: Sun 10.45am, Wed 11.15am, Fri 11.15am
There are no visiting hours on Jewish Sabbath, Jewish Festivals and Bank Holidays
Check website for admission prices
Aldgate or Liverpool Street tube

Opened in 1701, Bevis Marks is the oldest synagogue in England. It was established by Spanish and Portuguese Sephardic Jews in response to a surge in congregation numbers at the small synagogue in Creechurch Lane, when Cromwell unofficially re-admitted Jews into England after their expulsion in 1290 by Edward I.

Cromwell never formally revoked the expulsion, but made it clear that the ban would not be enforced. The government hoped to profit from their connections with the mercantile centre of Amsterdam as England grew into a global trader. The ultra-Protestant Cromwell believed that the conversion of the Jews to Christianity was essential before Christ's return to reign on Earth. However, it wasn't until 1858 that English Jews received formal emancipation.

The synagogue is tucked away in a courtyard approached through a stone archway, and is largely unchanged since its construction three centuries ago. It is the only synagogue in Europe that has held regular services continuously for over 300 years. Above its doors is inscribed A.M. 5461, the Hebrew year in which it was opened. Its interior resembles a Wren church, although its décor, furnishing and layout are clearly influenced by the 1675 Portuguese Synagogue in Amsterdam. Embedded in the roof is a beam from a royal ship presented to the congregation by Queen Anne. The Ark (which holds the scrolls of the Pentateuch) at the east end reflects the late 17th-century taste for classical architecture, again in the manner of Wren. The synagogue also has a very good collection of Cromwell-era and Queen Anne furniture, which remain in regular use.

Aldgate was the 19th-century centre of London's Jewish community. There are still vestiges such as the dirt-cheap, 24-hour bagel shops at the top of Brick Lane, but mostly there are ghosts: Jewish schools, bath houses, and soup kitchens, now converted into gracious flats for City workers. Look out for the colourful mural commemorating the Jews of the East End, opposite the Brune Street Soup Kitchen. The arch on Wentworth Street is the only survivor of the Four Percent Industrial Dwellings Company, founded in 1885 by Sir Nathaniel Rothschild to clear the area's slums and provide decent housing for Jewish residents – albeit with a 4% profit for investors. Now one of London's largest mosques, the synagogue at 59 Brick Lane used to be so busy that classrooms were built on the roof – look up and you can still see them.

TOWER BRIDGE BASCULE CHAMBER

Underwater engineering

Tower Bridge Road, SE1 2UP
0207 403 3761
www.towerbridge.org.uk
April-Sept 10am-5.30pm, Oct-March 9.30am-5pm. Check website for tour times
Check website for admission details
Tower Hill tube

Tower Bridge may be a preposterous structure – a colossal piece of Victorian engineering that someone has tried to disguise as a Gothic castle – but it's undeniably an eye-catcher. The standard tour of the bridge is pretty good, especially since the installation of the thrilling/ horrifying glass floors in the pedestrian walkways linking the tops of the towers. If you get your timing right, you can look straight down onto the bridge when it opens, its jaws widening below you like a giant mechanical shark. (Check the website for bridge opening times.)

But if you book a place on the Behind-the-Scenes Personal Guided Tour (that really is what it's called!), you can delve into the bowels of this monster. Like most of its contemporaries, Tower Bridge was massively over-engineered to avoid any possibility that this most easterly of London bridges should collapse.

The high point – or in fact, the low point – of the tour is to one of the bascule chambers beneath the bridge's twin towers. Bascule means seesaw: all 422 tons of counterbalance swing down into these giant, wedge-shaped spaces when the bridge is raised. There are hundreds of safety measures in place, but that weight still looms above your head when you stand at the bottom of the chamber staring up. Noise from the traffic overhead bounces around the space and you can hear clearly when a bus or truck rattles by. Accessed via steep, narrow stairs, most of the chamber is well below the surface of the river, on the other side of 20-foot-thick walls. Consequently, this is one of the few rat-free spaces anywhere along the Thames. There's nothing for rodents to survive on – a bonus for muriphobes.

The acoustics in these cavernous vaults are phenomenal, and they are occasionally used for classical and contemporary concerts during the Thames Festival. However, the difficulty of getting large numbers of people in and out means that events are restricted in scale and number – check out the Festival's website well in advance for pre-booking.

In its heyday, Tower Bridge employed an operating staff of 96; this is currently down to 12, including the six bridge 'drivers' who control the bascule chambers from the north-east cabin. The bridge opens around 1,000 times a year; river traffic takes priority – even the Queen has to wait.

TOWER SUBWAY

A lost passage under the Thames

Tower Hill, EC3N 4AB
Tower Hill tube

When Italian writer Edmondo de Amicis visited London in 1883, he described a '… gigantic iron tube, which seems to undulate like a great intestine in the enormous belly of the river'. This river monster was, in fact, Tower Subway, built beneath the Thames in 1869 to shuttle passengers between the north and south banks. All that survives of this engineering feat is a small, circular brick tower beside the Tower of London ticket office. This is not actually the original entrance to the Subway – it was built by the London Hydraulic Power Company, when they took over the defunct tunnel in 1897. The other entrance on Vine Street, south of the Thames, has been demolished.

Unlike its predecessor, Marc Isambard Brunel's Thames Tunnel, which cost £60,000, two lives and took almost eighteen years to complete, Tower Subway was built in ten months for £16,000 by a 24-year-old named James Henry Greathead. The tunnel's innovative structure, clad in an iron tube, was the template for London's first underground train, the City & South London Railway, built in 1890.

A dozen passengers were shuttled across the Thames in an 'omnibus' that ran along a single-gauge track. After a series of mechanical mishaps, this service folded after just three months and the tunnel was converted into a gas-lit walkway. Charles Dickens Jr warned: '… it is not advisable for any but the very briefest of Her Majesty's lieges to attempt the passage in high-heeled boots, or with a hat to which he attaches any particular value.' Though damp and claustrophobic, this did not deter the 20,000 pedestrians who used the Subway every week, paying a halfpenny each way.

When toll-free Tower Bridge opened in 1894, Tower Subway became redundant. It was sold to the London Hydraulic Power Company for a measly £3,000. The water pipes have since been replaced by TV cables.

NEARBY

Dead Man's Hole   ⑯

Before Tower Subway was built, Londoners relied on wherrymen to transport them across the river (see p. 260). One popular route ran from Horselydown Steps in Bermondsey to Dead Man's Hole on the north bank. As the name suggests, not all the passengers were alive. The boatmen didn't forfeit the corpses' fares: they sold them for medical research to Barts Hospital, which paid 6d more for bodies than Guy's Hospital on the south bank. A sign marks the spot beneath Tower Bridge, where mildewed steps lead into the murky river where countless corpses were dumped.

THE GARDEN
OF ST DUNSTAN-IN-THE-EAST

Beautiful bomb site

St Dunstan's Hill, EC3R 5DD
Open all year round, 8am-7pm or dusk, whichever is earlier. Closed Christmas
Day, Boxing Day and New Year's Day
Admission free
Monument tube

One of the few little green lungs in the City, this garden hidden within the walls of a bombed-out church is popular with office workers during their lunch hours. The high walls of the ruins trap heat in the summer, and the relative secrecy of the garden makes it ideal for a liaison or a nap. In good weather, the garden encourages idleness. In bad weather, it invites melancholy.

Twisting paths lead through the garden, whose walls are covered by ivy and shrubbery. A lawn and trees have been planted and a low fountain sits in the middle of what was once the nave. The park and its ruins give the impression of being one of those artful gothic follies beloved by the Victorians – its tight enclosure by office buildings on all sides heightens the effect of its secrecy. The church spire, one of the few examples of gothic-style architecture that Wren built, was added after the building was severely damaged in the Great Fire of London in 1666. Rather than being completely rebuilt, the damaged church was patched up between 1668 and 1671 – the spire was designed to complement the medieval church that had remained largely intact since 1100.

However, the church was bombed out in 1941, leaving only the tower and steeple intact, which now house the offices of the Wren Clinic, a complementary medicine centre. Surrounding the church tower are iron railings commissioned by Wren, with putti on the gate, an unusual decoration in London.

St Dunstan-in-the-West

Dunstan, an eccentric English scholar, has another church dedicated to him: St Dunstan-in-the-West on Fleet Street. The church is best known for its exterior clock from 1671, showing the biblical giants Gog and Magog, traditional guardians of the City. The churchyard also includes a statue of Queen Elizabeth I from 1586, the only one known to have been carved while she lived, and the only open-air statue of her that survives in London. There are also statues of King Lud, the mythical re-builder of London, and his sons. All of the statues originally stood in Ludgate, one of the historically sacred parts of London, so the church may have more than its fair share of voodoo. The celebrated London diarist Samuel Pepys used the church as a place to pick up serving-girls, generally with little success.

SKY GARDEN

Beauty on the beast

1 Sky Garden Walk, EC3M 8AF
https://skygarden.london
Mon-Fri 10am-6pm, weekends 11am-9pm
Admission free, but online booking essential. Bring ID
Monument or Bank tube

Londonʼs skyline has exploded upwards in the last ten years as property developers have sought to capitalise on the insatiable demand for housing. The City of London took the fight to Canary Wharf by building more ʻsignatureʼ skyscrapers. There are always more to come – 2008 mayoral candidate Boris Johnson promised the electorate that he wouldnʼt allow the building of Dubai-on-Thames, but then, you know, he kind of did. In 2016 alone, there were over 430 new tall buildings planned for the capital. Some of these are welcome, but many of them simply dwarf the place.

Among the most notorious of the new showpiece builds is 20 Fenchurch Street, known as the Walkie-Talkie because of its shape. Completed in spring 2014, it promptly won the 2015 Carbuncle Cup for the worst new building in the UK. The concave glass wall at the front directs sunlight downwards, and in 2013 the construction company had to pay the owner of a car parked in the street below whose bodywork was melted by the building. The bulbous behemoth looms menacingly over Eastcheap, an ogre of a building that makes passers-by feel like ants.

However, the beast has a beautiful secret. The developers have constructed a huge light- and air-filled atrium at the top of the tower, with a balcony and a 360° view of London. Unlike the Shard, which sits directly across the river, entry is free, although the limited number of spaces means that online booking well in advance is essential. There are a couple of bars, a brasserie and a restaurant placed between two rising terraces of plants: they include figs and other flowers, shrubs and ferns that flourish all year round. The whole thing is wrapped in glass, with excellent unobstructed views (unlike the Shard). The effect is as if a minor greenhouse from Kew Gardens had been dropped on top of a skyscraper.

A church full of shoes

At the foot of 20 Fenchurch Street is St Margaret Pattens, a minor Wren church with an odd name (Pattens wasnʼt the saintʼs surname). These wooden-soled overshoes, later soled with iron rings, allowed the wealthy to walk the streets of London without muddying their shoes. The sound supposedly made the streets seem as if they were filled with horses. The church has long been associated with The Worshipful Company of Pattenmakers, and there is a display of pattens in the vestibule.

LONDON BRIDGE MODEL AT ST MAGNUS THE MARTYR

London's first bridge

Lower Thames Street, EC3R 6DN
www.stmagnusmartyr.org.uk
Tues-Fri 10am-4pm
Admission free
Monument tube

St Magnus the Martyr, tucked away near the Monument, is a seldom-visited Wren church in the shadow of London Bridge. The road to the original bridge, pulled down in 1831, once ran through the churchyard. Inside the church is a 4-metre-long model of the original bridge in its medieval incarnation, complete with the houses and shops that once lined it. The model is beautifully made, and crowded with tiny figures, giving some idea of how chaotic it must have been. At its peak, there were 200 businesses on the bridge, as well as a church. Just 4 metres wide, it was the only river crossing in London for livestock, horses, wagons and pedestrians until Putney Bridge opened in 1729. Unsurprisingly, crossing the bridge could take up to an hour. All of the tiny figures are authentically dressed in medieval costumes, with one exception...

The model of London Bridge also includes the heads of traitors set on spikes above the southern gatehouse. These were dipped in tar to preserve them against the elements. Oliver Cromwell's head was on display for at least 20 years after he had been dug up, ceremonially hanged and then decapitated.

Vestiges of the first London Bridge

By the end of the 18th century, the bridge was clearly no longer fit for purpose as the city expanded – not only was it too narrow, but it obstructed the growing river traffic. The first step was to clear the bridge of its buildings: they were pulled down between 1758 and 1762. Several fragments remain, however: the coat of arms on the front of the King's Arms, in Newcomen Street south of the river, was once fixed above the entrance to the south gate of London Bridge. The arms are dated 1760, above the vigorous Lion and Unicorn; the pub itself dates back to 1890.

The bridge remained in use until its demolition, but the road was widened and both sides lined with stone cupolas to shelter pedestrians. Two of these are now in Victoria Park in Hackney; far closer is the one in the courtyard of the Counting House, in what was the original Guy's Hospital, but is now part of King's College London. Walk straight through the gates of Old Guy's House on St Thomas Street, then through the arches ahead of you, and the cupola is on the left. Sitting inside is a statue of the poet John Keats, who trained at the hospital as a surgeon-apothecary between 1815 and 1816.

ASCENT OF THE MONUMENT

Pillar of strength

Fish St Hill, EC3R 8AH
www.themonument.info
Oct-March 9.30am-5.30 daily (last admission 5pm), April-Sept 9.30am-6pm
daily (last admission 5.30pm)
Check website for admission prices
Monument or Bank tube

This oddity is much seen, but rarely visited. A single Doric column of Portland stone, the Monument contains an internal staircase of 311 steps winding up to a viewing balcony. When it was built in 1677, this would have afforded long-distance views; after 300 years of continuous building, the views are less spectacular. Once visible for miles, today visitors almost stumble across the column – the effect is like discovering a sailing ship in a canyon.

Designed by London's greatest architect, Sir Christopher Wren, and Dr Robert Hooke to commemorate the Great Fire of London, the 61-metre Monument is the tallest freestanding stone column in the world. The height is supposedly equal to the distance between the column and the baker's house in Pudding Lane where the fire reputedly began. It is topped by a flaming copper urn that symbolizes the Great Fire, but looks more like a flaming pudding. Originally, the column was to be topped with a phoenix (embodying the motto of London: 'Resurgam' – 'I am reborn'), then with a colossal statue of King Charles II. But the committee responsible opted for the gilt pudding instead.

The walk up inside the column is precipitous: a thin handrail is all that lies between you and oblivion. Many visitors are undone by the climb, but each receives a certificate after getting up the damn thing. The summit was a favourite place for staging suicides until the balcony was fenced in with a metal cage. This cage is strong enough to support vigorous gymnastics and pull-ups, a very effective way of terrifying your friends.

Look closely and you will see that the base of the column is wrapped with a finely executed relief by Caius Gabriel Cibber, depicting a personification of London grieving before a backdrop of flaming buildings. Peace and Prosperity hover in the clouds, promising renewal, and King Charles II is on the right, all dressed up. Cibber is most famous for two statues, *Melancholy* and *Raving Madness*, made for the gates of the infamous mental hospital Bedlam, which can still be seen at the Museum of the Mind (see p. 372). His son, Colley Cibber, a famously bad poet and actor, was the chief target of Alexander Pope's satirical poem *The Dunciad*.

THE ROYAL EXCHANGE AMBULATORY PAINTINGS

A pictorial history of England

Royal Exchange, between Cornhill and Threadneedle Streets, EC3V 3DG
Mon-Fri 10am-11pm. Closed weekends
Admission free
Bank tube

Sandwiched between the Bank of England and Mansion House, the Royal Exchange is a grand repository of the City's history. The current building, with its sweeping atrium and arcade of luxury shops, dates from 1844. The original Royal Exchange – twice destroyed by fire – was founded in 1566 'as a comely bourse for merchants to assemble upon' by Sir Thomas Gresham, a merchant who cannily offered to build London a stock exchange at his own expense, in return for a lifetime interest in its profits. The building doubled as an Elizabethan shopping mall. The apothecaries and wig makers have been replaced by the likes of Boodles and Hermès, but the courtyard bar still thrums with the energy of commerce.

The pinstriped powerbrokers lunching in the mezzanine restaurants lining the space seem oblivious to the 32 paintings hidden in the shadowy recesses of the ambulatory. The tables face the courtyard, rather than these patriotic interpretations of landmarks in English history. Lords and ladies, kings and queens, admirals, cardinals and ordinary Londoners are shown feasting and fighting, trading and signing treaties. There are also statues of Elizabeth I and Charles II tucked away in the corners, all of which underlines the financial and political might of the City.

Until the 1950s, these images were used to illustrate school history books, but today they are overlooked. Many precious works, commissioned from the likes of Edwin Austin Abbey, J. Seymour Lucas and Sir Frederic Leighton (see p. 206), are concealed behind the restaurant kitchens, doomed to be splattered with bacon fat. Even though the paintings are poorly lit and the titles are barely legible, they are still an awesome sight.

NEARBY

Gresham's grasshopper

The weathervane of the Royal Exchange is tipped with a gilded grasshopper, Gresham's crest, which survived both the Great Fire and another devastating blaze in 1838. A golden grasshopper also hovers above Gresham's former HQ in Lombard Street. Allegedly, his ancestor Roger de Gresham was abandoned in a field of long grass as a baby, but was rescued by a woman drawn to the spot by a chirping grasshopper. A more likely explanation is that the grasshopper is a rebus of Gresham, since gres meant grass in Middle English. Traditionally a symbol for the merchant, the grasshopper is also an ancient good luck charm.

THE ROMAN AMPHITHEATRE OF GUILDHALL YARD

23

Ancient arena

Off Gresham Street, EC2V 5AE
0207 332 3700
The amphitheatre can be visited via the Gallery on the east side of Guildhall Yard
Mon-Sat 10am-5pm, Sun 12pm-4pm
Admission free
St Paul's or Moorgate tube

In the courtyard of the Guildhall, the ancient administrative centre of London, is a curved line of dark stone that implies a great loop under the surrounding buildings. This circle marks the outline of the city's Roman amphitheatre; within the line was the sand of the arena. Around AD 43, the Romans established Londinum: within 30 years, they built a wooden amphitheatre, upgrading it in the early 2nd century. The amphitheatre, which had space for 7,000 spectators to watch fights and executions, is reconstructed inside the Guildhall Art Gallery.

London was less of a Roman backwater than many assume. Tacitus refers to the city as a mercantile hub, and there are significant remains all over the city. London Wall (see p. 166) is the most obvious, but there are others, and the existence of an amphitheatre like this suggests the scale of the city. After the Romans abandoned London in the 4th century, like much of the city, the site lay derelict for hundreds of years. The local inhabitants, descendants of the waves of barbarians from Germany that looked to colonise Western Europe, seem to have been afraid of living among the ancient buildings, which must have looked as though they were built by giants. Most of the remains of their settlements lie on the periphery of the Roman city.

It was only in the mid-11th century that overcrowding in London led to the reoccupation of the area. The first Guildhall was built in the early 12th century just north of the arena. But the amphitheatre was not rediscovered until 1988, after Museum of London archaeologists unearthed its foundations by chance. The Guildhall itself stands above the largest medieval crypt in the city.

ST STEPHEN AND THE LOST WALBROOK RIVER

24

A hidden river and Henry Moore

39 Walbrook, EC4N 8BN
0207 626 9000
ststephenwalbrook.net
Mon, Tues, Thurs, Fri 10am-4pm, Wed 11am-3pm
Bank tube /DLR, Cannon Street rail, Mansion House tube

Christopher Wren built many churches in the City of London. St Stephen is one of the hardest to find – and is getting even more so. As the City strives to compete with Canary Wharf as a commercial centre by throwing up more towering office buildings, this perfect little church is dwarfed by its neighbours. It stands on the edge of the Walbrook, one of London's many hidden rivers, which runs in a culvert past the front of the church.

Walbrook was the first river around which London was built, lying between the early settlements on Cornhill and Ludgate Hill. It was at the centre of Celtic and Roman life, and probably so-called because it

ran through London Wall – the defensive rampart built by the Romans. In the 3rd century AD, the Romans erected the Temple of Mithras on the east bank of the Walbrook, where soldiers would bathe in the blood of slaughtered bulls to rev themselves up for battle.

More than a hundred styli have been found in the Walbrook, suggesting Roman clerks simply threw their used pens into the stream. More ominously, at the end of the 19th century, large numbers of skulls were found in the river; many of these gruesome remnants are still being dredged up today. The victims may have been Roman prisoners ritually decapitated after the sacking of London by Asclepiodotus or Boudicca. But nobody really knows.

St Stephen's was Wren's own church, as he lived at 15 Walbrook. The church is almost anonymous from the outside; once inside, you find yourself in a miniature masterpiece. Somehow Wren created a light-filled cube with 16 Corinthian columns supporting a Roman dome (the prototype for St Paul's Cathedral) in a very limited space. The room immediately inspires a lifting of the heart. Most of the original fittings remain intact, as the church escaped the worst of the Blitz.

The only threat to this internal harmony is the altar – a huge, circular slab of marble designed by Henry Moore, which sits in the centre of the church. The monumental altar, cut from the same travertine marble used by Michelangelo, does look incongruous at first. But its bold statement makes sense for a church designed by Wren, who was not afraid to be controversial and experimental.

Try to time your visit with one of the frequent lunchtime recitals.

The original Samaritans telephone

Chad Varah was rector of St Stephen when he founded The Samaritans, which he called a '999 for the suicidal'. The original Samaritans telephone is on display in a glass box inside the church.

LONDON STONE

Rock of ages

111 Cannon Street, EC4N 5AR
Admission free
Cannon Street tube

L ondon Stone is back home again. This hunk of oolitic limestone was on display at the Museum of London while construction work took place at its traditional home, but was returned to a new case outside 111 Cannon Street in October 2018. It was originally larger and stood on the south of the street, but seems to have been damaged by the Great Fire of 1666. In 1720 what was left of it was housed in a stone cupola. In 1742 this was moved across the street, and later built into the wall of the new Wren church of St Swithin. Following the church's destruction in the Blitz, London Stone was placed in the Guildhall, before its 1962 return to Cannon Street. But where's it from?

Like many venerated objects, nobody really knows what London Stone is. One story has it brought to London by the Trojan Brutus, son of Priam, who fought and killed a race of giants led by Gog and Magog (whose images are still carried in the Lord Mayor's Parade) and erected a temple to Artemis with this stone as its altar.

Or it may be a Roman road marker. Or a Saxon one. Although there are no written Roman references to the stone, it was an important landmark after the city's foundation by the Romans. For hundreds of years, it was recognised as the symbolic heart of the City of London, before which deals were made, oaths taken, laws passed and official proclamations made. In 1450, the rebel Jack Cade struck his sword against it to signify his seizure of sovereignty after his forces had entered London.

London Stone has always attracted mystical enthusiasts. One legend has it as part of some kind of Druidic altar. William Blake, London's seer poet, imagined the groaning of the Druids' sacrificial victims in his poem, *Jerusalem The Emanation of the Giant Albion*. Some people believe it sits on a ley line linking St Paul's and the Tower of London, making it a psychic lodestone for London. The truth is probably more boring (it usually is) – but London Stone isn't saying.

The London Stone ley line

London's most powerful ley line – an alignment of ancient sacred places – runs along Cannon Street, connecting the churches of St Martin, Ludgate, St Thomas, St Leonard Milkchurch and All Hallows Barking, near the Tower of London. The hub of all ley lines in London is thought to be Ludgate Circus, where it is believed that a megalithic stone circle like Stonehenge once stood.

THE ORIGINAL GLOBE THEATRE

Footprint of the Wooden O

Park Street, SE1 9AR
Open during daylight hours
Admission free
London Bridge or Borough tube

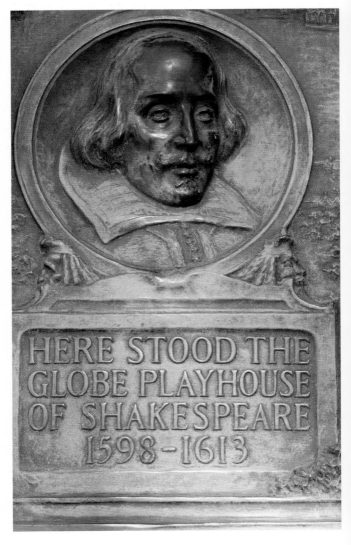

The reconstruction of Shakespeare's Globe Theatre is one of London's best-known tourist attractions; rebuilt with scrupulous scholarship and opened in 1997, it is as close to the Elizabethan experience as it can possibly be. However, its authenticity doesn't extend to its actual location. Walk out of the Globe's box office, turn right and head down New Globe Walk away from the river. Turn left onto Park Street, walk under the foot of Southwark Bridge and there, in the car park of a block of flats, is the original site of the Globe Theatre. The site is marked on the ground by a line of black marble that traces the perimeter of the theatre's outer wall.

The site of the new Globe is therefore far closer to the river, where the Beargarden, the popular venue for bear baiting and other animal torturing, stood. The concentration of playhouses in this part of Southwark made it the 16th- and 17th-century equivalent of the West End, and the Globe was built here in pursuit of the play-going public. The Lord Chamberlain's Men, the company that Shakespeare wrote and acted for, failed to negotiate a new lease for the Theatre, their East London base, and decided to relocate south of the river. One night at the end of December 1598, a troupe of actors and workmen began to secretly dismantle the theatre. They carried its timbers from Shoreditch across the frozen Thames to Southwark. The timbers were then used to build a larger and better theatre, the Globe.

NEARBY
Remains of the Rose Theatre ㉗
www.rosetheatre.org.uk

On Park Street, you can also see the remains of the Rose Theatre, the first theatre on Bankside. The Rose opened in 1587, but the arrival of the Swan in 1595 and the Globe in 1599 drove it out of business. The archaeological site was only discovered in 1989, during construction of an office block beside Southwark Bridge. The footprint of the Elizabethan playhouse is marked out with red rope lights, although the actual remains currently lie beneath nine feet of mud. Plans are in place to complete its excavation and open it to the public permanently. Currently, volunteers open the site every Saturday from 10am to 5pm. The Rose is also occasionally used as a stage, although space is limited.

CITY LIVERY COMPANIES

Descendants of the guilds

Various locations, various opening times
www.liverycompanies.info

London has 110 (and counting) Livery Companies. These are trade associations based exclusively in the City that were originally developed from guilds (hence Guildhall), which regulated their trades, controlling wages and labour conditions – a kind of proto-union. Medieval in origin, most are known as 'The Worshipful Company of …'. Many of them represent obsolete trades, such as Bowyers (longbow makers) and Girdlers (sword belt and dress belt makers). However, numbers are rising as modern trades become incorporated. In 1992, the Worshipful Company of Information Technologists became the 100th City of London livery company. The Worshipful Company of Arts Scholars is the most recent addition.

Nowadays, most Companies are primarily charitable organisations, but they still retain an aura of medieval pomp and circumstance; they have a strict order of precedence, and the first 12 are known as the Great Twelve. Around 40 have meeting halls, and many of these are open to the public on open days or by arrangement. Choice halls include the 1835 Goldsmiths' Hall, laid out in marble (www.thegoldsmiths.co.uk), the riverside Fishmongers' Hall (www.fishhall.org.uk), which contains the dagger that Sir William Walworth, the Lord Mayor of London – and a fishmonger – used to end the Peasants' Revolt by stabbing the rebel Wat Tyler to death in 1381. The difficulty with visits is that each hall has a different entry policy, and arrangements must be researched and made in advance with each Company's offices. The spectacular Drapers' Hall (www.thedrapers.co.uk), for example, admits no tours between the end of July and mid-September. Persistence is worthwhile, however; very few Londoners ever see inside the halls.

Doggett's Coat and Badge

The City Livery Companies are primarily involved in charities, schools and investment, but still operate longstanding historical traditions. The world's longest continually running sporting event, Doggett's Coat and Badge, is organised by the Fishmongers' Company; this is a four-mile rowing race against the tide, between London Bridge and Chelsea Bridge, which has been run since 1714. Irish comic actor Thomas Doggett gave money to endow the race between 'young watermen'. The prize is a red coat with a silver badge on one arm. There is a horrible pub of the same name south of Blackfriars Bridge. Best avoided.

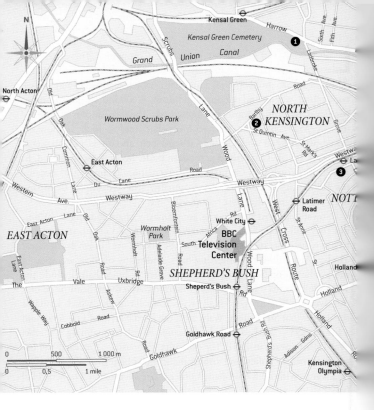

Marylebone to Shepherd's Bush

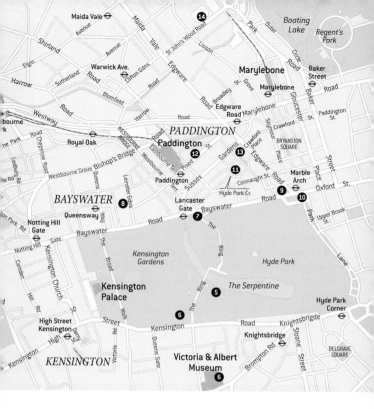

KENSAL GREEN CATACOMBS

Dead and buried

Kensal Green Cemetery, Harrow Road, W10 4RA
07530 676151
www.kensalgreen.co.uk
1 April-30 Sept: Mon-Sat 9am-6pm and Sun 10am-6pm; 1 Oct-31 March:
Mon-Sat 9am-5pm and Sun 10am-5pm; bank holidays 10am-1pm. Guided
tours every Sunday at 2pm from 1 March to 31 Oct, and on the first and third
Sunday of each month in Nov, Dec, Jan and Feb
Check website for tour prices
Kensal Green tube/rail, Ladbroke Grove tube, Kensal Rise rail

The first of the 'Magnificent Seven' cemeteries that sprang up around London in the mid-19th century (see p. 380), Kensal Green is also the largest and most opulent. The Grand Union Canal runs along the cemetery's southern border, so you could even have a waterborne cortège.

Inspired by the Père Lachaise Cemetery in Paris, Kensal Green Cemetery became intensely fashionable after the Duke of Sussex was buried there in 1843. Other notable graves include those of Charles Blondin, who crossed Niagara Falls on a tightrope, pausing midway to cook and consume an omelette, and the fifth Duke of Portland.

A paranoid recluse, the Duke built miles of gaslit tunnels, including a ballroom and billiards room, beneath his Nottinghamshire estate. He was so averse to human contact that his servants sent his roast chicken into his room on a model railway.

The Friends of Kensal Green, a conservation charity, offer regular tours of the cemetery, which include a descent into the extensive catacombs beneath the Anglican Chapel. The musty chapel contains the only working catafalque in the country, a hydraulic winch used to lower the coffins to the catacombs at a suitably funereal pace.

The catacombs are everything you might expect: damp, cold and dark. The brick avenues are lined with coffins stacked on shelves, sometimes behind glass, or iron grilles – mourners liked to be able to commune with the dead. Each coffin is triple shelled: a wooden casket inside a lead one, encased in an outer shell covered in scarlet velvet or metalwork. Most are covered in a powdery bloom where rot has set in. Some coffins are outlandishly huge, as if giants were buried within; others are instantly recognisable as children. Look out for a pair of glass domes containing immortelles – beautiful, lifelike flowers made from the finest porcelain and copper. The catacombs are still functioning, and there is shelf space for sale if you're interested. Vacancies are marked with a grubby sign: 'Available'.

The catacombs are currently closed for essential conservation work. Until they reopen, visitors can peek into the smaller subterranean chambers beneath the Dissenters' Chapel.

West Norwood Catacombs

Founded in 1837, West Norwood was the world's first Gothic cemetery. Popular with millionaires, it contains the graves of Sir Henry Doulton, Baron de Reuter and Sir Henry Tate. The Greek Necropolis, where shipowners and merchants could flaunt their wealth even after death, contains the highest concentration of listed funerary monuments in Britain. The Friends of West Norwood Cemetery (www.fownc.org) organise monthly tours and occasional forays into the splendid Gothic catacombs.

WEST LONDON BOWLING CLUB

Roll up, roll up

112a Highlever Road, W10 6PL
www.westlondonbowlingclub.com
Membership fee applies
Latimer Road tube

I lived around the corner from this bowling green for a year before I realised it was there. Hidden at the end of a narrow alley wedged between two ordinary houses, the West London Bowling Club has been around since 1903. (It moved to the present site in 1920.)

Bordered by low-rise cottages, it was one of five 'backlands' created as communal recreation grounds for the residents of the St Quintin Estate, a leafy patch of West London that was a model of social and affordable housing long before former Prime Minister David Cameron and his ilk moved in. None of the other backlands has survived with its original use intact.

During the Second World War, while other backlands were turned into allotments, the club's members doggedly continued to bowl despite near misses by bombs and land mines. Men always wore whites. Their wives, who were not welcome on the green, had to make do with providing tea and cakes.

As one of the first female bowlers recalls: 'The year that man walked on the moon was the year that women were first allowed to walk on the green.' However, strict rules regarding the length of skirts were enforced for many years.

The popularity of bowling has waned since the club's mid-20th-century heyday. Membership dwindled, the green was unkempt and the prize-winning rose gardens became overgrown. The little clubhouse became a cheap drinking den, to the annoyance of the neighbours. Eventually the bowling club lost its licence and closed in 2013, but it has now been revived by a group of volunteers. Thanks to their efforts, the bowling club has been designated a 'local green space' that cannot be built over by developers.

Under new management, the bowling green has been relayed, a croquet lawn and petanque pitch installed, and the surrounding garden is gradually being spruced up.

The bowling season runs from mid-April to the end of September, with play from noon until one hour after sunset. Most afternoons, a few members show up for 'roll-ups' – casual games of barefoot bowls. There are occasional matches against other clubs, and experienced bowlers are usually on hand to coach beginners.

The bar is currently open on Fridays and Sundays in season, with film nights and social events year round. On a sunny summer evening, with the fragrance of freshly mowed grass and the thwack of croquet mallets hanging in the air, you could be back in the 1920s.

MUSEUM OF BRANDS

A catalogue of consumerism

111-117 Lancaster Road, W11 1QT
0207 243 9611
www.museumofbrands.com
Tues-Sat 10am-6pm, Sun 11am-5pm. Closed Mondays, except bank holidays.
Last entry 45 mins before closing time
Check website for admission prices
Ladbroke Grove tube

Avisit to the Museum of Brands is like leafing through a picture book of Britain's social history over the last two centuries. Collector par excellence Robert Opie has assembled over half a million everyday objects, from Victoriana ('harness liquid' for carriages and 'wind pills' for sea sickness) through to royal memorabilia. Toys, cosmetics, candies and cleaning products – it's all here, artfully arranged by decade or theme. It's a time tunnel that takes you through the changing fashions and consuming passions of British society.

Once upon a time, banal products like shoe polish and cough syrup came in ornate jars and dainty decanters. Housekeepers stocked up on Vermin Killer ('Mice eat it readily and die on the spot!') and Desiccated Soup ('My dear, buy it!'). How times have changed from the days when 'Servants' Friend' stove polish was in vogue to the invention of the servants' friend: the first vacuum cleaner.

Opie's impressive hoard includes souvenirs from the Great Exhibition of 1851. There are wireless radios and wind-up gramophones, saucy postcards and cigarettes with 'guaranteed 22-carat gold tips'. From the art deco glamour of the 1930s, it's a jarring leap to the ration cards and trench football games of the Second World War, when people were exhorted to eat 'health salts' in lieu of fruit. The *Win the War Cookery Book* promises 'complete victory – if you eat less bread'. The 1950s bring a kitschy optimism, all colourful Formica, pin-ups in bikinis, and convertible cars for beach holidays. The '60s are summed up by the arrival of portable TVs and, of course, the Beatles. And what a decade the 1970s was: *Planet of the Apes* and platform shoes.

Graphic designers will delight in the Brand Hall, which revisits the evolution of classic British products like Cadbury's chocolate, Colman's mustard, and Kellogg's All-Bran (which has wisely changed its selling line from 'natural laxative' to 'high fibre').
The shop sells scrapbooks themed by decade, a useful source of inspiration for designers and illustrators.

The rather dreary café overlooks one of the museum's best features: a secret memorial garden that flowers all year round. Brimming with rambling roses and curious squirrels, the garden is the last vestige of The Lighthouse, a residential and day care centre for people living with HIV and AIDS, which occupied the premises until 2015. Many of the former patients' ashes are scattered in this lovely memorial garden.

THE ARAB HALL OF LEIGHTON HOUSE

④

Arabian maximalism

12 Holland Park Road, W14 8LZ
0207 371 2467
www.leightonhouse.co.uk
Daily 10am-5.30pm. Closed Tues. Guided tours every Wed and Sun at 3pm
Check website for admission prices
High Street Kensington, Kensington Olympia, or Holland Park tube

Many of the Victorian mansions around Holland Park were built by artists who gravitated to this urbane neighbourhood towards the end of the 19th century. The 'Holland Park circle' included Lord Frederic Leighton (1830-1896), President of the Royal Academy, whose red brick show home looks fairly unassuming from the outside, apart from its dome.

Inside, Leighton House is designed to make a very big impression. Mary H. Krout, an American who visited in 1899, remarked: '…it was like a bit of Aladdin's palace, which some obliging genius might have set down in London and have forgotten.' The entrance hall is clad in dazzling peacock blue tiles, while a real stuffed peacock guards the wooden staircase. To the left is the Arab Hall, a floor-to-ceiling vision of rare Islamic tiles, inlaid mosaics, and Arabic inscriptions, with a black marble fountain as its centrepiece. The rest of the house is decked out in equally opulent style. Flock wallpapers, oriental carpets, and ornate fireplaces create an orgy of patterns and textures, against which the pre-Raphaelite paintings by Leighton and his contemporaries look positively sedate. By contrast, Leighton's bedroom is unexpectedly austere – perhaps he too needed a respite from so much oriental exotica.

Among Leighton's extensive art collection are works by Edward Burne-Jones, Albert Moore, and George Frederic Watts, who lived around the corner on Melbury Road. Leighton's own light-filled studio appears to be decorated with friezes filched from the Parthenon. This magnificent room was the setting for Leighton's annual music recitals; the tradition continues today with occasional chamber music and jazz concerts, with a smattering of socialites in attendance.

THE SERPENTINE SOLARSHUTTLE ⑤

Solar-powered pleasure cruise

Serpentine Lake, Hyde Park, W2 2UH
0207 262 1989
www.solarshuttle.co.uk
Check website for admission prices
Cruises operate approximately every half hour from noon until dusk at
weekends, school and public holidays between March and September. Daily
service during June, July and August

With its miserable weather, London is not an obvious choice for innovations in solar power. Yet the Solarshuttle glides silently across the Serpentine in Hyde Park, powered entirely by the sun. The journey between the north and the south banks of the Serpentine Lake takes about half an hour, as the boat doesn't go much faster than five miles (8km) an hour. The whole world seems to slow down as you drift past pedaloes and rowing boats, ducks and swans.

With its graceful glass and stainless steel design, the Solarshuttle feels more like a yacht than a miniature ferry. The wooden deck is lined with slatted steel benches, which afford unbroken views of the park. All the architectural details emphasise light and transparency. Detachable glass panels protect passengers from the elements during the winter. Overhead, a curved canopy of 27 solar panels attached to a simple steel frame glints in the sunlight. Not much thicker than a credit card, these photovoltaic cells are embedded into Plexiglas tiles that are layered between a transparent membrane. The solar energy produced is stored in batteries that power two electric engines. When the boat is docked, any surplus electricity generated by the solar panels is fed back into the national power grid.

The Solarshuttle took seven months and cost £237,000 to build – a worthwhile investment given that a diesel-powered boat of this size would produce 2.5 tons of carbon dioxide every year. Even on those overcast days so depressingly familiar to Londoners, there's enough sunlight to keep the Solarshuttle cruising. If the weather gets really dire, the batteries provide enough reserve power to drive the shuttle for 20 miles in pitch darkness.

NEARBY
V&A pet memorials ⑥

Set into the wall of the Victoria and Albert's beautiful John Madjeski garden are two unusual memorials: the plaques commemorate a pair of 'faithful dogs' named Jim and Tycho. Jim was the beloved Yorkshire terrier of Sir Henry Cole, the museum's first director. Cole and Jim were inseparable, and the pooch was a regular fixture at the museum. In his diary, on 11 January 1874, Cole wrote: 'In Museum with Jim, who barked as usual'. Tycho – perhaps named after the Greek for 'lucky' – belonged to Cole's son, Alan.

HYDE PARK PET CEMETERY

Bestial burial ground

Victoria Gate, Hyde Park, W2 2UH
By appointment only. Call 0300 0612000 or
email hyde@royalparks.gsi.gov.uk at least one week in advance to book a tour
Admission charges apply
Lancaster Gate, Marble Arch or Queensway tube

Mad dogs and Englishmen have always been inseparable. The members of the Victorian upper crust were so obsessed with their pets that they buried them in special cemeteries. Barely visible behind the railings of Hyde Park, on the corner of Bayswater Road and Victoria Gate, hundreds of miniature, mildewed gravestones stand testament to this morbid tradition.

This particular pet cemetery was founded in 1880 by George, Duke of Cambridge, who had flouted royal convention by marrying an actress, Louisa Fairbrother. When his distraught wife's favourite dog, Prince, was run over, the Duke – who doubled as Chief Ranger of Hyde Park – asked the gate-keeper, Mr Windbridge, to give the poor creature a proper burial in the back garden of his lodge. By 1915, the graves in Mr Windbridge's garden were so tightly packed that the cemetery was closed.

Over 300 animals are laid to rest here – dogs, cats, birds, and even a monkey. Drowned, poisoned, or run over, Flo, Carlo, and Yum Yum's miniature gravestones bear epitaphs that range from the touching to the maudlin. Quotes from the Bible and Shakespearean couplets are sprinkled among personal tributes: 'To the memory of my dear Emma – faithful and sole companion of my otherwise rootless and desolate life.' The unlikeliest epitaphs are to pooches named Smut and Scum. Some posh dogs even had bespoke coffins. One lady who buried her Pomeranian in a locked casket allegedly wore the keys around her neck until she went to her own grave.

This bestial necropolis received one last canine resident – also named Prince – in 1967, when the Royal Marines were granted special permission to bury their 11-year-old mascot in the southern corner. Today, the place George Orwell called 'perhaps the most horrible spectacle in Britain' can only be viewed by prior appointment.

NEARBY

The fake houses of Leinster Gardens ⑧

When London's first Tube line was extended westwards, inevitably some houses had to be demolished. The owners of 23/24 Leinster Gardens in Bayswater sold up, but local residents demanded that the façades of these five-storey terraces be rebuilt to keep up appearances. At first glance, the fake façades are indistinguishable from their neighbours; but look closer and you'll see that all 18 windows are blacked out with grey paint. Although there are no letterboxes, the address is predictably popular with conmen. In the 1930s, unsuspecting guests turned up to a charity ball at 23 Leinster Gardens in full evening dress. They never got their money back.

TYBURN CONVENT

A cloistered existence

8-12 Hyde Park Place, W2 2LJ
0207 723 7262
www.tyburnconvent.org.uk
Guided tours of the crypt at 10.30am, 3.30pm and 5.30pm daily
Admission free
Marble Arch tube

The highly desirable townhouses along Bayswater Road overlook Hyde Park, but the residents of Nos 8-12 can only enjoy these green vistas from a distance. Around 20 Benedictine nuns are cloistered here, maintaining a 24-hour vigil in the ground-floor chapel of Tyburn Convent. Though just moments from the bustle of Oxford Street, the nuns only venture out for medical emergencies. Food is delivered, but they don't do takeaways. The nuns spend most of their time in silence, broken by Mass, which is sung seven times a day, the ethereal music wafting through the chapel. Worshippers can hear, but cannot see the nuns: the altar is screened by a metal grille.

Tyburn Convent was founded in 1901 to commemorate the Roman Catholics hanged nearby on the Tyburn Tree gallows during the Reformation (1535 - 1681). The crypt contains a shrine to over 350 Catholic martyrs, including gruesome relics of their bones, hair, and bloodstained clothing. You can get a good look at these creepy appendages and keepsakes on one of the three daily tours of the shrine. Over the altar is a replica of the infamous Tyburn gallows, which stood just east of here, on what is now a traffic island at the junction of Bayswater Road and Edgware Road. A small, circular plaque in the paving stones marks the site where around 50,000 people were executed between 1196 and 1783. Hangings were so popular that execution days were declared public holidays. However, Mayfair's posh residents didn't like this barbaric spectator sport on their doorstep, and forced the authorities to move the gallows to Newgate (see p. 114) in 1783.

The smallest house in London

Now part of Tyburn Convent, the red brick 'house' at 10 Hyde Park Place is just over one metre wide. Apparently the ground floor consists entirely of a corridor, while the first floor contains nothing but a bathroom. Dating from 1805, it was probably erected to block a passageway leading to St George's graveyard – popular with body-snatchers at the time.

NEARBY

Marble Arch surveillance rooms ⑩

Marble Arch was built by John Nash in 1828 as a monumental entrance to Buckingham Palace. To this day, only senior royals and their guards are permitted to pass through its central arch. No matter: since it was moved in 1851, Marble Arch has been marooned at the junctions of Oxford Street, Park Lane and Edgware Road, making access impossible to all but the most foolhardy pedestrians. Legend has it that there are three small rooms inside the arch, used for police surveillance until the 1950s.

HORSEMAN'S SUNDAY

Equestrian blessings

St John's Hyde Park, Hyde Park Crescent, W2 2QD
0207 262 1732
http://stjohns-hydepark.com/
Open after morning mass on the penultimate Sunday of September
Marble Arch, Paddington, or Lancaster Gate tube

At noon on the penultimate Sunday of September, Connaught Village celebrates a bizarre ritual dating back to 1968, when the riding stables nearby were threatened with closure. Outside St John's Church, a neo-Gothic pile on Hyde Park Crescent, locals tuck into tandoori chicken while children pelt coconuts. It feels like a village fete, complete with tombola, home-baked cakes, and a jazz band tinkling away.

As the Sunday service draws to a close, the Vicar appears on horseback in an emerald green cape and Napoleonic hat, followed by an orderly procession of about 100 horses. There are squat Shetland ponies with pint-sized riders, sleek stallions, and posh blondes in skin-tight jodhpurs. There's even a Harrods carriage, its poker-stiff passengers kitted out in the store's distinctive green livery. An impatient stallion lets out a torrent of urine, frightening the toddlers and titillating the teenagers. The Reverend Stephen Mason gives 'thanks to all the animals that give us pleasure in our homes and in the world.' He even quotes John Wayne: 'Courage is when you're scared to death and still get into the saddle.'

How Rotten Row got its name

After moving his court from Whitehall to Kensington Palace, King William III discovered that the route back to St James's palace through Hyde Park was thick with 'footpads', or muggers. So in 1690 he installed 300 oil lamps – the first artificially-lit highway in Britain – along the Route de Roi (Route of the King), soon corrupted by the British to Rotten Row. This was where 19th-century kings and courtesans paraded in all their finery. There are still five miles of bridleways in Hyde Park. Ross Nye Stables (8 Bathurst Mews; 0207 262 3791; www.rossnyestables. co.uk) and Hyde Park Stables (63 Bathurst Mews; 0207 723 2813; www.hydeparkstables.com) offer horseback jaunts along them.

London's mews

In 1900, there were 300,000 working horses in London. These days, Jaguars and Bentleys are parked behind the stable doors of London's mews. These cobbled cul-de-sacs housed London's many stables when the most common form of transport for ladies and gentlemen was the horse and carriage. The Queen has her own Royal Mews behind Buckingham Palace, where she keeps the Gold State Coach, covered in four tons' worth of bling. Queen Victoria refused to ride in it. Apparently, it gave her 'distressing oscillations'.

ALEXANDER FLEMING LABORATORY MUSEUM

Mouldy microbes

St Mary's Hospital, Praed Street, W2 1NY
0203 312 6528
www.imperial.nhs.uk/about-us/who-we-are/fleming-museum
Mon-Thurs 10am-1pm or by appointment
Check website for admission prices
Paddington tube/rail, Edgware Road tube

Ablue plaque outside St Mary's hospital alerts passers-by that Alexander Fleming (1881-1955) discovered penicillin in the second-storey room above it. Few visitors venture up to the tiny museum, accessible via a dingy entrance on Norfolk Place.

When Fleming was born, antibiotics did not exist. Minor infections often proved fatal and a quarter of all hospital patients died of gangrene after surgery. When Fleming enrolled as a medical student at St Mary's in 1900, he dreamed of becoming a surgeon; but – luckily for the rest of us – he was given a temporary position in the Inoculation Department, where he remained until his death.

The poky laboratory where Fleming worked between 1919 and 1933 (when it was converted into a bedroom for students of midwifery) has been painstakingly recreated. The wooden counter is cluttered with vials and test tubes containing mysterious fluids, tattered leather-bound medical tomes, a couple of antique microscopes and countless glass culture dishes. One day in 1922, Fleming was hunched over his bacteria cultures as usual, despite suffering from a nasty cold. A drop of snot landed on his Petri dish, which led to his discovery of the antiseptic properties of mucus, saliva and tears.

In September 1928, Fleming made another chance discovery that changed the course of medical history. When one of his cultures was contaminated with mould from a lab downstairs, Fleming hit on the healing properties of fungus – and effectively invented penicillin. Fleming's assistant, Stuart Craddock, ate some of this 'mould juice' to prove that it was not poisonous. Craddock claimed that it tasted like Stilton, prompting a flurry of sensational headlines about mouldy cheese being a miracle cure for disease.

'It couldn't have happened anywhere but this musty, dusty lab, as the mould would not have grown in a more hygienic environment,' says the museum's curator, Kevin Brown. The mouldy Petri dish in the museum is actually a replica – the original is in the British Library, along with several of Fleming's notebooks.

Alexander Fleming's grave in St Paul's Cathedral is decorated with the Scottish thistle and the fleur de lys, symbol of St Mary.

THE HANDLEBAR CLUB

Wax factor

The Heron Tavern, 1 Norfolk Crescent, London W2 2DN
www.handlebarclub.co.uk
Members meet at 8pm on the first Friday of the month
Admission free
Edgware Road tube, Marylebone tube / rail

London is full of odd members' clubs such as the Veteran-Cycle Club, the Time Travel Club, and the Eccentric Club (whose patron, appropriately, is HRH Prince Philip, Duke of Edinburgh). Perhaps the oddest of them all is the Handlebar Club of Great Britain. It was founded in 1947 by Jimmy Edwards, a popular post-war comedian, who once sang: 'Every girl loves a fella with a bush upon his mush!' The Handlebar Club originally had ten members; today, it has around 100 acolytes from all over the world. The club's mission was and remains 'to bring together moustache wearers socially for sport and general conviviality'.

The criterion for membership is simple: prospective members must have 'a hirsute appendage of the upper lip, with graspable extremities'. Beards of any kind are banned; this includes 'soul patches', 'chin strips', 'closely-trimmed goatees', and any hair growing on the chin. The other essential qualification is 'to be able to drink plenty of beer' at the club's monthly get-togethers.

For years, the club's monthly knees-up took place at the Windsor Castle, an old-fashioned boozer rammed to the rafters with royal memorabilia. Since this rare gem was bought up by a Saudi conglomerate hell bent on converting the pub into more luxury flats, it was forced to close in August 2016. So the Handlebar Club has decamped to the Heron Tavern, just across Edgware Road. Though it lacks the surreal charm of the Windsor Castle, the Heron is a suitably old-school establishment with a small beer garden and incongruous Thai restaurant in the basement. (The food is outstanding, if you can handle eating authentically fiery Thai cooking to the sound of karaoke.)

About a dozen members of the Handlebar Club usually show up at these monthly gatherings. Most are dressed in 'member's regalia' – maroon ties emblazoned with a white moustache and matching sweaters – and all have redoubtable chops. Bushy, twirly, waxed or curled, their moustaches are eminently graspable. These self-confessed 'facial hair fanatics' don't appear to do much other than 'furry fraternising', which involves frequently raising their pint glasses with the toast: 'To the last whisker!'

Members occasionally engage in charitable stunts such as finding out how many moustaches fit into a Mini. They do at least pay lip service to the Handlebar Club's Constitution, a copy of which is available to prospective members. For instance, anyone who lets their sideburns merge with their moustache is fined.

MARYLEBONE CRICKET CLUB MUSEUM

The world's oldest sporting museum

Lord's Cricket Ground, St John's Wood Rd, NW8 8QN
0207 616 8658
www.lords.org
Tours run several times a day, except on match days. The MCC Museum is free for ticket-holders on match days
Check website for admission prices
St John's Wood, Warwick Avenue, or Marylebone tube

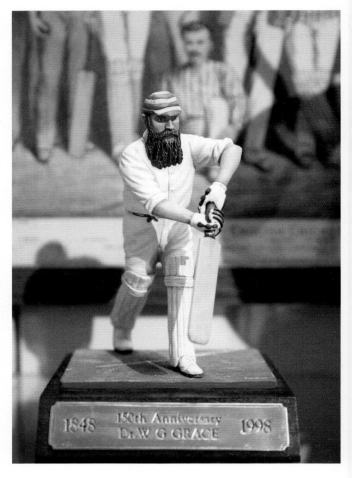

1848   150th Anniversary   1998
Dr W G GRACE

Although it has somehow acquired a reputation as a 'gentleman's game', at least to outsiders, early cricket fans were all chronic gamblers. In the 19th century, the wicket was prepared before a match by inviting sheep to graze on the grass. There is a waiting list of 18 years for membership of Marylebone Cricket Club (MCC). These are just a few of the surprising facts you'll learn if you 'take a tour of Lords', probably the world's most famous cricket ground. It's certainly one of the oldest, founded on a former duck pond in 1814 by a wine merchant named Thomas Lord.

The guided tour starts in the MCC Memorial Gallery, the world's first sporting museum. Among the signed bats, smelly boots, and old photographs spanning 400 years of cricket history, are oddities such as the stuffed sparrow that was 'bowled out' by Jehangir Khan in 1936.

The prized exhibit is a small Victorian perfume jar, containing 'the Ashes'. The term was coined after England lost to Australia on home soil for the first time on 29 August 1882. The next day, the *Sporting Times* published an ironic obituary to English cricket, concluding that: 'The body will be cremated and the ashes taken to Australia'. When the English team set off to tour Australia weeks later, Captain Ivo Bligh vowed to return home with the Ashes. After Bligh's team beat Australia, his future wife, Florence Morphy, gave him this miniature urn as a token of his victory. When Bligh died in 1927, he bequeathed the Ashes to the MCC where they have been on display ever since.

Visitors also have a rare opportunity to sneak around the 19th-century club rooms reserved for the 22,000 members of the MCC. On match days, at least 200 VIPs are crammed into the elegant Long Room, with its picture windows and paintings of celebrated cricketers. Players make their way to and from the field through the Long Room's double doors – either to rapturous ovation or deadly silence, depending on their performance. When the Queen cares to watch a match, she sits in the Committee Room, where the worldwide laws of cricket are still thrashed out. But the best seats are undoubtedly in the Media Centre, a sleek white capsule that hovers 15 metres above the ground.

'The worst-behaved crowd of the season'

The annual fixture between the pupils of Eton and Harrow has been played out since 1805. According to the tour guide, it's 'the worst-behaved crowd of the season.'

CAB SHELTERS

Knowledgeable diners

*Locations: Embankment Place, Charing Cross WC2 - Grosvenor Gardens,
Victoria SW1 - Chelsea Embankment SW3 (currently closed) - Hanover
Square, Mayfair W1 - Kensington Park Road, Notting Hill W11 - Kensington
Road (north side), South Kensington W8 - Pont Street, Belgravia SW1 - Russell
Square (west corner), Bloomsbury WC1 - St George's Square, Pimlico - Temple
Place, Victoria Embankment WC2 - Thurloe Place, South Kensington SW7 -
Warwick Avenue, Maida Vale W9 - Wellington Place, St John's Wood NW8*

The London Hackney Carriage Industry was first licensed by an act of Oliver Cromwell in June 1654, and Londoners can be justly proud of the city's characteristic black cabs, the direct descendants of these horse-drawn carriages. This is one of the few really pleasurable travel experiences in the city, where the congestion charge deters motorists and public transport is overcrowded, unreliable, and overpriced. The cabs have so much legroom that you can sit back almost horizontally and watch the city slide by.

London's cab drivers are equally impressive, as all of them are required to have 'the Knowledge'. This exam, introduced in 1865, means cabbies must remember every street within six miles of Charing Cross (the official centre of London, see p. 75). This formidable feat can take years to achieve. If you keep your eyes peeled, you can see students of the Knowledge everywhere – people riding mopeds around the city with a clipboard and map on the handlebars are usually prospective cabbies learning routes before their exam, which involves a flawless rendition of a route between any two points chosen at random.

Originally, cab drivers weren't allowed to leave their horse and carriage when parked. They would have to sit up top, exposed to the elements, while awaiting their next fare. Instead, they often took refuge in the nearest pub. So in 1874 the Earl of Shaftsbury set up the Cabmen's Shelter Fund to construct shelters to provide cabbies with 'good and wholesome refreshments at moderate prices'. The result was a flourishing of green wooden sheds around the capital. Because the shelters stand directly on a public highway, they could be no bigger than a horse and cart – even so, they still manage to squeeze in a working kitchen and space for a dozen strapping men. Many of them still have black rails running along the outside, originally intended for tethering horses.

The philanthropists who set up the shelters were typically high-minded Victorians: gambling, drinking and swearing were strictly forbidden. There were originally 61 of these cabmen's shelters, but numbers have now dwindled to 13, and not all of these are open. However, they still stand, as they are now listed buildings. Many of them still thrive as a place for colleagues to meet and eat. Only cabbies are allowed to sit inside, but anyone can get a take-away – bacon roll, brown sauce, tea, four sugars, thanks love – through the serving hatch.

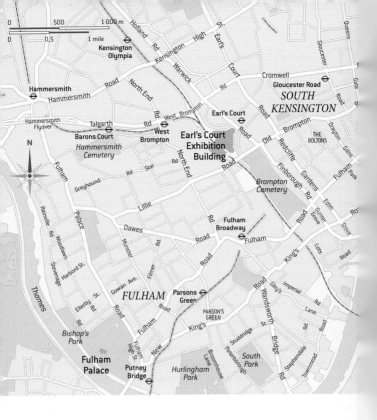

Westminster to Hammersmith

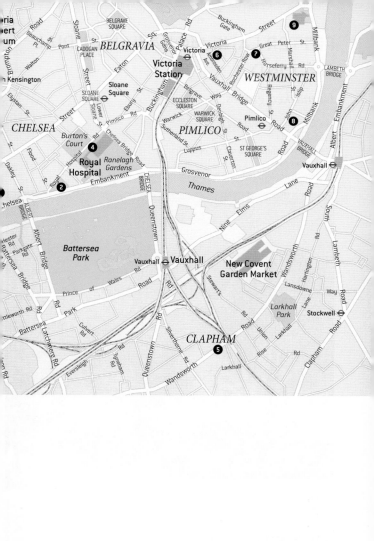

FETTER LANE MORAVIAN BURIAL GROUND ①

Unmarked graves

381 King's Road, SW10 0LP
0208 4829363
Times vary, contact church for details
Admission free
South Kensington, Fulham Broadway, or Sloane Square tube

World's End sounds like a good location for a graveyard. Hidden from the bouffant shoppers of King's Road by a high brick wall, this small cemetery adjoins the evangelical Moravian church. Established in 1742, the chapel looks like a country cottage transplanted into the heart of Chelsea. But the back garden is actually a burial ground. Known to the congregation as God's Acre, it contains a handful of 18th-century graves, marked only by flat, white stones. Traditionally, Moravians are buried separately in simple graves, men on one side and women on the other. The deceased are also sub-divided into those who are married and unmarried.

Originally from Bohemia and Moravia (now the Czech Republic), Moravians first came to Britain in the 1730s. The congregations created settlements with their own farms, businesses and schools. In 1750, their filthy rich leader, Count Zinzendorf, bought Lindsey House, a riverside mansion built by Henry VIII's ill-fated chancellor Thomas More, for £750. After a lavish renovation, the house became the international headquarters of the Moravian church and a resting place for missionaries. Its grounds stretched all the way from the waterfront to what is now the King's Road. Thomas More's former stables were converted into a church and the stable yard became the congregation's graveyard. However, the Moravian brethren never really took hold in London. After Zinzendorf's death in 1760, the property was divided into five townhouses and the church sold off most of the land, apart from this modest burial ground. Zinzendorf's son, Christian Renatus, is interred here, commemorated in a tablet on the south wall of the chapel.

Little remains of Thomas More's vast riverside estate, apart from the Tudor brick walls enclosing the Moravian burial ground. Roman Ambramovich and Mick Jagger have since occupied Lindsey House (now 100 Cheyne Walk). The Georgian mansion allegedly contains some religious murals painted by the Moravians. Owned by the National Trust, the gardens (subsequently re-designed by Edwin Lutyens) are accessible to visitors on Open House weekend.

A feline Sloane Ranger

During the 1960s, the Moravian graveyard became the playground of Christian, a pet lion belonging to John Rendall, an Australian antiques dealer who bought the cub over the counter at Harrods. (Fittingly, Rendall's furniture shop on Kings Road was called Sophistocat.) The obliging vicar allowed Christian to play football in the safe confines of the parish grounds. Christian was later taken to Africa and rehabilitated into the wild.

CHELSEA PHYSIC GARDEN

Bankside botanicals

66 Royal Hospital Road, SW3 4HS
0207 352 5646
www.chelseaphysicgarden.co.uk
The Garden, café and shop are open Tues, Fri and Sun 11am-6pm
Only the Garden is open on Mondays, 10am-5pm
Check website for admission prices
Sloane Square tube

Horticulturalists and herbalists will delight in this enchanting walled garden containing around 5000 plant species from all over the world. The collection was founded in 1673 by the Society of Apothecaries to study the medicinal properties of plants. In 1712, Dr Hans Sloane, a wealthy physician, purchased the entire Manor of Chelsea. Ten years later, he leased some four acres of land to the apothecaries for £5 a year in perpetuity – a bargain even back then. The deed of covenant is on display, stating the garden's purpose, that 'apprentices and others may the better distinguish good and usefull plants from those that bear resemblance to them and yet are hurtfull.'

The location on the banks of the Thames created a warmer microclimate so that exotic plants could survive the biting British winter. Tropical plants are still cultivated in fetid greenhouses. The apothecaries' botanical experiments were influential in developing the American cotton industry and the tea trade in India. Given the 21st-century trend for natural medicine, the Garden of World Medicine and Pharmaceutical Garden were way ahead of their time. Look out for the bizarre pond rock garden, partially built with Icelandic lava and stones from the Tower of London. The café is also notable for its home-made cakes and lavender scones.

Dr Hans Sloane: inventor of milk chocolate

As well as giving his name to Sloane Square, Dr Hans Sloane invented milk chocolate. After discovering locals drinking cocoa mixed with water in Jamaica, Sloane improved on the recipe by mixing it with milk. Back in England, his formula was sold as medicine until the Cadbury brothers cottoned on and began selling tins of Sloane's drinking chocolate.

NEARBY
Carlyle's House ③

Boasting the most blue plaques in a single street, Cheyne Walk is one of London's most exclusive addresses. These genteel surroundings have been an unlikely refuge for rock stars Mick Jagger, Keith Richards, Kylie Minogue, and Bob Geldof. Around the corner, at 24 Cheyne Row, you can snoop around the home of a Victorian celebrity, Thomas Carlyle, historian, essayist, and founder of the London Library (see p. 56). Dickens, Tennyson and Browning were regular visitors at this literary sanctuary, which is preserved exactly as it was left in 1895. In the attic, Carlyle built a specially sound-proofed study. When it was completed, his wife Jane declared: 'The silent room is the noisiest room in the house!' (www.nationaltrust.org.uk/carlyles-house. Open March-Oct Wed-Sun 11am-4.30pm.)

ROYAL HOSPITAL CHELSEA

Retirement home designed by Christopher Wren

Royal Hospital Road, Chelsea SW3 4SR
0207 881 5200
www.chelsea-pensioners.co.uk
The Museum is open Mon-Fri 10am-4pm (excluding bank holidays). Guided tours Mon, Wed, Fri at 10am and Mon, Tues, Thurs at 1.30pm (minimum of 10 people); tours must be booked at least 4 weeks in advance
Admission free to visit the Museum. Check the website for details about guided tours
Sloane Square tube

Renting a small flat on Chelsea's Royal Hospital Road would set you back a small fortune. For the price of their monthly pension, the lucky 300-odd army veterans who live at the Royal Hospital Chelsea get to live in glorious digs designed by Christopher Wren, enjoy three meals a day served in an oak-panelled Great Hall lined with royal portraits, and have access to a clubhouse, library, bowling green, croquet lawn, billiard rooms, and 66 acres of gardens beside the Thames. They also get to wear snazzy uniforms – scarlet jackets and tricorne hats for special occasions, smart navy blazers and 'shako' caps for everyday wear.

King Charles II founded the baroque, redbrick Royal Hospital in 1682 as a refuge for 'the succour and relief of veterans broken by age and war'. Back in the 17th century, when recruits joined the army at the age of 11 or 12, only one in ten pensioners were literate. These days, the charming old boys are happy to show visitors around the small museum, which tells the history of this miraculous time warp through paintings, historical artefacts, and over 2,000 medals. There's even a model wooden berth, snug as a ship's cabin. Nine foot square, with no windows, these cubicles originally had no lights at all, let alone plugs for modern appliances.

Since 2015, the Chelsea pensioners' lodgings have been upgraded to include a private study and wet room. Women were welcomed for the first time in 300 years after en-suite bathrooms were installed.

The Royal Hospital's residential halls are laid out around three immaculate quadrangles. At 10:30 on Sunday mornings, from April to November, pensioners parade through Figure Court in their ceremonial finery. Only about a dozen have the energy or inclination these days.

Listen carefully, and you might hear the master of ceremonies mumbling: 'Shuffle about, boys!' An infirmary was built some years ago. The only drawback is that rooms overlook their last posting – the cemetery.

Chelsea pensioners must be over 65, 'of good military character', and have no dependents. When a pensioner applies for admission, they are invited to stay for four days to see whether the Royal Hospital suits them. Who would turn down the chance to live out their days in such magnificent surroundings?

575 WANDSWORTH ROAD

Dreamy DIY

575 Wandsworth Road, SW8 3JD
0207 720 9459
www.nationaltrust.org.uk/575-wandsworth-road
Tours for a maximum of six people run March-Nov: Wed, Fri, Sat and Sun. Call
0844 249 1895 or email 575wandsworthroad@nationaltrust.org.uk to book
Admission charges and a booking fee apply. Entry is free for National Trust
members, but they still need to book a place
London Overground/rail to Wandsworth Road

First things first. If you want to visit this singular house, book well in advance – ideally, months in advance. Visitors are strictly limited to 54 a week, with tours in groups of six people at a time. Since opening its doors to the public in 2013, the house of Khadambi Asalache, bequeathed to the National Trust, has attracted more visitors than it can accommodate.

From the outside, this unassuming house doesn't look like much. When the exiled Kenyan poet, novelist and philosopher of mathematics Khadambi Asalache bought it in 1981, the small, terraced house was in a bad way. Asalache, who trained as an architect but worked at the Treasury, fixed pine floorboards to the persistent damp patches on the walls and floors. He went on to cover almost every wall, ceiling and door in the house with delicate fretwork that he hand-carved with a plasterboard knife from pine doors and floorboards scavenged from skips. This pragmatic approach to his art characterises the whole project, and the National Trust has been careful to maintain it, retaining the Polyfilla used on the ceilings and a taped-up broken windowpane in the sitting room.

Asalache carved out this private sanctuary compulsively for the rest of his life. (He only once employed a carpenter, but dismissed his work as sub-standard.) Delicate ballerinas, angels, giraffes and birds dance over every surface. The astonishing fretwork was inspired by a mixture of the Moorish art of Andalusia, carved doors in Asalache's native Lamu, panelled interiors in Damascus, and the wooden mansions along the banks of the Bosporus in Istanbul. During conservation, over 2,000 pieces of woodwork were catalogued. The woodwork is juxtaposed with the painted decoration of the walls, doors and floors, hand-carved furniture and carefully arranged collections, including pressed-glass inkwells, postcards, and the poet's collection of pink and copper 19th-century English pottery.

The amount of stuff crammed into the house ought to be overwhelming, but the effect is quietly soothing. As the director of the Sir John Soane's Museum has said, it is 'an extremely serious and carefully worked-out exercise in *horror vacui* (fear of the void)' – and it works. In fact, 575 Wandsworth Road shares the compulsive nature of its interior with the Soane Museum. There is a huge amount to see in such a small space. The best bit? Possibly the main bedroom, with its shutters decorated with the initials of Khadambi and his partner Susie Thomson, and the kennel carved for Thomson's Tibetan spaniel next to the bed.

WESTMINSTER CATHEDRAL BELL TOWER

Look out across London's skyline

Ambrosden Avenue, SW1P 1QW
0207 798 9055
www.westminstercathedral.org.uk
Mon-Fri 9.30am-5pm, Sat and Sun 9.30am-6pm
Check website for admission prices
Victoria tube

With its neo-Byzantine copper domes and terracotta bell tower striped with Portland stone, Westminster Cathedral is surprisingly less visible than Westminster Abbey, just half a mile down Victoria Street. A market, fairground, maze, bull-baiting ring and children's prison once stood on the site, before the Catholic Church bought the land in 1884. Built between 1895 and 1903, the cathedral's interior was never actually completed. Its rich marbles and mosaics shimmer in the shadowy gloom.

In the northwest corner, concealed behind a gift shop, a lift whisks visitors up to the seventh floor of the 83-metre bell tower. (Originally, visitors had to climb the 375 steps to the top.) From viewing platforms on all sides, you can look across London from this great height and marvel at how the ugly modern office blocks have dwarfed the landmarks of a lost empire. Look carefully and you will spot the Union Jack fluttering atop Buckingham Palace, the dome of St Paul's, the spindly skeleton of the Crystal Palace transmission tower. The industrial bulk of the BT Tower, Canary Wharf, and Battersea Power Station make more of a statement. You can contrast today's skyline with blown-up photographs of the same views from 1912.

Don't be alarmed if Big Edward, the 2.5-ton bell named after Edward the Confessor, suddenly strikes overhead. When the lift was installed in 1929, Big Edward had to be relocated above the belfry, which explains why the bell now sounds faintly muffled.

In Alfred Hitchcock's 1940 thriller *Foreign Correspondent*, an assassin plunges to his death from Westminster Cathedral's bell tower as the Requiem Mass is chanted inside. Hitchcock's own Requiem Mass was held at Westminster Cathedral after his death in 1980.

Eric Gill's stations of the cross

Eric Gill was a prolific sculptor, typeface designer, and printmaker who helped design the font for London Underground. Gill also carved the colossal and controversial Stations of the Cross in Westminster Cathedral, which has the widest nave in England. In many ways, they jar with the Byzantine ornamentation of the building. Gill's work has great simplicity of line, a cold, almost depersonalised style of figuration, and his relief work is almost medieval in its blankness. But he was an odd choice of artist for this hallowed site. Despite being an enthusiastic convert to Catholicism, who wrote extensively on the relationship between art and religion, Gill sexually abused his own children, had an incestuous relationship with his sister, and experimented sexually on his dog.

THE LONDON SCOTTISH
REGIMENTAL MUSEUM

From kilts to camouflage

95 Horseferry Road, SW1P 2DX
0207 630 1639
www.londonscottishregt.org
By appointment with the curator only. Email curatorlonscot@aol.com or call
the number provided above
Admission free, but donations welcome
Pimlico or St James's Park tube

Behind the sombre façade of this Territorial Army headquarters on Horseferry Road is a soaring drill hall, whose red and blue balconies are decorated with memorabilia from the London Scottish Regiment's colourful history. A volunteer corps set up by a group of influential Scots in London in 1859, its distinguished members have included Sir Alexander Fleming, travel writer Eric Newby, and movie star Basil Rathbone.

Access is by appointment, which means that visitors get an exhaustive tour from the zealous archivist – though he may reprimand you if your military history is sketchy. Some of the army acronyms might be rather arcane for the non-expert, but only the coldest of heart will be unmoved by the memorials to the hundreds of untrained soldiers who served and died in the South African War (1900-2) and the Great Wars.

Around the upper floor balconies are all manner of medals, machine guns, bagpipes, uniforms, and photographs of 'old soldiers' going into battle in kilts and spats. There is even a scrap of Lieutenant-Colonel Lord Elcho's grey overcoat, which inspired him to invent the first form of camouflage. Fed up with soldiers from different clans bickering about tartans, Elcho decreed that the regiment should wear Hodden Grey, a coarse cloth typically worn in Scotland. This canny move also made the troops less of a target.

On Tuesday evenings, between 7pm and 9pm, the magnificent hall is used for drill practice, which must be a stirring sight.

NEARBY
Millbank buttress and tunnels ⑧

Opposite Tate Britain is an innocuous-looking bollard bearing a tiny plaque that reads: 'Near this site stood Millbank Prison, which was opened in 1816 and closed in 1880. This buttress stood at the head of the river steps from which, until 1867, prisoners sentenced to deportation embarked on their journey to Australia.' These prisoners would be shuffled through a series of underground tunnels beneath the prison. A section of the tunnel survives in the cellars of the nearby Morpeth Arms (www.morpetharms.com), a pub built to serve the prison warders and now allegedly haunted by the ghost of a former inmate. Millbank, the first national penitentiary, was designed as a pentagonal 'panopticon' by Jeremy Bentham (see p. 34), whose revolutionary design did not live up to his ideals of social reform. Novelist Henry James called Millbank 'a worse act of violence than any it was erected to punish'. The Tate Gallery was built on this inauspicious site in 1897.

FUNERARY IMAGES
OF WESTMINSTER ABBEY

Dog's eyebrows and stuffed parrots

Westminster Abbey, 20 Deans Yard, SW1P 3PA
0207 222 5152
www.westminster-abbey.org
Usually open Mon-Sat throughout the year, though times vary according to church services. On Sundays and religious holidays, the Abbey is open for worship and entrance is free.
Check website for admission prices
Westminster or St James's Park tube

Westminster Abbey's tombs and monuments give it the atmosphere of a fetish house for the Establishment. Worst of all is the co-opting of people deemed to have added to the lustre of England. The poet Shelley, despite being an avowed anti-Establishment artist and buried in Rome, is memorialised in Poets Corner, just across the transept from Viscount Castlereagh, (of whom Shelley once wrote: 'I met Murder on the way – He had a face like Castlereagh'). There is an unseemly huddle of political statuary next to the northern door, inclusion here apparently constituting the height of ambition for the great and good working over the road in Parliament.

The Abbey is a Royal Peculiar; that is, a church that falls directly under the jurisdiction of the British monarch, rather than a bishop's diocese. Given that, it is surprising that the Crown cannot do more to alleviate the gouging at the ticket office. Or perhaps not.

If you can stomach the prices and steel yourself to fight the tour groups, then the Undercroft museum is really worth a visit. It contains some of the oddest exhibits in London: a collection of royal funerary effigies. Until the Middle Ages, British monarchs were traditionally embalmed and left to lie in state for a set period of time. Eventually, the corpse was substituted for a wooden figure of the deceased, fully dressed with clothes from the Great Wardrobe and displayed on top of the funeral carriage during the final journey. As the clothes were expected to fit the effigy perfectly, these likenesses are probably fairly accurate.

All are surprisingly tiny, even fatboy Henry VIII. Edward III's face has a strange leer, a recreation of the stroke that he suffered in his final years. His eyebrows supposedly came from a plucked dog. The collection also includes the effigies of Edward III, Henry VII, Elizabeth I, Charles II, William III, Mary II and Queen Anne. Later wax effigies include Nelson, William Pitt, and several soldiers known as the Ragged Regiment, due to their decrepit state. Take a close look at Frances, Duchess of Richmond and Lennox: she's holding what may be the world's oldest stuffed bird, an African Grey parrot that died in 1702. Samuel Pepys wrote in his diary that Frances was the greatest beauty he'd ever seen. Sadly, she was disfigured by smallpox in 1668.

The Triforium of Westminster Abbey

In 2018, the Triforium of Westminster Abbey reopened for the first time in 700 years. With giddying views of the church, 21 metres below, the gallery shows off relics stashed in the Abbey's cluttered loft for centuries.

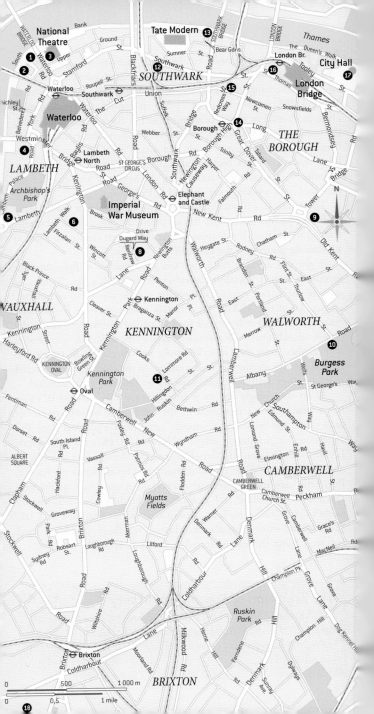

South Bank to Brixton

BFI MEDIATHEQUE

Movie jukebox

BFI Southbank, Belvedere Road, South Bank, SE1 8XT
0207 928 3232
www.bfi.org.uk/Southbank
Tue-Sat 12-8pm, Sun 12.30-8pm
Admission free
Waterloo or Embankment tube

Since it re-launched to great fanfare in summer 2007, the re-branded Southbank Centre has lived up to the hype. But one of the most intriguing additions, the BFI Mediatheque, is overlooked by most visitors. Perhaps that's because it is hidden behind the café and cinemas.

In a sleek, steel grey screening room designed by architect David Adjaye are 14 flatscreen viewing stations, where anyone can access hundreds of hours of footage from the British Film Institute's digital archive for free. Some of the viewing stations hold multiple viewers, some are only singles. The BFI's celluloid archives are huge: over 230,000 films and 675,000 television programmes, and counting. Until now, this material could only be seen on request or at special screenings. As the collection is slowly digitised, new material will be added to the Mediatheque every month.

From wartime propaganda films (*So Clever Are the German Spies in Their Disguises That Even Nuns Have to Have Their Passports Examined*, 1914) to early pornography (*Strip! Strip! Hooray!!!*, 1932), the material provides an eclectic overview of British history through footage spanning more than a century. The Essentially British strand ranges from Queen Victoria's Diamond Jubilee in 1897 to suffragettes rioting in Trafalgar Square in 1913, *Tea Making Tips* from 1941, to the 1960s Carnaby Street scene. *London Calling* showcases the capital's hidden charms and faded glories. Today's Kensington of Russian oligarchs and Arab billionaires bears little resemblance to the squalid slum it was in 1930. In *The London Nobody Knows*, James Mason guides viewers around the city's more esoteric sights in 1967. Many of them have vanished forever. The highlight for many British viewers will be another distant dream: the World Cup final in 1966.

To use the Mediatheque, just show up and book a two-hour slot. You can stay longer if there is no queue – and there usually isn't.

NEARBY
Poetry Library   ②
0207 921 0943; www.poetrylibrary.org.uk
Tues-Sun 11am-8pm. Admission free
Another underrated collection on the South Bank is the Poetry Library, the most comprehensive collection of modern poetry in Britain. Located on Level 5 of the Royal Festival Hall, it holds over 200,000 items and is growing all the time. Audio recordings of poets reciting their work are especially rewarding.

NATIONAL THEATRE BACKSTAGE TOURS

Sneak preview

Upper Ground, South Bank, SE1 9PX
0207 452 3400
www.nationaltheatre.org.uk
75-minute tours run several times a day, Mon-Sat. Book online or email tours@
nationaltheatre.org.uk
Check website for current admission prices
Waterloo or Embankment tube

A modernist colossus sat squarely on the South Bank, Britain's National Theatre opened in 1976 (the National Theatre Company was previously based in the nearby Old Vic). Designed by architect Denys Lasdun (who had never built a theatre before), the theatre is loved and loathed in equal measure. Lasdun integrated the horizontal design with Waterloo Bridge, with one terrace actually built into the bridge to create the impression of an umbilical cord linking the West End theatres across the river with this monument to concrete.

The National Theatre produces up to 25 new plays a year on its three stages, which always pull in big crowds. But few take advantage of the backstage tours held several times a day. Guides whisk visitors behind the scenes, their commentary occasionally drowned out by sound checks for the evening's performances. In the warren of backstage corridors and studios, you can spy on carpenters and portrait painters, wig makers and welders at work. You might catch a glimpse of period sets being painted, rubber vol-au-vents being created, or orchestras warming up.

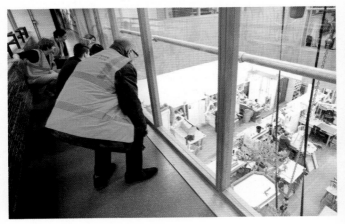

Cutting edge back in 1976, some of the stage technology now seems archaic. In the Lyttleton Theatre, the traditional 'fly tower', used for moving sets, lighting, and microphones, is still operated by 75 'flymen', rather than controlled by computer. The most extraordinary piece of stage equipment is buried deep beneath the Olivier Theatre. Five storeys high and 150 tonnes in weight, the vast 'drum revolve' allows lavish sets to emerge from the bowels of the theatre at dramatic moments.

Sherling High-Level Walkway

You don't have to book a tour or pay a penny to take a peek backstage. Above the Dorfman Theatre, the Sherling High-Level Walkway overlooks some of the workshops where props are made and sets are built. A permanent exhibition by theatre designer Vicki Mortimer takes you through the design process from scale model to curtain up. (Open Mon-Sat 9.30am-7.30pm)

National Theatre Costume Hire

Chichester House, Kennington Park Business Estate, 1-3 Brixton Road, SW9 6DE

The huge trove of costumes and props from past productions is stored at a depot in Brixton. At the National Theatre Costume Hire, you can try on corsets and chainmail for size and hire a ball gown or a bishop's cassock for weddings and fancy dress parties.

FLORENCE NIGHTINGALE MUSEUM

To the bedside manner born ④

St Thomas' Hospital
2 Lambeth Palace Road, SE1 7EW
0207 188 4400
www.florence-nightingale.co.uk
Daily 10am-5pm (last entry 4.30pm)
Check website for admission prices
Westminster or Lambeth North tube, Waterloo tube/rail

A hospital car park isn't the most obvious location for a museum – even one with a medical theme. But that's where you'll find this homage to Florence Nightingale, the genteel rebel who invented the nursing profession.

'There is nothing like the tyranny of a good English family,' Florence once sniped. She came from wealthy but liberal stock: her grandfather campaigned to abolish slavery and her father taught both his daughters mathematics, philosophy and science, then considered strictly male pursuits. The Nightingales also loved to travel; their honeymoon lasted so long that they produced two daughters (in Naples and Florence) before they returned home.

Devout and scholarly, Florence was not expected to do anything much apart from marry and procreate. She was certainly not supposed to work, but her ambition was to become a nurse. Her parents were aghast; in the Victorian age, nurses were known for being devious, dishonest and drunken. Hospitals were filthy, dangerous places exclusively for the poor; the rich were treated in the privacy of their own homes.

Undeterred, Florence set off for the Crimean War at the age of 34, with no formal training and very little experience. She spent two years nursing injured soldiers at the Scutari military hospital in Turkey, where she had to contend with rats, lice, cockroaches and an absence of sewage. In Britain, penny papers popularised the image of the 'lady with the lamp' patrolling the wards.

Although Florence hated the 'buzz fuzz' of celebrity, her famous lantern is the prize exhibit at the Florence Nightingale Museum. Dimly lit and curiously curated, with circular display cases covered in fake grass or wrapped in bandages, the small museum is packed with fascinating exhibits, from Florence's hand-written ledgers and primitive medical instruments to pamphlets with titles like *How People May Live and not Die in India.*

The most bizarre item is Athena, Florence's stuffed pet owl, whom she rescued on a visit to the Parthenon. Athena always perched on Florence's shoulder or in her pocket, with a specially designed pouch to catch her droppings. When the bad-tempered owl died, Florence wrote: 'Poor little beastie, it was odd how much I loved you.'

After contracting 'Crimean fever', Florence suffered ill health until her death aged 90. Unable to continue nursing, she devoted herself to health reform, founding the first training school for nurses at St Thomas' Hospital, campaigning to improve hospital ventilation, sanitation and nutrition, and championing the cause of midwives. Florence never married. She rejected several suitors, including one Richard Monckton Milnes, a devotee of the Marquis de Sade with an extensive collection of erotica.

GARDEN MUSEUM

Admire a rare cucumber straightener

Lambeth Palace Road, SE1 7LB
0207 401 8865
www.gardenmuseum.org.uk
Check website for admission details
Westminster or Lambeth North tube

The Garden Museum, which reopened in 2017 after undergoing redevelopment, may be one of London's best connected museums. Created from the former church of St Mary-at-Lambeth, it sits in the shadow of Lambeth Palace, residence of the Archbishop of Canterbury since 1200 and across the river from Westminster. This closeness to the heart of the UK establishment is probably about right for it – gardening is a British obsession from top to bottom, and this is the first gardening museum in the world.

The museum was founded by John and Rosemary Nicholson, after tracing the tomb of the 17th-century royal gardeners John Tradescant the Elder and Younger to this churchyard. Both men travelled widely and introduced a huge variety of trees and plants to British gardens.

The redevelopment, which included an expanded mezzanine inside the church, has allowed more of the vast collection to go on display. Jewels of this inlcude a cucumber straightener and a collection of garden gnomes. The café, one of the best in any London museum, also got an overhaul.

The museum's beautiful, if small, grounds include a 17th-century-style knot garden. These geometric and highly formal compositions were typically lined with clipped low hedges. The churchyard contains some noteworthy graves, including the tyrannical Captain 'Breadfruit' Bligh of the mutiny on The Bounty.

A plaque to the left of the church's front door commemorates Brian Turbeville, Gent., who bequeathed £100 to St Mary-at-Lambeth for the apprenticeship of two poor boys each year. The museum also hosts occasional concerts and lectures. Education is set to become a more prominent part of the museum's brief – watch out for talks and evening symposia.

Lambeth Palace

Lambeth Palace contains some of the few surviving Tudor buildings in the capital, notably the red brick gatehouse built in 1495, as well as the Lollard's Tower, visible from the outside. Although the Lambeth Palace garden was split in two to create Archbishop's Park in 1901, it is still the second-largest garden in London after that of Buckingham Palace. Lambeth Palace is open to the public for the annual Lambeth Parish Fete and on Open House weekends. Check the Archbishop's website (www.archbishopofcanterbury.org/pages/visit-the-lambeth-palacegardens-.html) for details.

ROOTS AND SHOOTS

Grassroots garden

Walnut Tree Walk, SE11 6DN
0207 587 1131
www.rootsandshoots.org.uk
Mon-Fri 10am-4pm and occasional open days. Check website for details
Admission free
Kennington, Lambeth North or Elephant & Castle tube

Despite the onslaught of high-rise apartments, some pockets of central London have managed to hang onto their village vibe. Kennington is one such neighbourhood. MPs and spies skulk in the handsome garden squares, while commoners rub shoulders on cheek-by-jowl council estates.

Owing to its proximity to Westminster, Kennington took a pummelling during the Second World War. Empty plots were commandeered by the Civil Defence, including this site, where engineers built parts for fighter planes and military vehicles. By the 1980s, it had become a dumping ground, with a lone white lilac tree and three derelict buildings. Roots and Shoots, an environmental education charity, stepped in and started digging. Gradually, they have transformed the disused land into a refuge for young people struggling with mainstream education. They spend a year learning horticulture, floristry, beekeeping, and other basic skills to prepare for the world of work.

With a microclimate comparable to Cornwall, the hidden, half-acre garden is also a sanctuary for foxes, frogs, newts, 25 species of bees and many migrating birds. Open to the public during office hours, it's a magical place to lose your kids – or yourself – for a few hours.

NEARBY
Vauxhall Park Model Village ⑦
Vauxhall Park, Off Fentiman Road, SW8 1PU

Like so much of the surrounding area today, Vauxhall Park was earmarked for development in 1886. Thanks to the efforts of local campaigners, the land was preserved as a public park. In a corner of this Victorian oasis, six miniature, mock-Tudor houses squat among the flowerbeds. No more than 2 feet high, they might be *pieds-à-terre* for elves or a hamlet for Smurfs. In fact, these teeny dwellings were built in 1949 by Edgar Wilson, a retired engineer from West Norwood. Originally located in Brockwell Park (where the rest of this model village still stands), these houses were relocated to Vauxhall Park in the 1950s. Made of lead and hand-painted concrete, the cottages were restored by local resident Nobby Clark in 2001.

Camouflaged in the lavender garden nearby is a human sundial. Stand on the right month on the flat stone and your shadow will tell you the time – as long as the sun is out. The community orchard also contains a rare Vauxhall apple tree.

THE CINEMA MUSEUM

Stars in your eyes

The Master's House, 2 Dugard Way, SE11 4TH
0207 840 2200
www.cinemamuseum.org.uk
By appointment
Admission varies for guided tours, talks, events and screenings
Kennington or Elephant & Castle tube

Hidden down a cul-de-sac in Kennington is one of the world's most extensive collections of film-related images and artefacts. Fittingly, the Cinema Museum has found a temporary home in the former Lambeth workhouse where a nine-year-old boy named Charlie Chaplin and his half-brother Sydney were 'processed' in 1896.

The building was once divided into wings for men and women of 'good' or 'bad character'. Today, the musty corridors and dormitories are crammed with mechanical projectors and Art Deco cinema signs, original lobby cards, piles of periodicals dating back to 1911, and around 17 million feet of film.

This extraordinary collection was amassed by Ronald Grant, whose lifelong passion for cinema began when he helped out at his local picture house in Aberdeen as a boy. Since then, Grant has accumulated over one million cinematic images dating back to 1895, the year the Lumière brothers screened the first 'actualités' in Paris. This vast anthology of production stills and portraits of movie stars keeps the Cinema Museum afloat: the images are hired out to the media. The archive is divided by subject matter, from abattoirs to ventriloquists. Leafing through the 'P' drawer, Grant offers up pictorial material on practical jokes, pratfalls, prisons and private eyes.

But it's the artefacts that really bring the early days of cinema to life. There are silent film scores and song lyrics that were projected onto the screen so that audiences could sing along as the organist played during the interval. Before X-rated movies, there was Category H: 'horrific'. There's a 1917 ticket machine that issued metal tokens of various shapes depending on the price, so ushers could feel the difference in the dark. These nattily dressed ushers would use floral sprays 'to disguise the smell of 1,000 wet raincoats and cigarettes on a Saturday night'. Cinemas may have had fancy fittings and names like the Majestic or the Picture Palace, but audiences could be rowdy. One old notice warns patrons: 'No shouting or whistling allowed – applaud with hands only. In the interests of public safety please do not spit.'

The Cinema Museum has led a precarious life, and is still struggling to maintain a permanent home here on Dugard Way. To raise funds, it has launched regular film nights and talks, held in a screening room with vintage cinema seats and illuminated signs. All proceeds go towards maintaining this glorious anachronism. A great night out for a good cause.

MANDELA WAY TANK

(9)

The right kind of tank on the street

Stompie Garden, 105 Page's Walk, SE1 4HD
Elephant & Castle tube

Take a brief stroll down the Old Kent Road from the Tower Bridge end, swing left onto Mandela Way and there, precisely where it shouldn't be, is a decommissioned Soviet-built T-34-85 battle tank. It's called Stompie. To add to the surprise, you're never quite sure what colour it will be painted when you next see it. Over the years, it's been pink, gold, tricked out in tiger skin or covered in geometric designs à la Bauhaus. The point is, it doesn't look like the threat it once was, sitting placidly in a little garden and rusting away, and that's a good thing.

How did it end up on this scrap of land just off the Bricklayers Arms roundabout? The story goes that the tank, which was allegedly used to suppress the Prague Spring in 1968, was brought to London to feature in Ian McKellen's *Richard III*. Filming finished, and the tank was bought by businessman Russell Gray, who had recently been denied permission by Southwark council to build on the plot of land where the tank now squats. However, the council hadn't said anything about decommissioned military vehicles, and Gray installed the tank on the plot, claiming it was a present for his 7-year-old son. Hmmm. The council attempted to force its removal, but this time, Gray's paperwork was all in order. There the tank sits, with its gun reputedly trained on Southwark council's offices.

Films that wander way off the beaten track

Stompie was used in filming at the then derelict Battersea Power Station, now being turned into a huge residential area. London is a popular film location, but in general, it's the tourist sites that crop up again and again – Buckingham Palace, Big Ben, the London Eye. However, there are plenty of films that wander way off the beaten track – Patrick Keiller's *London and Robinson in Space*, which defy description and meander all over the city, are soaked in its alternative history and cannot be recommended highly enough; Jules Dassin's *Night and the City*, shot on location in 1950 when London was rebuilding after the war, and which features a frankly insane performance by a young Richard Widmark; and *The London Nobody Knows*, a short documentary from 1969 featuring James Mason poking around the underbelly of the city. Drunks, Salvation Army bands, huge queues of people waiting to buy live eels, and street entertainers all feature. "I'm a genius and I felt I'm psychologically unfit for normal work," says one of the buskers. Well, we all feel like that sometimes.

CHUMLEIGH GARDENS

Absence of humbug

Burgess Park, off Albany Road, SE5 0RJ
Daily 9.30am - 5pm
Admission free
Elephant & Castle tube, then bus 12, 42, 63, 136, 343, 363, 468

Burgess Park is evolving from an unloved non-descript expanse of stubby lawns off Camberwell's unlovely Walworth Road into a well-planned public space. This includes a killer BMX track, lots of wild planting and an adventure playground.

At the heart of the park is a square of almshouses, the first asylum built by the Female Friendly Society in 1821 (there's a copy of the dedication on the central block). Run 'solely by love, kindness and absence of humbug', the Society provided social housing for single ladies who were 'destitute of a husband's industry, a husband's counsel, a husband's sympathy', as long as they were 'of good and pious character'.

Hidden away behind these is an L-shaped 'multicultural garden', laid out as a tribute to the area's diverse population.

The little walled garden surrounded by hedges provides a microclimate that allows a variety of aromatic herbs, flowering plants and fruit trees from the Orient, Africa, the Caribbean, Australia and the Mediterranean to survive. The centrepiece is the Islamic Garden, built around a raised pond wrapped in blue tiles with a jelly palm tree sprouting out of the middle.

Chumleigh Gardens is also home to Art in the Park workshops, so you may stumble upon sculptors working in the grounds. It's a serene, unpretentious little place with a real sense of community – a perfect spot to sit while your kids make a beeline for the poisonous plants. The Metropolitan Police funded the gates to the Heart Garden, tended by those with recent or ongoing health issues. Afterwards, take tea at the Parklife Café just outside the gardens.

The old almshouse currently serves as a temporary home for the Cuming Museum, a quirky collection of ordinary artefacts and ancient relics, which was partially destroyed by a fire at its former base in Walworth Town Hall in 2013. It is due to reopen in 2019.

NEARBY

Henry Moore's 'Two Piece Reclining Figure No. 3' ⑪

Brandon Estate, Cooks Road, SE17 3PJ

Built in the late 1950s, Kennington's Brandon Estate is visible for miles thanks to its six 18-storey tower blocks. On a hillock of grass at its centre is a sculpture by Henry Moore, donated to the residents of Brandon Estate in 1961. Its bronze contours have since turned gangrenous green and there is some half-hearted graffiti on the concrete base. But there's a peculiar magic to this lonely figure marooned in such an incongruous setting, especially at dusk when the lights in the tower blocks are flickering on.

KIRKALDY TESTING MUSEUM

Giant ball-breaker

99 Southwark Street, SE1 0JF
www.testingmuseum.org.uk (No telephone)
Open first Sunday of every month, with guided tours on the third Sunday of every month
Check website for admission prices
Waterloo, Southwark, London Bridge or Borough tube; Waterloo, London Bridge, Blackfriars rail

This little – or not so little – gem of Victorian engineering is tucked away between the modern glass monoliths that have sprouted around Tate Modern. Opened in 1874, Kirkaldy's Testing and Experimenting Works was built to house David Kirkaldy's monstrous Universal Testing Machine: a vertical hydraulic ram, 48 feet long and weighing 116 tons, that can pull, push, bend, twist and bulge metal beams to breaking point, recording just how much pressure they can take before shattering.

Smashing things to pieces hardly feels like rocket science to 21st-century visitors, but this machine represented the cutting edge of Victorian engineering. The 19th century saw an explosion in the use of metal for construction, but designers were not always certain of the capabilities of their materials. One example was the collapse of the Tay Rail Bridge in 1879, just 19 months after it opened; the bridge's beams were tested at Kirkaldy's after being retrieved from the riverbed. On the other hand, buildings, bridges and ships were often over-engineered because their architects feared failure.

Kirkaldy introduced the greatest possible accuracy to this pioneering technology. His rigorous approach is summed up in the inscription above the workshop: 'Facts, not opinions'. Among other projects, he tested steel for the Eads Bridge over the Mississippi, one of the first steel structures in the world and still in use today, as well as materials for London's Blackfriars Bridge and Hammersmith Bridge. Originally, the works housed a Museum of Fractures, showing hundreds of different samples that had been torn apart. These are long gone, but Kirkaldy's office is still there, as well as a collection of smaller machines, including the splendidly named Cement Dogbone Briquette Machine. In the basement stands a Denison chain tester, used to find weak links – presumably best viewed at a safe distance.

If there are enough visitors, a tour of the works includes a demonstration of the giant testing machine. Tension mounts surprisingly quickly as the big beast hisses into life. The demonstrator slips an ingot of steel into the jaws of the ram and gradually cranks up the power. As the pressure rises, the ingot stretches imperceptibly. Just before its explosive failure, it sheds its coat of rust and the true metal appears beneath, before snapping loudly. Worth the admission price alone.

THE FERRYMAN'S SEAT

⑬

A little seat with a long history

Bear Gardens, Bankside, SE1 9HA
London Bridge or Southwark tube

The Ferryman's Seat

The Ferryman's seat, located on previous buildings at this site, was constructed for the convenience of Bankside watermen, who operated ferrying services across the river. The seat's age is unknown, but it is thought to have ancient origins.

Historic Southwark

Wedged into a wall not far from Shakespeare's Globe Theatre, and before Southwark Bridge, is a small chunk of flinty stone. This is the last surviving example of the boatmen's seats that once lined the South Bank. Until 1750, London Bridge was the only means of crossing the Thames in central London; so 'wherrymen' ferried passengers across in narrow water taxis, or 'wherries'. The boatmen waited on these rough stone benches until their vessels filled up with rowdy patrons spilling out of the nearby Rose and Globe theatres (see p. 194), the bear-baiting rings and brothels (evocatively known as 'stews' because of their origins as steam baths) that littered the unsavoury suburb of Southwark.

The wherrymen must have been lean, as the seat is a tight squeeze for even the trimmest of 21st-century buttocks. It can't have been a pleasant resting place: the area reeked of open sewers and the stench of the surrounding tanneries.

Bear-baiting: 'a very rude and nasty pleasure'

This street is still called Bear Gardens after the Davies Amphitheatre, the last bear-baiting pit on Bankside. Banned in 1642, bear-baiting was a popular pastime in Tudor times, frequented by roughnecks and courtiers alike.

NEARBY
The black-faced clock
(14)

Borough High Street, SE1 1JA
www.stgeorge-themartyr.co.uk

Sleazy Southwark was home to many famous literary figures, including Geoffrey Chaucer, William Shakespeare and Charles Dickens. Dickens immortalised the area in *Little Dorrit*, whose fictional father – like the novelist's own – is imprisoned in Marshalsea prison for failing to pay his debts. The last remaining wall of this infamous jail now forms the northern boundary of the churchyard of St George the Martyr, where Little Dorrit is married at the end of the novel. Inside the church, in the east window behind the altar, is a stained-glass memorial to Little Dorrit, kneeling at prayer. St George's steeple has four clocks, but one of them – facing Bermondsey – is black and is not illuminated at night. Allegedly, this was because Bermondsey's Victorian parishioners refused to cough up their share of funds for the clock.

CROSSBONES GRAVEYARD

A burial ground for misfits

Redcross Way, SE1 1TA
www.crossbones.org.uk
Garden open weekdays 12-3pm. Vigil for the Outcast at 7pm, 23rd of each
month. Check website for details and events
Admission free
Borough tube

This piece of wasteland owned by Transport for London (TfL) contains the bodies of over 15,000 people, over half of them children. But there is no evidence of their passing – this was unhallowed ground, first for prostitutes and then for paupers. In early local records, Crossbones was referred to as a graveyard for 'Single Women' – the whores working in the nearby 'stews' or brothels of the Liberty of the Clink. This was an area of Southwark, south of London Bridge and outside the jurisdiction of the sheriff of London, where Londoners could legally enjoy theatre, bear-baiting and whoring.

In 1161, the Bishop of Winchester was granted the power to licence prostitutes and brothels in the Liberty, which persisted for 500 years until Oliver Cromwell closed down the whole area. Clink prostitutes were known as Winchester Geese (one of many euphemisms for prostitutes in London including trulls, buttered buns, squirrels and punchable nuns). They were refused burial in the local St Saviour's parish – an irony given that they owed their jobs to the church. After the closure of the Liberty, Crossbones graveyard served for the poor, and was closed in 1853 as it was 'completely overcharged with dead'.

The site is evolving into a memorial space. The gates (opposite the cosy Boot and Flogger wine bar) are a kind of spontaneous tribute; they are covered with ribbons and other totems in sympathy with the dead. There is a vigil there to honour the outcast, dead or alive, on the 23rd of every month. In 2014, TfL signed a temporary lease for the Friends of Crossbones to create a garden on the site, and the small but perfectly formed Crossbones Garden of Remembrance is now open to the public. However, there's a strong feeling that this site is hanging on by its fingernails, with developers eyeing the site as London's property market explodes.

> The Boot and Flogger is supposedly the only bar in the country not to require an alcohol licence, because of special dispensation from James I in 1611.

The George Inn courtyard

Little remains of the Liberty of the Clink; the rebuilt Globe Theatre is its best memorial. However, it's not the only courtyard theatre in the area. The George Inn, just off Borough High Street, would originally have offered plays; this pub was built on three sides around a courtyard, and its wide, double-tiered balconies were perfect for heckling the actors below. British theatre evolved from places like this, and their design influenced purpose-built venues such as the Globe, the Rose and the Cockpit.

THE OLD OPERATING THEATRE

No pain, no gain

9a St Thomas Street, SE1 9RY
0207 188 2679
Mon-Sun 10.30am-5pm
Check website for admission details
London Bridge tube/rail

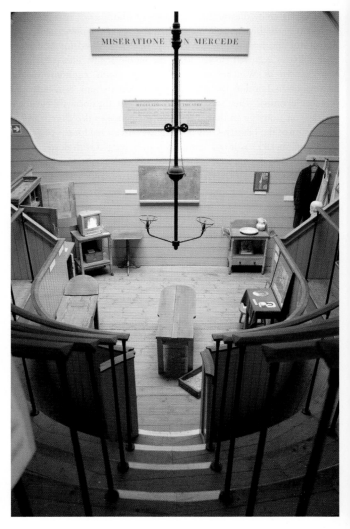

This little oddity was rediscovered by chance in 1957, during repairs in the eaves of St Thomas' Church in Southwark, on the original site of St Thomas' Hospital. This is the oldest surviving operating theatre in the country, and was used in the days before anaesthetics and antiseptic surgery. The garret also served to store the hospital apothecary's medicinal herbs. The museum that stands there now displays a collection of terrifyingly primitive medical tools, including instruments for cupping, bleeding and trepanning, a hair-raising practice of perforating the skull to 'alleviate pain.'

The operating theatre was built in 1822, after the 1815 Apothecary's Act, which required apprentice apothecaries to watch operations at public hospitals. Prior to this, operations took place in the patient's bed right on the ward, which must have been a blood-curdling ordeal – all that blood and bellowing in such a confined space. The operating theatre was annexed to the women's surgical ward, so patients could be carried straight in via what is now the fire escape. Students crammed the viewing platforms to watch the operations, carried out without anaesthetic prior to 1847. Patients, who were typically from the poorer strata of London society, submitted willingly, as this was the only way to get the best medical treatment, which they otherwise could not afford. The wealthy underwent operations in the relative comfort and privacy of their home.

Open surgery

Surgeon John Flint South described the pandemonium on the sidelines of an operation here: 'Behind a second partition stood the pupils, packed like herrings in a barrel, but not so quiet, as those behind them were continually pressing on those before and were continually struggling to relieve themselves of it, and had not infrequently to be got out exhausted. There was also a continual calling out of "Heads, Heads" to those about the table whose heads interfered with the sightseers.'

Florence Nightingale was indirectly responsible for the operating theatre's closure. In 1859, she set up her nursing school at St Thomas', but on her advice the hospital moved to a new site opposite the Houses of Parliament in 1862. There is still a small Florence Nightingale Museum at St Thomas' Hospital (see p. 246).

LONDON'S LIVING ROOM

The Mayor's penthouse

City Hall, The Queen's Walk, SE1 2AA
0207 983 4100
www.londonslivingroom.co.uk
Open usually one weekend every month; check website for details. Limited
access to other parts of City Hall Mon-Fri 8am-8pm
Admission free
Tower Bridge or London Bridge tube

Though sometimes fondly referred to as 'the Mayor's testicle,' Norman Foster's City Hall is a stunning building. Completed in 2002, the wonky glass sphere is a brilliant icon for transparent government. To endorse the notion of open politics, some restricted access areas of the Greater London Authority's HQ are opened up to the public on occasional weekends.

As you enter City Hall's hollowed-out reception area, look over the glass railing onto the exhibition space on the lower ground floor. The floor covering may at first glance seem to be merely a grubby green and grey carpet, but in fact it's the London Photomat, an aerial view of Greater London. Covering an area of 1,000 square miles, the 16 x 10-metre image is a collage of 200,000 photos, taken from four planes flying at an altitude of 5,500 feet over London, which were then printed onto the floor tiles. The result is so detailed that it is possible to pinpoint individual houses as well as major landmarks. The project took three years to complete, but you can now walk all over London in just minutes.

The heart of City Hall is a sweeping spiral ramp, half a kilometre long, leading all the way up to the ninth floor. It is like an asymmetrical version of New York's Guggenheim museum, but instead of galleries you look in at open-plan offices and out at sweeping views of London. The purple and grey Assembly Chamber on the second floor, with seating for 250 members of the public to watch London's government in action, creates the slightly disturbing impression that you are floating on the Thames.

The Mayor's office is on the 8th floor. Above it is London's Living Room, a spectacular setting for political fundraisers, parties, and premieres with a 360° panorama of the London skyline. The minimalist design lets the view dominate. From the wraparound balcony, you can look down on the boats bobbing along beneath Tower Bridge and feel on top of the world.

The basement café looks out onto The Scoop, a sunken amphitheatre of grey limestone where outdoor screenings and concerts are staged during the summer.

Designed to consume 25% less energy than the average office building, City Hall is a great advertisement for eco-architecture. Heat generated by computers and lights is recycled and the building is cooled using water extracted from the water table beneath London.

BRIXTON WINDMILL

Relic of rural London

Windmill Gardens, Blenheim Gardens, Off Brixton Hill, SW2 5EU
www.brixtonwindmill.org
Guided tours from April to October, usually on the second weekend of every
month, plus a few extra dates. Check website for details
Admission free
Brixton tube, then 45, 59, 109, 118, 133, 159, 250 or 333 bus

As London continues to spread across South East England – it now covers around 1,600 square kilometres – it is hard to imagine that until relatively recently the city was dominated by the countryside. Evidence of the city's agricultural past is limited, having been concreted over at a time when the idea of putting preservation before progress was unthinkable.

Sitting in the shadow of Brixton Prison, this flour mill is a relic of rural London. It was built in 1816 before the mid-19th-century urbanisation along Brixton Hill. What is remarkable is that it exists in the middle of one of the most densely populated parts of the capital. Brixton as farmland is hard to imagine, but there are comparatively modern agricultural references to the area – in the Sherlock Holmes story 'The Blue Carbuncle', Holmes tracks the criminal to a goose farm on Brixton Hill.

Originally the windmill sat in open fields with others; up to twelve sites in Lambeth have been detected, with evidence of milling dating back to the Middle Ages. As the city grew around it, new housing shielded the mill from the strong winds needed for its operation.

In 1862, the owners moved their milling business to Mitcham. The windmill was used for storage until 1902, then fitted with a steam engine, after which it resumed milling until 1934. In its current incarnation it sits in a small park, a short distance from the high street on Brixton Hill. Visitors pick their way through residential side streets until, after turning a corner, the windmill suddenly appears. The windmill was fully restored in 2010. It is still used for milling demonstrations, although the sails are yet to be fully operational.

Just over the wall squats Brixton Prison. The oldest correctional facility in the UK, it opened in 1820. One of the first prisons to introduce treadmills in 1821, it was first a women's prison, then a military prison, and now a remand centre with a terrible reputation.

Also worth checking out in the immediate vicinity is The Windmill pub, not for its looks (it has none), but rather for its gigs. The pub has a great tradition of alternative live music, often featuring bands on the verge of a breakthrough.

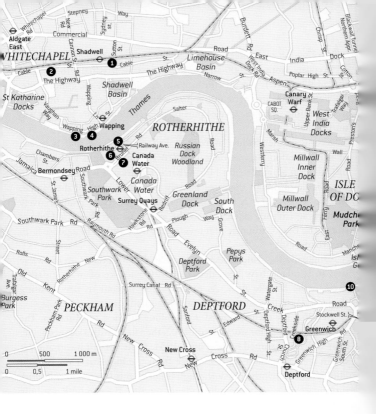

Whitechapel to Woolwich

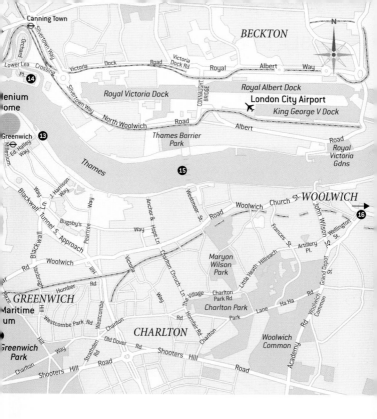

CABLE STREET MURAL

The art of resistance

236 Cable Street, E1 0BL
Admission free
Shadwell DLR/Overground

Reminiscent of the social paintings of the great Mexican artist Diego Rivera, the Cable Street Mural commemorates the 'Battle of Cable Street' in 1936, when the aristocrat Oswald Mosley, in a spiffy outfit of black military jacket, grey riding breeches, jackboots, black peaked hat and a red arm band, led the British Union of Fascists (BUF) on a march into the East End, at that time the centre of London Jewish life. Having secured the protection of the police, the BUF felt safe. However, large numbers of anti-fascists, including Jewish, Irish, socialist, and communist groups, came out in protest. Most of the fighting was between the protesters and the 10,000 police, some on horseback, who had been deployed in record numbers to secure a route for the BUF, who were forced to abandon the march.

Some argue that this protest deepened anti-Semitism in the area; the so-called Pogrom of Mile End, in which Jews and their properties were attacked far more violently, took place a week afterwards. The BUF were proscribed in 1940, and Mosley was interned with his wife Diana Mitford for most of the war in a house in the grounds of Holloway prison.

The mural is a treat. Started in 1976, it is the work of a number of local artists, who finally finished it in 1993, and restored it in 2011, after a long-running battle against vandalism and graffiti. The picture is wildly full of movement, and gives a strong sense of the almost tidal surges of large-scale street demonstrations. A propeller whirling in the top right of the picture is echoed in other eddies and vortices in the mural: a man throwing leaflets into the wind, men surging around barricades, horses turning in confined spaces. Comically, a figure who appears to be Hitler is borne aloft away from the action, wearing only his underpants. It's not an especially nuanced or subtle piece of art, but its energy makes it leap off the wall.

Other murals around town

Cable Street is probably the most iconic of all London's murals, although Nuclear Dawn on Brixton's Coldharbour Lane, which shows Death sowing the world with bombs, is a close contender. Brixton is fertile for murals – check the giant children painted on the back of the Academy music venue (Stockwell Park Road), the market mural in the railway station, and the slightly wistful river mural (corner of Strathleven and Glenelg Roads). Outside Stockwell tube, a portrait of French Resistance heroine Violette Szabo dominates the deep shaft ventilator. In Soho, look out for strange trees on the corner of Poland Street and Noel Street, and portraits of famous residents on the corner of Carnaby and Broadwick streets.

WILTON'S MUSIC HALL

World's oldest surviving music hall

1 Graces Alley, E1 8JB
0207 702 2789
https://wiltons.org.uk
John Wilton Room: Mon-Fri 11am-6pm
Mahogany Bar: Mon-Sat 5pm-11pm
Cocktail Bar: Tues-Sat 6pm-11pm
Auditorium: ticketed access only. Check website for tours
Tower Hill tube, Shadwell DLR

There is so little left of London's music halls, yet they were central to many people's lives in the capital in the days before television. These venues, popular from the early Victorian era and lasting until 1960, offered a mixture of popular songs, comedy, speciality acts and variety entertainment. Wilton's was one of the grandest.

Like many East End music halls, Wilton's was originally built as a concert venue. It stood behind a pub called the Mahogany Bar. John Wilton bought the business around 1850, enlarged the concert room three years later and replaced it with his 'Magnificent New Music Hall' in 1859. Wilton was determined to bring West End glamour, comfort and entertainment to his predominantly working-class audience and invested heavily in fitting out a 'sun-burner' chandelier of 300 gas jets and 27,000 cut crystals that illuminated a mirrored hall. He also installed the best available heating, lighting and ventilation systems and strove to make sure that the acoustics in the hall were perfect.

Some of the biggest stars of the day performed here, including George Ware (writer of the song, 'The Boy I Love is Up in the Gallery'), Arthur Lloyd and George Leybourne, better known as Champagne Charlie. Part of Leybourne's schtick included living the life of a swell on and off the stage – this involved the consumption of plentiful free champagne from wine merchants looking to promote themselves. Leybourne died of liver disease aged 42.

Wilton's was only a music hall for 30 years. It was destroyed by fire in 1877, was rebuilt and then became a mission of the Methodist Church for nearly 70 years. It then became a warehouse, but was scheduled for demolition as part of the slum-clearance schemes of the 1960s. A campaign was started to save the building, with supporters including John Betjeman, Peter Sellers and Spike Milligan, and it reopened as a theatre and concert hall in 1997. The place has an elegantly decayed feel to it and shows off its scars beautifully.

EXECUTION DOCK

Where timbers were shivered

Wapping Old Stairs, off Wapping High Street, E1W 2PN
Shadwell DLR, then 15-minute walk, or Wapping Overground

L ondon's connection with piracy is hardly surprising, given the city's history as one of the world's greatest ports. Pirate life seems to have been pretty desperate, despite all the fighting and drinking; pirate death seems to have been even worse, either killed in action, or more likely by picturesque diseases (Vomito Negro? Flux? The Itch? Yellow Jack?). Worst of all was to be dispatched at Execution Dock.

Policing the sea was left to the Admiralty, and for 400 years it executed pirates on the foreshore of the Thames at Wapping, at a site far enough offshore as to be near the low-tide mark. Typically, prisoners were publicly executed en masse after being paraded from the Marshalsea Prison across London Bridge and past the Tower of London.

The hanging was unusual in that the rope was too short for the drop to break necks, so the condemned would 'dance' as they strangled. Their bodies were left in place until three tides had washed over them. The more notorious corpses were then tarred and hung in cages along the Thames estuary to encourage other sailors to behave themselves. Captain Kidd, inspiration for Robert Louis Stevenson's *Treasure Island*, stepped off here, and George Davis and William Watts were the final two hanged for piracy at the docks on 16 December 1830.

The actual site is disputed, as the gallows are long gone; three pubs on Wapping High Street claim it as an attraction. The Prospect of Whitby, London's oldest riverside pub formerly known as the Devil's Tavern, is one, the Captain Kidd another; but the likeliest location is behind the Town of Ramsgate. Go down the alley at the side, descend Wapping Old Steps and you are on the river bed (obviously wait until the tide is out). Walking on the foreshore is well worth it; the river is constantly turning up weird flotsam and jetsam. However, to actually dig you need a special licence from the Port of London Authority.

Mudlarking

Sounds like a filthy habit, but mudlarking is actually the word used for beachcombing along the Thames – named after a bird, apparently. Access to the river is surprisingly easy (especially along the south bank), either through ancient water-steps such as Pelican Stairs or down modern steps from the Embankment. The highlight of the mudlark's year is the annual opening of the beach in front of the Tower of London in conjunction with National Archaeology Week.

THAMES RIVER POLICE MUSEUM

The world's first police force

Wapping Police Station, 98 Wapping High Street, E1W 2NE
www.thamespolicemuseum.org.uk
To arrange a visit, send a written request to the police station, enclosing
stamped self-addressed envelope
Admission free
Wapping Overground

ondon is home to the world's first police force. Established in 1798, the Thames River Police were recruited by the West India Merchants and Planters Committees to protect their cargo from river pirates. Magistrate Patrick Colquhoun had worked out that half a million pounds' worth of freight was being filched each year. The original force had about 50 members: watermen, who rowed the boats; surveyors, who checked cargo; and lumpers, who supervised the offloading of vessels. Armed with cutlasses, pistols and truncheons, they had to monitor the 33,000 workers on the Thames, a third of whom – according to Colquhoun's calculations – were felons. In its first year of operation, the river police saved £122,000 worth of cargo.

The force was absorbed into London's Metropolitan Police in 1839. Now known as the Marine Support Unit, high-speed launches have replaced the rowing galleys and officers are more concerned with counter-terrorism than brigands. But the 78-strong force still operates from the original police station on Wapping High Street. The workshop where boats were repaired was converted into a museum in 1974. Visitors are treated to an expert commentary by curator Robert Jeffries, a retired marine policeman and City of London guide.

Motorised launches were introduced after the 1878 Princess Alice disaster, in which 640 day-trippers died after two ships collided. The Thames is now one of the cleanest rivers in Europe, but back then most of the passengers were killed by swallowing raw sewage. The ship's tattered ensign is on display in the museum, a gift from the captain's son, who joined the river police soon afterwards.

There is an impressive collection of handcuffs, uniforms, telescopes and rattles, used before whistles to sound the alarm. The most remarkable objects are the 18th-century handwritten ledgers, detailing everyday crimes and punishments. The first page of a tattered inspector's pocketbook from 1894 details the discovery of a baby's severed head in the Thames. Most of the policemen's misdemeanours involve drinking on duty. Some 30 pubs lined the riverbank in Wapping, including the Turk's Head, where those condemned at nearby Execution Dock (see p. 276) could enjoy their last pint.

The origins of police stations
The term "police station" derives from the police craft "on station" (anchored) at various points in the Thames. The phrase "on the beat" comes from the beating of the oars in river police boats.

THE BRUNEL MUSEUM

Underworld echo chamber

Railway Avenue, Rotherhithe, SE16 4LF
0207 231 3840
www.brunel-museum.org.uk
Daily 10am-5pm
Check website for admission prices
 Rotherhithe tube

sambard Kingdom Brunel, builder of the Saltash Bridge, the Clifton Suspension Bridge, and the Great Western Railway, is a towering legend in the history of engineering. However, the Brunel Museum focuses on another Brunel – his father, Marc Isambard Brunel. Brunel père was born in Normandy, and initially seemed destined for priesthood, but became a naval cadet instead. In 1793, Brunel fled the French Revolution for the US, where he became chief engineer of New York. He moved to Britain in 1799, hoping to exploit the possibilities of the Industrial Revolution. This museum is based around his most famous achievement, the Thames Tunnel, the only project that father and son ever worked on together. Completed after 18 years' labour in 1843, it was hailed at the time as the eighth wonder of the world.

Like most things Brunel, the construction is ingenious. The shaft was formed by building a brick tower, and then digging the earth out until the tower sank under its own weight to line the shaft. A patented tunnel shield was forced through the soft clay under the river to reduce the risk of collapse. Conditions were appalling – miners would work four-hour shifts with short handled spades until they were overcome by gas fumes, and then replaced. The tunnel flooded five times, almost drowning young Isambard. Although originally designed for horse-drawn traffic, the development company ran out of money to build access for carriages.

Despite a fundraising dinner at which the band of the Coldstream Guards played patriotic airs under the Thames so loudly that no-one could speak, the tunnel was only ever used by pedestrians. After great initial success, including a parade of shops, public interest faded and the tunnel was bought by the East London Railway Company and converted to rail use. It still carries the East London Line under the Thames.

The museum itself has a small collection of tunnel and Brunel related items. However, a ticket also gets entry to the reopened Grand Entrance Hall. The world's first underground theatre, where acrobats and tightrope walkers once wowed spectators, now doubles as a music venue. The hall is a surprise – through a nondescript door outside the museum, a vast chamber reveals itself. Descending to a floor suspended above the railway, you can still make out traces of the original staircases. The museum also organises tours, including boat and train tours of Brunel sites along the Thames.

NEARBY
The Old Mortuary   ⑥
St Marychurch Street, SE16 4JE
Now a community centre, this was the mortuary for the river – suicides, dockers and drunks who drowned all washed up here. Erected in 1895, it still retains many of its original features.

FINNISH CHURCH

Prayers and sweat

33 Albion Street, SE16 7HZ
0207 237 4668
www.finnishchurch.org.uk
Tues-Fri 2-8pm, Sat and Sun 10am-8pm
Check website for sauna prices
Canada Water or Bermondsey tube, Rotherhithe rail

This is probably the only church in London with a sauna. The current building – the latest incarnation of the Finnish Seamen's Mission, established in London in 1882 – was opened in 1958. The whole complex is an extremely active social and cultural focal point for Finns in London, with a café (Finns seem to drink a mind-boggling amount of coffee) and a small supermarket for anyone who needs tinned *hernekeitto* or a bag of *täysjyväohrajauhoja* in a hurry. It also offers very reasonable hostel accommodation. The small sauna (a maximum of seven people at a time) is in the basement.

The church itself is beautiful. As you might expect from a Scandinavian country, there's a lot of blonde wood, light and open space. The congregation is Lutheran, and therefore there is a focus on simplicity. The entire end wall behind the altar is plain rough stone, and the absence of decoration focuses the attention on what little is there.

There are still plenty of seamen's missions in London, despite the terminal decline of the city as a port since the 1960s – there's even a Norwegian mission just up the road from the Finnish one. The huge, and expanding, Queen Victoria Seamen's Rest on East India Dock Road is probably the best known of them. It's hard to understand how important the merchant navy was to London, now that so much of the docks is buried under new housing, but the city is full of their ghosts. The Tower Hill Memorial in Trinity Square, designed by Lutyens to commemorate 24,000 non-military sailors who died during both world wars, with 'no grave but the sea', is a good place to start.

A very unfriendly tunnel

If you're in the mood to do something horrible, the church sits above the mouth of the Rotherhithe Tunnel, opened in 1908 for road traffic between Rotherhithe and Limehouse. Raised pavements mean you can walk (or cycle) through it as the cars howl past – it's the last road tunnel in London where you can still do this. You can safely say that few people will have made the trip. Perhaps the sensible thing is to start at Limehouse, and then go for a sauna at the church to get rid of the grime.

CREEKSIDE DISCOVERY CENTRE ⑧

Mud, glorious mud

14 Creekside, Deptford, SE8 4SA
0208 692 9922
www.creeksidecentre.org.uk
Check website for admission prices and opening dates/times
Deptford rail, Greenwich rail / DLR

The Creekside education centre looks as though it has washed up on the shores of the Thames along with the driftwood. Built right next to Ha'penny Hatch, on the edge of Deptford Creek, this showcase of sustainable riverside architecture was set up to raise awareness of the creek's unique environment. Deptford Creek is the tidal reach of the Ravensbourne, one of the Thames' tributaries, and among the last of them not yet tamed to make room for the city – the Fleet runs via a sewer under Farringdon Road, the Westbourne is piped over the platform at Sloane Square tube, and the Effra enters the Thames via a storm drain next to the headquarters of the British intelligence agency, MI6.

Deptford Creek is uncovered, and refreshed each day by the surge of the tide up the Thames. This, as well as its location in an abandoned industrial landscape, has produced a lively local wildlife habitat, including one of the country's rarer birds, the Black Redstart. The industries and businesses along the creek provide this bird with an environmental paradise, as they nest in power stations, gas works, industrial plots, railway yards and old wharves.

Visitors to the centre are issued with waders; when the tide ebbs, the riverbed becomes a mile-long, firm path of black mud, embedded with the skeletons of old boats and docks. At low tide, expeditions are led by centre staff, pointing out both the wildlife and the history of the creek, which may include anything from Russian tsars to the mating cycle of eels. Volunteers are also invited to join the frequent creek clean-ups, which are exhilarating – and very muddy – affairs.

There is a pleasing aura of decrepitude about the creek itself, although it is now being buried between new housing developments. This will eventually chase out the artists that fill the area, working from an estimated 100 studios. Like much of the South Bank, Deptford has always attracted the gamier parts of the art world, as it is cheaper and far from prying eyes. Not for long. There is also a colony of houseboats, a far more piratical-looking fleet than the one at Chelsea.

Christopher Marlowe's grave

Playwright Christopher Marlowe, author of *Dr Faustus* and *The Massacre At Paris*, was stabbed in the face in a private house near Creekside, and is buried in an unmarked grave in nearby St Nicholas. The church is also worth visiting for the two glowering skulls that sit atop its gateposts.

THE FAN MUSEUM

Miniature masterpieces

12 Crooms Hill, Greenwich SE10 8ER
0208 305 1441
www.thefanmuseum.org.uk
Tues-Sat 11am-5pm, Sun 12-5pm
Check website for admission prices
Greenwich rail/DLR, Cutty Sark DLR

The Fan Museum in Greenwich is another of London's many specialist museums reflecting the obsessive, collecting side of the English. It claims to be the only museum in the world devoted to every aspect of fans and fan making (although a similar venture exists in Paris), and there may be good reason for this – the craft does seem limited. But the collection works as a set of miniatures and the building itself is worth visiting. Housed in a pair of listed Georgian buildings from 1721 that have been restored to their original state, the museum contains over 3,500 mostly antique fans from around the world. These date from the 11th century to the present day. However, the bulk of the collection is based around fans from the 18th and 19th centuries, when mass production of folding fans saw their use spread throughout society. Demand was such that the fan makers had their own livery company, which still exists, although its membership now mainly derives from the heating and air-conditioning industry.

Fans may be practical objects, but the blank canvas of the 'leaf' meant that they became a highly decorative form of display. Fans often directly referred to contemporary events and allegiances, with Nelson's victories a particularly popular subject in mass-produced fans. They also served as a kind of primitive advertising hoarding. At the fancier end of the market, leading society artists painted fans for clients – the museum holds a fan painted by Walter Sickert. The functions of the fans on display thus vary wildly: ceremonial tools, fashion accessories, status symbols, political flags, or advertising giveaways.

On the first Saturday of the month, the Fan Museum holds fan-making workshops. At the rear is an Orangery covered in delicate murals, overlooking a Japanese garden, with a fan-shaped parterre. Afternoon tea is served on Tuesday, Friday, Saturday and Sunday.

Fan language

The practical use of a fan is clear. However, at the apogee of their popularity at the turn of the 19th century, a whole language was involved in their use, much of which can be seen in contemporary paintings. A fan resting upon the lips, for example, means 'I don't trust you'; placed on the heart it declares, 'My love for you is breaking my heart'; hiding the sunlight implies that 'You are ugly'; and fanning with the left hand says, 'Don't flirt with that woman'. Go to the museum, buy a fan, and reinstate these practices in polite society.

GREENWICH FOOT TUNNEL

Tunnel under the Thames

Cutty Sark Gardens, Greenwich / Island Gardens, Isle of Dogs
Open 24 hours
Admission free
Island Gardens or Cutty Sark DLR

The Greenwich Foot Tunnel, an underwater passageway linking Cutty Sark Gardens in Greenwich and Island Gardens on the Isle of Dogs, is one of the great engineering feats of 19th-century London. Lined with 200,000 glazed white tiles, which give it the unfortunate acoustics and ambience of a public toilet, the tunnel opened in 1902. Designed by Sir Alexander Binnie, it was commissioned to alleviate the overcrowded ferry service used by commuters who worked at the docks on the Isle of Dogs. Once barely populated, the marshy Isle of Dogs grew with the success of the British Empire. By the end of the 19th century, the population had risen to 21,000. International shipping poured into the new docks, which once stretched all the way from Tower Bridge to Barking, making London the largest port in the world. All of this is long gone. The Isle of Dogs still maintains its reputation as one of the tougher parts of town, but 'The Docklands' is now synonymous with the executive housing that services the City of London to the west and Canary Wharf to the east.

The entrance shafts at both ends of the tunnel are topped by glazed cupolas. Lifts (not running at night) and spiral staircases allow pedestrians access to the tunnel, which is 370 metres long, with an internal diameter of about three metres. The tiled walls make the tunnel echo eerily, especially when you creep into it in the dead of night – the tunnel is a public highway and therefore by law is open 24 hours. At such times of low traffic, it feels like the loneliest, most desolate place in London, until the sound of approaching heels ring down the tunnel like bullets.

Hidden river crossings

Greenwich Tunnel is actually the third tunnel constructed under the Thames. The Thames Tunnel, designed by Brunel (see p. 280), opened in 1843. It came to be regarded as the haunt of prostitutes and 'tunnel thieves' who lurked under its arches and mugged passers-by. Greenwich Tunnel was duplicated about three miles downstream at Woolwich Crossing, which runs between Silvertown and Woolwich, one of the few areas in London to escape gentrification. The ferry across the river is also a treat. Unlike any of the other boats on the Thames, the ferry crossing here is free, and gives an idea of the river's scale.

STARGAZING AT THE ROYAL OBSERVATORY

Secrets of the stars

Royal Observatory, Blackheath Avenue, Greenwich Park, SE10 8XJ
0208 312 6565
www.rmg.co.uk/royal-observatory
Observation events on selected evenings throughout the year
These events must be booked in advance and often sell out early
Check website for admission prices
Cutty Sark DLR, Greenwich or Maze Hill rail

The Royal Observatory in Greenwich Park may have been designed for surveying the stars, but the views of London from this hilltop landmark are equally spectacular. The dazzling towers of Canary Wharf and the distant glow of the London Eye are most dramatic at night, but the park closes at dusk. To enjoy this view – and see the stars, too – book a place on one of the Royal Observatory's special 'Evenings with the Stars'. These are held in the autumn and winter – check online for availability from September.

After an illuminating zoom into the night sky overhead in the high-tech Planetarium, with live commentary from one of the resident astronomers, visitors climb up a tower crowned with a bulging dome. As E. Walter Maunder wrote in 1900: 'This dome – which has been likened according to the school of aesthetics in which its critics have been severally trained, to the Taj at Agra, a collapsed balloon, or a mammoth Spanish onion – houses the largest refractor in England, the "South-east Equatorial" of twenty-eight inches aperture.'

This colossal feat of Victorian engineering is still the UK's largest refracting telescope. Built by Sir Howard Grubb in 1893, it took eight years to complete and weighs 1.4 tons. The lens alone weighs 102 kg. The telescope is tilted parallel to the Earth's axis of rotation, so you can follow a star from east to west by simply rotating the mount. This isn't quite as clever as it seems: the mount doesn't actually fit inside the dome.

Despite the addition of a GPS system, moving the telescope involves cumbersome manoeuvres of the dome's retractable shutters and crawling about on the floor. Early astronomers often had to lie flat on the floor to look through the lens. What you see depends on the time of year and the weather. The experience will be enjoyable even if it's overcast, as enthusiastic astronomers explain the mysteries of the solar system and point out stars with fantastical names, from Aspidiske to Zubenelgenubi.

Meridian line laser

As the official starting point for the New Millennium, a bright green laser was turned on at the Royal Observatory in December 1999, illuminating the path of the Prime Meridian Line across the London sky. It is visible for 10 miles on a clear night.

PRINCESS CAROLINE'S SUNKEN BATH

Bubble trouble

Near Chesterfield Gate in the southwest corner of Greenwich Park, entrance from Charlton Way, SE10 8QY
Admission free
Blackheath or Greenwich rail, then bus 53, 386

In 1795, Princess Caroline of Brunswick married her cousin George, the Prince of Wales (later King George IV). It was not a happy marriage. Fat George (known as Prinny) was pressured into marrying Caroline and secure the succession as part of a deal to get his massive debts cleared by the government, and had, in fact, already (secretly and illegally) married his mistress, Maria Fitzherbert. On first sight of Caroline, George staggered off to the other end of the room and said to the Earl of Malmesbury: 'Harris, I am not very well, pray get me a glass of brandy'. He then spent the next three days before the wedding drinking, and collapsed into the bedroom fireplace on the wedding night.

Not an auspicious start. The philandering prince started spreading rumours about Caroline's sluttish and slovenly ways – apparently, she was adulterous, never washed, rarely changed her underclothes, and had bad breath because of her fondness for raw garlic and onions.

After giving birth to a daughter, the couple were formally separated and Caroline went to live in Montague House in Greenwich, where she allegedly consoled herself with wild orgies and scandalous affairs. When Caroline finally tired of Britain and went into self-imposed exile in 1814, in a fit of pique George had Montague House torn down. The site is now part of Greenwich Park.

Between the Ranger's Lodge and the Rose Garden, however, a little piece of Caroline's pleasure palace survives: a sunken bath complete with a staircase. Used as a flowerbed for decades, the white-tiled plunge pool was unearthed in 1909. A small plaque commemorates the scorned princess, proving that although she may have been unfaithful at least she wasn't unhygienic.

The Greenwich gnomes

Just inside Blackheath Gate are some public toilets. Hiding in the cisterns on the maintenance buildings behind them is a family of garden gnomes.

SLICE OF REALITY
AND QUANTUM CLOUD

Radical riverside sculptures

Thames Path (by the Millennium Dome), Greenwich Peninsula, SE10
Admission free
North Greenwich tube

The Millennium Dome may have been a failure in its initial function (a glorified big top, dreamed up by politicians), and the estimated £1 billion development costs makes its current use as a concert venue hard to stomach. The tube station that serves it, North Greenwich, was money better spent: the blue-tiled and glazed interior and raking concrete columns were designed by Will Alsop, and merits a visit in their own right.

In addition to the Dome, the government also threw cash at artists to create municipal art in the surrounding area. Two of the most successful results are right by the river and are easily viewed from the Thames Path. (This stretch is best accessed from Greenwich proper; the short walk reveals the Thames as a more obviously tidal river.)

Slice of Reality is by Richard Wilson, a sculptor who works with volume. His most famous work is 20:50, a room half-filled with sump oil that leaves the viewer feeling like they are embedded in a liquid black mirror. *Slice of Reality* is equally disorientating: a 20-metre-high cross-section of a 600-ton dredger set in the Thames riverbed. Seen at low tide, the sculpture looks as though it will keel over from its dainty little plinth. The effect close up is unnerving – only 15% of the ship remains, yet the slice overwhelms. It serves admirably as a memorial to the maritime past of London.

Quantum Cloud is by Anthony Gormley, probably the most high-profile creator of public art in Britain. At first sight, this giant work appears to be a cloud created by thousands of square, hollow sections of steel. Focus, and at the centre of the cloud the outline of a human form emerges. The river as a backdrop makes perfect sense; the sculpture appears to echo the whirling seabirds of the Thames and the static form is full of movement.

These two sculptures now form part of The Line, London's first dedicated contemporary art walk. The route runs between the Queen Elizabeth Olympic Park and The O2, following the waterways and the Meridian line (the-line.org). Work in the immediate vicinity of the Dome includes Alex Chinneck's playful *A Bullet from a Shooting Star*, an inverted electricity pylon. Other attractions along the walk include Damien Hirst's *Sensation*, installed at Cody Dock.

LONGPLAYER

Music for a millennium

Trinity Buoy Wharf, 64 Orchard Place, E14 0JY
longplayer.org/
Every weekend 11am-5pm (except Oct-March 11am-4pm)
Admission free
East India Dock DLR, then 10-min walk

Housed in London's only lighthouse, Longplayer is probably the most protracted celebration of the third millennium. Launched on January 1, 2000, this musical installation features a composition for Tibetan singing bowls and gongs, digitally remixed so that the same sequence of sounds will not be repeated for 1000 years. On December 31, 2999, Longplayer will return to its starting point – and begin all over again. That is, as long as the technology that powers it survives or evolves, or some very dedicated musicians volunteer to perform the score in perpetuity.

Creator Jem Finer, a founding member of The Pogues, is exploring the possibility of building six two-armed turntables six to 12 feet in diameter, with automated mechanisms to raise and lower the arms. Even if Finer figures that out, he will have to build a device capable of cutting 12-foot records. A likelier solution is a dedicated global radio frequency, or a 'small computational device' along the lines of those used in deep space missions. The possibility of endless live performance is also being explored.

Listening to this mesmerising soundscape in a disused lighthouse, with views across the Thames to the docks and the Dome, is both captivating and slightly creepy. Built in 1864, Trinity Buoy lighthouse was used to develop lighting for Trinity House, an association founded in 1514 to safeguard shipping and seafarers. Its headquarters are still located in the City (www.trinityhouse.co.uk).

Container City

Trinity Buoy Wharf was named for the wooden buoys made and stored here in the early 19th century. Urban Space Management, using the huge metal shipping conatiners that helped kill off London's docklands, built the first prototype Container Cities here in 2000 and 2002. They consist of stacked, recycled containers, whose brightly coloured, corrugated walls and porthole windows conceal low-cost studios and homes for a community of artists and designers. Most of them open their studios for Open House weekend. A few more containers have been sound-proofed and can be hired as music studios.

THAMES FLOOD BARRIER

High and dry

1 Unity Way, Woolwich, SE18 5NJ
The Thames Barrier is operated every month for maintenance and testing. Once a year, they also test the barrier at a high spring tide (normally Sept or Oct). Call 0208 305 4188 to check opening times or see: www.gov.uk/guidance/the-thames-barrier
Admission charges apply for the Information Centre exhibition and guided talks
Charlton or Woolwich Dockyard rail, or North Greenwich tube, then bus 161 or 472

About eight miles downstream from Tower Bridge is the Thames Flood Barrier, a row of ten movable gates across the river that protect London from flooding. The effect is that of ten gleaming sails moving upstream, line abreast. On a sunny day, viewed from the river or the shore, they are a pleasingly modern feature in an otherwise run-down part of London. Measuring 520 metres wide, the flood barrier consists of a set of semi-cylindrical gates that rotate upward from the riverbed, closing the river to traffic. When closed, the four largest gates stand as high as a five-storey building.

The need for the flood barrier seems to escape most Londoners, who prefer not to think about the implications of its construction. But the barrier has been raised 176 times since 1982, and the frequency is rising.

Global warming and rising sea levels are partly responsible for a rise in tide heights in the Thames, while the movement of tectonic plates in the Mid-Atlantic Ridge is gradually causing South East Britain to sink seaward. The wide mouth of the River Thames and its position at the foot of the North Sea also make the river vulnerable to surge tides. The construction of the Embankment has constrained the swollen river even more tightly – witness the height of the Thames during high tide at Blackfriars Bridge. So when the river siren sounds, run for the hills.

The Information Centre on the south bank contains a working model of the barrier and exhibits about its construction and the Thames. There are good views of the Barrier from the café. Also worth a look is the Thames Barrier Park, 14 hectares of public space built on what was one of the country's most polluted sites, the former PR Chemicals factory.

Access to the barrier is a little awkward. It is best viewed as part of a walk along the Thames Path, which stretches 184 miles from the river's source in Gloucestershire. Pick up the trail by the Cutty Sark in Greenwich and walk downstream past the Millennium Dome to the barrier. Then press on to Woolwich, cross the river by ferry or foot tunnel, and catch a train back into central London from North Woolwich.

CROSSNESS PUMPING STATION

Healer of the Great Stink

The Crossness Engines Trust, Thames Water S.T.W., Belvedere Road, SE2 9AQ
0208 311 3711
www.crossness.org.uk
Tues and Fri 9.30am-4pm and second Sunday of every month 10.30am-2pm.
Check website for details of other open days
Check website for admission prices
Abbey Wood rail. On open days, a minibus usually operates from Abbey Wood
to the Crossness site every 30 mins. Otherwise it's a brisk 30-minute walk from
the station through an industrial wasteland

There aren't many opportunities to make a trip to a sewage farm, but Crossness Pumping Station – opened in 1856 by Edward, Prince of Wales – offers the chance. The obsolete Pumping Station is located in the middle of the Crossness Sewage Treatment Works, which is still very much operational: if you miss the shuttle service from the station, simply follow your nose.

The Pumping Station was part of legendary engineer Joseph Bazalgette's innovative sewage system for London. By the mid-19th century, London's exploding population meant the Thames had effectively become an open sewer. The contaminated water caused cholera outbreaks that killed over 30,000 Londoners. Plans to address this were finally put into action following the 'Great Stink' of 1858, when an unusually warm summer and clogged-up River Thames made the House of Commons unusable. Bazalgette built 1,100 miles of brick-lined, underground sewers that diverted untreated sewage downstream.

Crossness was the business end of the southern half of the system (a similar station at Beckton performs the same function for North London). Sewage arrived at the site and was pumped up into a 17-foot-deep reservoir, which could hold 27 million gallons of waste. The reservoir gates were opened twice a day, and the contents were swept out to sea on the Thames' ebb tide. Eventually, only liquid waste was disposed of in this way; the prosaically named 'sludge boats' dumped solid, untreated waste beyond the mouth of the river until 1998.

Crossness Pumping Station is an incredible place. The Beam Engine House, home to four steam-driven pumping engines, contains some of the most spectacular ornamental ironwork in the capital. At the heart of the building is the Octagon, an exuberant framework for the engines made of brightly coloured iron columns and screens. This is characteristic of the Victorians' love of Gothic adornment in the unlikeliest places.

The building was abandoned in the 1950s after it became obsolete. Ongoing restoration work, largely by unpaid volunteers, began in 1987. The scale of the engineering is unnerving: the four engines (each weirdly named after a member of the royal family) are the largest rotative beam engines in the world. They have 52-ton flywheels and 47-ton beams,

and were capable of pumping around 20 milk lorries of sewage a minute into the reservoir. Only one – the 'Prince Consort' – is currently restored, but the Crossness Engines Trust is now focused on bringing 'Victoria' back to her former glory.

Greater London (North)

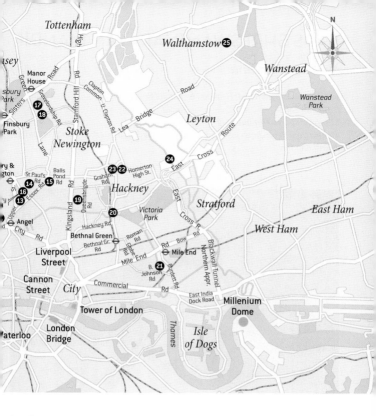

BAPS SHRI SWAMINARAYAN MANDIR

Neasden Nirvana

①

105-119 Brentfield Road, Neasden NW10 8LD
0208 965 2651
http://londonmandir.baps.org
Temple 9am-6pm daily. Free guided tours available. Modest clothing is required
Admission free
Neasden tube

Scarcely believable at first sight, this is the largest Hindu temple outside India. This spectacular edifice was opened in August 1995 by His Holiness Pramukh Swami Maharaj. It is but a stone's throw from the grim North Circular, the drab ring road circling London's northern suburbs. To build it, 5,000 tonnes of Indian and Italian marble and Bulgarian limestone were hand-carved into 26,300 pieces by 1,526 skilled craftsmen in India, then shipped to London and assembled like a giant jigsaw puzzle in less than three years. The finished building includes seven shikhars (or pinnacles), six domes, 193 pillars, and 55 different ceiling designs.

Deities and motifs representing the Hindu faith spring from the walls, ceilings and windows. The heart of the mandir, or temple, is its murtis, or sacred images of the deities, who are revered as living gods. In total, there are 11 shrines with 17 murtis, including Ganesh, Hanuman, and Swaminarayan – to whom the temple is dedicated. The deities are ritually served by dedicated sadhus (monks) who live in the temple. Before sunrise, the murtis are woken by the sadhus and the shrine doors opened for the first of five daily 'artis' (prayers). Feeding and bathing of the murtis continues throughout the day.

The best time to visit is just before 11.45am, when the rajbhog arti ceremony is performed daily. Lit candles are waved in front of the embodiments of the deities, accompanied by a musical prayer performed by drums, bells, gongs and a conch-shell. A haunting and uplifting experience.

PADDOCK

Churchill's spare bunker

109 Brook Road, NW2 7DZ
0208 782 4239
www.networkhomes.org.uk/paddock/
Open two weekends a year – check website
Admission free
Neasden, Dollis Hill tube

Paddock is an incongruously rural name for this horrible concrete warren next to a reservoir at the top of Dollis Hill. Built as an alternative command centre to the Cabinet War Rooms in Whitehall, which would not have survived a direct hit, this bunker system was designed to offer protected accommodation for the Cabinet and the Chief of Staff of the air, naval and land force had it ever been used.

However, Churchill did not care for Paddock, supposedly describing it as 'dank, dark, far away from the light … somewhere near Hampstead'. He might have been talking about Kentish Town. He also took the view that if the government abandoned the centre of London, the people would have no reason to stay. Anyway, if he didn't like it then, he'd have liked it even less now. Even in its heyday, it was an airless hole in the ground under many feet of concrete. The years have not been kind to it – wearing a hard hat, visitors descend into a series of rooms that look like something from a horror film. Water drips down the walls, forming puddles everywhere. There is spectacular mould, long spidery stalactites and desolate machinery covered in rust. Piles of wet wood lie against the walls next to broken furniture. But with the skilled guides from Subterranea Britannica – literally an underground society – the place comes to life.

Even though the bunker was only ever used twice by the Cabinet (and one of these was a dress rehearsal followed by a 'vivacious luncheon', according to Churchill's memoirs), it was operational until 1944 just in case things got too hot in the Cabinet War Rooms. The top secret Map Room is interesting – it was lined with wall-sized maps of all the theatres of war and lit with fluorescent tubes, cutting-edge technology when Paddock was built.

The bunker originally lay within the grounds of Chartwell Court, a highly sophisticated wartime communications research station, where the Enigma code-breaking machine Colossus was built, and where the Speaking Clock was also invented. This explains the enigmatic sign for Floor 28 in Paddock's entrance hall – the numbering was part of the system for the whole complex, and does not mean that there are daleks, mole-men or secret tunnels to Whitehall underneath the bunker. Unfortunately.

FENTON HOUSE

Comfortable country house

Hampstead Grove, Hampstead, NW3 6SP
0207 435 3471
www.nationaltrust.org.uk/fenton-house-and-garden
Mar-Oct, Wed-Sun 11am-5pm
Check website for admission prices and events
Hampstead tube

Few people seem to know of or visit this large, well-appointed National Trust property near Hampstead tube station. As a result it has the feel of a trip to the countryside, despite its central location.

Dating from 1686, it was bought by merchant Philip Fenton in 1793. The house remained largely untouched over the years; it has a huge walled formal garden, a rose garden, a kitchen garden and a 300-year-old orchard. Apple Weekend, held every year in late September, gives members of the public the chance to try old English varieties of apples.

The garden is worth the trip alone. However, the house's real glory is the interior. In 1936, the house was bought by Lady Katherine Binning, who filled the house with her collections of porcelain, 17th-century needlework pictures (known as stump work) and Georgian furniture. Lady Binning lived alone in this pile – and very comfortable she made it too – before bequeathing it to the National Trust following her death in 1952. Subsequent additions include an impressive collection of paintings, notably a selection of the Camden Town Group of English Post-Impressionists, which includes work by Walter Sickert. Elsewhere, paintings by Sir William Nicholson also stand out.

In the attic there is a painting of Mrs Jordan, the Irish actress who bore the Duke of Clarence ten illegitimate children. He shamefully abandoned her once he had a sniff of the throne and was crowned as William IV. His portrait hangs in the hall, next to his appalling brother, George IV. One of William's daughters also lived in the house for a while.

If harpsichords are your thing, the Benton Fletcher Collection of Early Keyboard Instruments is also worth a look. The house hosts musical events exploring different aspects of these instruments.

NEARBY

Fake bridge on Thousand Pound Pond ④

Once you're finished at Fenton House, roll down the hill to Hampstead Heath, which is full of wonderful things. Possibly the oddest is the 18th-century fake Palladian bridge at the end of Thousand Pound Pond, next to Kenwood House. This was part of the landscaping done by Robert Adam. The idea is that, when seen from the house, the bridge gives the illusion that the water continues beyond it.

BURGH HOUSE
& HAMPSTEAD MUSEUM

Ode to North London

Burgh House, New End Square, NW3 1LT
0207 431 0144
www.burghhouse.org.uk
Wed, Thurs, Fri, Sun 12-5pm. The Buttery Café is open Wed-Fri 11am-5pm, Sat & Sun 9.30am-5.30pm
Admission free
Hampstead tube or Hampstead Heath Overground station

Built in 1704, Burgh House is one of the oldest houses in Hampstead, a leafy suburb in North London whose walled lanes and wonky cul-de-sacs are ripe for strolling. Despite its exclusive character, this Georgian enclave still has the charm of a sleepy village whose steep slopes afford fine views across London. In its 18th-century heyday, the spa at Hampstead Wells was fashionable for its fetid, iron-rich water, reportedly good for afflictions such as hysteria and neurosis, as prevalent today as they were then. Dr William Gibbons, the spa physician, lived at Burgh House. His initials are carved into the wrought-iron gate although the house is now named after Reverend Allatson Burgh, a wildly unpopular vicar who bought the house for £2,645 in 1822.

During Burgh's sloppy tenure, the property fell into ruins. After successive occupants, ranging from an independent militia to Rudyard Kipling's daughter, Elsie Bambridge, Burgh House was abandoned in 1937. In 1979, it was finally restored and leased to the Burgh House Trust who set up a small museum here. Founder Christopher Wade, a local historian, presided over this living memorial to his community until his death in 2015 at the age of 95.

Exhibitions and recitals are held in the beautifully restored drawing rooms. Upstairs, you can trace the history of Hampstead in the small but intriguing museum, from the first silent film footage of London to Bauhaus furniture from the iconic Isokon flats. There are tributes to local luminaries John Constable, who painted the Heath before houses began to obscure the view, and John Keats, whose soppy odes were inspired by its wild landscapes.

Burgh House's Buttery is a favourite tea break for silver-haired visitors. Tables are set in the garden in summer, where you can glare at the lucky devils who live in the covetable council flats next door.

The fountain of Hampstead Wells

Nearby, on Wells Passage, is the fountain from which Hampstead Wells' 'chalybeate' water was pumped. History survives in the local place names: the foul-tasting water was bottled at Flask Walk, and the nearest section of parkland is called the Vale of Health.

NEARBY
A theatre with a morbid history ⑥

The New End Theatre nearby was a cult platform for emerging playwrights until its closure in 2011. Now converted into a synagogue, the theatre was built in 1890 as the mortuary of New End Hospital across the road; an underground tunnel allowed corpses to be discreetly transported to the morgue.

HAMPSTEAD OBSERVATORY

Stargazing and weather reading

Lower Terrace, Hampstead NW3 1DU
www.hampsteadscience.ac.uk/astro
Fri & Sat 8-10pm, Sun 11am-1pm (to observe the sun), from mid-Sept to mid-April, as long as the weather is clear
Admission free. Donations welcome
Hampstead tube

Y ou could live in Hampstead all your life without spotting this little oddity. Ringed by trees, the miniature dome of Hampstead Observatory is almost invisible from the street, although it's perched on one of London's highest points. Unlike the gated mansions that encircle it, the mildewed entrance to the observatory is so discreet you could easily miss it. Ignore the Metropolitan Water Board notice warning that trespassers will be prosecuted and climb to the top of the grassy hillock. You are actually standing on a giant reservoir containing millions of gallons of water, which has been pumped to local residents since Victorian times.

This observatory has been open to the public since 1910. The Hampstead Scientific Society (founded in 1899) originally set up a telescope near the swimming ponds on Hampstead Heath, which afforded marvellous views of the heavens – but stargazers risked falling into the ponds. So a wooden observatory was established on top of the reservoir instead. A small hut was added in 1933.

The 6-inch refracting Cooke telescope, mounted on a concrete pier that goes all the way to the bottom of the reservoir, has been in constant use since 1923. The rotating dome opens up so you can track the stars across the sky. Douglas Daniels, President of Hampstead Scientific Society, has been showing visitors the stars since 1965. 'Back then we could show people star clusters and remote galaxies,' says Daniels. 'Now, because of light and airplane pollution, we're mainly confined to the solar system.'

Seeing Saturn's rings, Jupiter's cloud belts, and the Moon's craters is still a thrill for novices, especially kids. Crowds of up to 250 will gather when there is a comet or eclipse. There's also a solar telescope through which you can safely look at the sun. But don't go if it's raining, cloudy, or blowing a gale. As the Society says: 'If the sky isn't clear then there's no point standing about looking at a dull orange glow, getting cold and wet. Bar heaters and fires have the same basic hue and will be superior companions on such nights.'

London's most long-suffering weather man

A meteorological station was set up alongside the observatory in 1910. Eric Hawke, an eager 17-year-old, volunteered to take a daily meteorological record. He kept up these manual readings from 1910 to 1965, only missing one day because of an air raid. The tiny weather station is now operated by a solar-powered computer.

2 WILLOW ROAD

A modernist show home

2 Willow Road, Hampstead NW3 1TH
0207 435 6166
www.nationaltrust.org.uk/2-willow-road
Wed-Sun 11am-5pm (March to October). Guided tours take place at 11am,
12pm, 1pm and 2pm. Self-guided viewings 3-5pm; last entry 4.30pm. Tickets
are available on the day on a first-come first-served basis. Group tours by prior
arrangement
Check website for admission prices
Hampstead tube or Hampstead Heath rail

Ernö Goldfinger is most famous as the architect of Trellick Tower, a 1960s high-rise council block in West London, once as notorious for brutal crimes as its Brutalist design. Trellick Tower is now a listed building, where small flats come with sky-high prices. The first house the Transylvanian émigré ever built was this low-key, low-rise Hampstead home, where he lived with his family for almost fifty years.

What makes this modernist show home unique is that everything is exactly as Goldfinger designed it in 1939 – and exactly as he left it on his death in 1987, from the prototype door handles on his desk to the baked beans in his wife Ursula's kitchen. The house is as fascinating for its ingenious, daring design as its insight into Goldfinger's life and work. The art collection is impressive, too: works by Bridget Riley, Max Ernst, and Marcel Duchamp hang alongside Ursula's surrealist paintings. In the 1930s, rural Hampstead had replaced Chelsea as the epicentre of a lively, left-wing arts scene. Lee Miller, Roland Penrose, and Henry Moore attended the Goldfingers' glamorous parties.

Although the house is relatively small – at least by Hampstead standards – folding doors, hidden storage, and vast windows with unbroken views of Hampstead Heath create a sense of space and light. Passionate volunteers offer guided tours several times a day. A graceful spiral staircase (designed by Ove Arup) leads to a lacquered scarlet landing. The house's Cubist colour palette – midnight blue, tomato red, mustard, terracotta – is oddly soothing. The furniture – mostly designed by Goldfinger himself – still looks thoroughly modern.

The house faced intense opposition when it was built. Goldfinger, who retorted that 'only the Eskimos and Zulus build anything but rectangular houses', was forced to cover the concrete frame in brick cladding to blend in with its Georgian neighbours. One of the main objectors was the Tory Home Secretary, Henry Brooke. Ironically, it was his son, Peter Brooke, then Heritage Secretary, who took possession of the house on behalf of the National Trust. Goldfinger's children could not afford the whopping death duties.

Goldfinger's nasty namesake

By all accounts, the dashing Goldfinger was a difficult man, mitigated by his generosity and charisma. But the anti-Semitic author Ian Fleming took such a dislike to Goldfinger's radical designs and Marxist principles that he named his infamous Bond villain after him. When the real Goldfinger threatened to sue Fleming's publisher, the author offered to change his character's name to Goldprick.

LONDON ZOO AVIARY CLOCK

Kinetic cuckoo clock

London Zoo, Outer Circle, Regent's Park, NW1 4RY
0344 225 1826
www.zsl.org
Every day from 10am, except Christmas Day. Seasonal closing times, check
website for details
Check website for admission prices
Camden Town, Baker Street or Regent's Park tube

Okay, so you have to buy a ticket to London Zoo to see this, and tickets aren't cheap. But as zoos go, it's a very good one. So if you do happen to be visiting, make a detour to the Blackburn Pavilion.

Originally built in 1883 as a reptile house, this Victorian building was restored and reopened as a home for the zoo's tropical birds in 2008. In keeping with the 19th-century ornithological theme, the zoo commissioned a clock from the singular genius Tim Hunkin, an engineer, artist and cartoonist.

Like much of Hunkin's work, the aviary clock is fitted with automata – lots of them: a pair of toucans peck the pendulum to keep it swinging; on the hour, small birds disappear from the display case at the front of the clock and pop up elsewhere; a Victorian couple – he with a covered dish, she with a birdcage – are astonished as first their dinner and then their pet fly away; finally, the toucans desert their posts to reappear squawking at the top, and the pendulum and clock stop running. Then it all happens again. Hunkin reportedly wanted to express something of Victorian attitudes to animals, which this amazing clock does very neatly.

Hunkin also designed the entrance to the children's area at the zoo, best described as a goat tug-of-war arch. Children turn wheels at the base of a pillar, driving aluminium goats to tug on a rope, from which hang the letters for the sign. When the rope is taut, the goats give up and release the tension, making the letters fall. Whew. It's harder to explain than it looks.

In fact, you don't have to go to the zoo to see Hunkin's work in London. Probably his most well-known piece is the Neal's Yard Water Clock on Short's Garden – currently stopped, but hopefully soaking pedestrians again at some point soon. He also built a steam clock for Chelsea Farmers Market (still there, but also out of action), as well as automated collection boxes for a variety of places across London, including St Thomas' Hospital. Hunkin's most exciting new addition to the capital is Novelty Automation (see p. 98), an adult arcade of tongue-in-cheek slot machines. In truth, Hunkin's work needs a fairly high level of maintenance, but they add to the gaiety of the city and should be encouraged. What the man needs is a wealthy benefactor . . . if there's one reading.

RUDOLF STEINER HOUSE

Eurythmic architecture

35 Park Road, NW1 6XT
0207 723 4400
www.rsh.anth.org.uk
Mon-Fri 1-6pm. Café open Sat 9am-5pm
Admission free to library and café; prices for lectures and performances vary
Baker Street tube, Marylebone rail

At first glance, this curious landmark looks like a 1920s office block; but behind the austere grey façade Rudolf Steiner House is as iconoclastic as its namesake. The rounded door and stained glass portholes hint at Art Nouveau flourishes. Inside, it's more like a habitat for hobbits. The entrance is dominated by a sculptural staircase that snakes all the way up the heart of the building, creating the curious sensation of entering a cocoon or a womb. Organic forms and distorted shapes suggest movement and fluidity. Pastel surfaces are painted in lazure, a glazing technique using translucent plant pigments that creates the effect of sunlight shimmering across water. It feels as though the architect was on acid; in fact, the trippy design is inspired by nature.

This is the first and only example of Expressionist architecture in London. One of the earliest proponents of Expressionism was Rudolf Steiner (1861-1925), an Austrian philosopher who developed the spiritual science of anthroposophy, or 'wisdom of the human being'. Depending on your point of view, Steiner was either a visionary who pioneered holistic education and biodynamic farming, or a racist crackpot who believed that mistletoe could cure cancer and that 'blonde hair actually bestows intelligence.' Like fellow occultist Aleister Crowley, Steiner was prone to wearing flouncy bow ties.

Rudolf Steiner House was purpose built for The Anthroposophical Society between 1924 and 1935 by Montague Wheeler, a fellow believer. The space positively radiates a sense of touchy-feely community. As well as workshops on spiritual development, meditation, and Rosicrucianism, the society offers classes in eurythmy. Derived from a Greek word meaning 'harmonious rhythm', eurythmy is part performance art and part dance therapy. In the café (biodynamic, naturally) the wooden beams, inlaid with seven different hardwoods, echo the Goetheanum, the Swiss headquarters of anthroposophy designed by Steiner himself in 1914. Originally built from wood, the Goetheanum burned down in 1922 and was rebuilt in poured concrete.

The small library is open to the public, should you wish to delve into Steiner's oeuvre. He wrote over 330 books.

THE ICE WELLS
OF THE CANAL MUSEUM

The history of London's waterways

12/13 New Wharf Road, N1 9RT
0207 713 0836
www.canalmuseum.org.uk
Tues-Sat 10am-4pm
Check website for admission details
King's Cross tube/rail

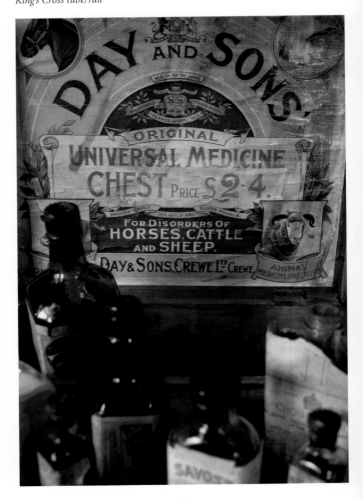

Today, stolen bicycles and supermarket trolleys clog London's murky canals. But until the 'great freeze' of winter 1963 finally killed off commercial canal traffic, barges cruised these waterways weighed down with bulk cargo of all kinds. London's network of canals remained the cheapest means of transporting goods across long distances well after the arrival of railways. Regent's Canal was built in the early 19th century to link the Grand Junction Canal at Paddington with the Docklands. At first, canal boats were drawn by horses, but a steam tug was introduced in 1826. By the 1840s, there was talk of turning the canal into a railway, but luckily this never happened.

Converted from an old ice-house used to store ice imported from Norway, in the days before refrigeration, the London Canal Museum is an old-fashioned, offbeat little venue that tries to capture this forgotten history. Some details are slightly cheesy – a fake horse, clothed dummies – but you can nose around a reconstructed narrowboat decorated with traditional roses and castles patterns, and peer down into the impressive ice wells, where hundreds of tons of ice were stored.

From the canalside terrace, spot the cranes and loading doors where barrels of Guinness were unloaded at the bottling factory on the other side of Battlebridge Basin, now transformed into trendy offices.

NEARBY

Narrowboat tours of Islington Tunnel ⑫

The Canal Museum organises occasional narrowboat tours of Islington Tunnel on Regent's Canal. When it first opened, this spooky tunnel, around ¾ of a mile long, could only be navigated by 'legging': men lay on their backs and walked the boat through by pushing against the slimy walls with their feet. Their hob-nailed boots would echo through the tunnel like the clapping of hands. A lantern at the prow lit this cumbersome operation.

Islington Tunnel cost nearly £40,000 to build, using explosives, horses and hard labour. When the renowned engineer Thomas Telford inspected the results in 1818, he reported: 'Materials and workmanship excellent, and its direction perfectly straight.' The tunnel opened in 1820, when Regent's Canal was completed, facilitating the transport of goods to the city centre. Its architect, James Morgan, travelled on the leading barge of a grand procession from St Pancras all the way to the Thames. Accompanied by a band, they were met by cannon fire as they emerged from the tunnel.

LITTLE ANGEL THEATRE

Theatre on a string

14 Dagmar Passage, Islington N1 2DN
0207 226 1787
www.littleangeltheatre.com
Times vary depending on performances and workshops
Admission varies
Angel or Highbury & Islington tube, Essex Road or Highbury & Islington rail

Long before Islington was colonised by overpriced cafés and designer boutiques, its backstreets harboured a secret venue. The setting is like something out of a fairy tale: on a pedestrian passage overgrown with creepers, the Little Angel Theatre has been staging puppet shows since 1961.

It was founded by John and Lyndie Wright, South African émigrés (and parents of movie director Joe Wright) who converted a derelict temperance hall, bombed during World War II, into this enchanting theatre for moving marionettes and pint-sized punters.

Everything about the theatre, with its bright blue door, pews for seats, and doll's house proportions, seems designed to delight children, who make up the biggest part of its audience. From re-workings of Shakespeare to operettas performed by marionettes, there's plenty to captivate adults as well.

All the puppets, props, and sets are created in the Little Angel Studios around the corner, which also runs puppetry workshops for all ages. Lyndie Wright (who still lives in the cottage next door) and her daughter Sarah continue to design many of the puppets and shows.

The puppet barge

In 1982, one of the Wrights' protégés, Juliet Rogers, established an even more unusual venue devoted to puppet theatre. Unable to afford London property prices even then, Rogers and her partner Gren Middleton bought a rusty Thames lighter – one of the iron barges originally used to transport goods from the Docklands to Henley and Oxford.

With its red and yellow striped awning, the Puppet Theatre Barge stands out among the colourful houseboats in Regent's Canal. Up to 50 children can squeeze inside the scarlet hold of this floating venue, which drifts down the River Thames to Richmond during the summer.

From October to June, the barge is moored opposite 35-40 Blomfield Road in Little Venice, W9 2PF; 0207 249 6876; www.puppetbarge.com.

CANONBURY TOWER

Through the Tudor keyhole

Canonbury Place, N1 2NQ
0207 226 6256
www.ciga.org.uk
Clerkenwell and Islington Guides run tours of the tower twice a month
Email info@ciga.org.uk to book
Check website for admission details
Highbury & Islington tube /rail, Essex Road or Canonbury rail

One of the few Tudor buildings still standing in London, Canonbury Tower has been home to all sorts of movers and shakers. First there was Prior William Bolton of St Bartholomew's in Smithfield, a short ride across what was then rolling farmland. (The tower enjoyed views of the whole of London in the 16th century; the rooftop still commands sweeping views of the city skyline.) Then came Thomas Cromwell, who was given this plush pad by Henry VIII in 1539 as a thank-you gift for masterminding the dissolution of the monasteries. However, Cromwell's Islington idyll didn't last long: a year later, he fell out of favour at court and was beheaded.

Sir John Spencer, the obscenely rich Lord Mayor of London, moved into Canonbury Tower in 1570 and stayed until his death in 1610. It was Spencer who commissioned the intricate wood panelling, decorated with Masonic and Rosicrucian symbols, on the second floor. On the top floor is a mysterious inscription, listing every king and queen from 'Will Con' (William the Conqueror) to Charolus (Charles I). Perhaps it was the handiwork of Sir Francis Bacon, the prominent Freemason, philosopher and statesman, who lived here for nine years, and allegedly planted the mulberry tree in the back garden in the early 17th century.

Other distinguished residents included Ephraim Chambers, who compiled the first encyclopaedia in 1728, writer and gambler Oliver Goldsmith, who hoped to evade his creditors in suburban Islington, and Washington Irving, author of *Rip Van Winkle*, who promptly moved out after his landlady invited excitable fans to peer through his keyhole.

The Canonbury Masonic Research Centre, an organisation devoted to 'the study of mystical and esoteric traditions, in particular Freemasonry' moved out a few years ago. Owned by the Marquess of Northampton, whose family have held onto it since 1618, the Tudor tower is only open to the public on bi-monthly tours run by excellent Clerkenwell and Islington Guides.

You can still see Bolton's Rebus (see p. 110) of a bolt (arrow) piercing a tun (barrel) at 6 Canonbury Place, once part of the property's extensive grounds. According to local legend, subterranean passages linked Canonbury Tower to the priory at Smithfield.

However, the brick arches that led to this supposition were probably conduits that provided the priory's water supply.

NEW RIVER WALK

Last trickle of a great waterway

Canonbury N1 2PU. The best entry point is on Canonbury Road.
Daily 8am to dusk
Admission free
Essex Road or Canonbury rail, Highbury & Islington tube

With its Georgian mansions built around leafy squares, Canonbury is one of the lushest and loveliest corners of London. Only developed as a residential area in the early 19th century, Canonbury retains the feel of an exclusive country retreat. Running through the vast – and vastly expensive – houses of Canonbury Grove is a little stream, hidden from view by weeping willows and luxuriant shrubbery. This sleepy waterway is one of the last remaining sections of Hugh Myddelton's New River, an aqueduct built in 1613 to bring drinking water from springs in Hertfordshire to a reservoir in Myddelton Square, near Sadler's Wells (see p. 328).

Before 1600, London's water supply was sourced from the River Thames and local streams, wells and springs. Often contaminated, water was distributed by sellers sloshing wooden buckets. Hugh Myddelton, a goldsmith and serial entrepreneur, persuaded King James I to cover half the costs of creating a 39-mile aqueduct, on condition the King received half the profits and that the waterway ran through his palace grounds at Theobalds. Over 200 labourers were paid the equivalent of 4p a day to dig out the New River. The water was channelled throughout the city through hollowed out elm trunks. Although the aqueduct still supplies about 8% of London's water, most of the New River has been covered over by buildings.

Created in 1954 and maintained by volunteers from the Canonbury Society, New River Walk meanders for about a kilometre through fragrant gardens crossed by wooden footbridges. Water is pumped upstream to preserve the effect of a moving river. Hungry herons and ponderous ducks drift along the mossy surface of the shallow waterway. After your stroll, refresh yourself with a pint and a roast at the exceptionally cosy Myddleton Arms, named (but misspelled) after the self-taught engineer.

NEARBY

The Estorick Collection

39a Canonbury Square, N1 2AN
0207 704 9522
www.estorickcollection.com

The Estorick Collection is named after Eric Estorick, an American collector with a brilliant moniker and a fondness for Futurist art. After moving to England after World War II, Estorick (1913-93) snapped up drawings by Picasso, Gris, Léger and Braque. But it was during his honeymoon in Switzerland and Italy in 1947 that Estorick discovered Futurism; enthralled, he bought practically the entire works of Mario Sironi. In a converted Georgian townhouse, his collection includes works by Amedeo Modigliani, Giorgio de Chirico and Zoran Mušič. The peaceful garden café serves proper cappuccino. On a sunny afternoon, you could almost be in Italy.

WEST RESERVOIR

Sailing in the city

Green Lanes, Stoke Newington N4 2HA
0208 442 8116.
www.hackney.gov.uk/west-reservoir.htm
Daily 9am-5pm
Admission free. Cost of watersports courses varies
Manor House tube

I t may seem like one of the world's wettest cities, but London has less rainfall than Madrid, Rome or Dallas. That doesn't stop every resident using an average 155 litres of water a day. Back in the 19th century, for most Londoners the only water supply was a communal standpipe that churned out a brackish trickle for a few hours a day. After several cholera outbreaks, the East and West Reservoirs were built between 1831 and 1833 in Stoke Newington as a water reserve and purification plant. Stone from the recently demolished London Bridge was used to shore up the reservoirs' banks.

Surprisingly few locals know about this rural idyll in the heart of Hackney. A muddy footpath surrounded by meadows circles the West Reservoir, where swans and seagulls swoop among colourful sailing boats. After a long campaign to save the reservoirs from property developers, a water sports and environmental education centre opened in the former pump station in 2001. You can take sailing, kayaking, and canoeing classes, go open water swimming (wetsuit required), or just marvel at the old hydraulic machinery, which apparently handled 'a weight of water equivalent to that contained by 4,366 bathtubs or 3,492,800 glass fulls dropped from a height of seventeen metres up to six times each day.'

After your nautical exertions, pull up a chair on the waterside deck of the Reservoir Cafe. The food is terrible, the service is laughable, but the view is sensational.

The not-so-New River

Stoke Newington has been instrumental in bringing clean water to London since the early 17th century, when the New River first ran through the area. Almost 400 years old, the New River is not technically a river at all. It is an artificial aqueduct constructed to transport water from springs in Hertfordshire to London, and is still used to transport water today. Determined walkers can follow its course along a 45-km footpath from Clerkenwell to the countryside (see p. 326).

NEARBY
Castle climbing centre
⑱

As its name suggests, gritty Green Lanes was once a lush rural retreat. Very few houses stood nearby when the Stoke Newington Water Pumping Station was built in 1856. But the contractors opted to appease local objections by disguising the main building as a medieval fortress. Today, this flamboyant monument to Victorian engineering has been reinvented as one of the largest indoor climbing centres in Britain.

CLOWNS' GALLERY AND MUSEUM ⑲

Fool's paradise

*Holy Trinity Church, Beechwood Road, Dalston E8 3TF (entrance on
Cumberland Close)*
0207 608 0312
http://clowns-gallery.wix.com/clowns-gallery
Open first Friday of every month 12-5pm, or by appointment
Admission free
Dalston Junction Overground

The Holy Trinity has been London's Clowns' Church since 1959. The only clue to this curious association is a stained-glass window in the main hall, depicting scenes from the life of Joseph Grimaldi (1778-1837), the godfather of all jesters. In a tiny room at the rear of the church (accessed via Cumberland Close) is one of London's smallest museums: the Clowns' Gallery. Over a tinkling soundtrack of fairground tunes, a clown/curator entertains visitors to the monthly open day with uproarious anecdotes. Among the clown stamps, cartoons and tributes are a few religious references to 'The Holy Fools': a tapestry proclaiming 'Here we are fools for Christ' and The Clown's Prayer (a slightly cloying ode to laughter). The real highlight is the collection of clown portraits painted on over 200 porcelain eggs. A tradition that originated in the late 1940s, these eggs are faithful representations of the trademark make-up worn by each clown – a suitably humorous way of patenting their personal face-paint. In addition to paint, the artist uses samples of each clown's costume and wig to produce an 'eggs-act' miniature portrait.

Traditionally held at Holy Trinity, but recently relocated to All Saints Church on nearby Livermere Road, the annual clown service takes place on the first Sunday in February. Among the local congregation in their Sunday best, a 'pratfall' of clowns in full 'motley and slap' cause havoc in the pews – blowing bubbles, honking horns, wearing stilts, and singing along to 'Send in the Clowns'. One popular hymn at the Holy Trinity goes like this: 'When we are tempted in our pride to dizzy heights of sin, beneath our feet, oh Lord, provide a ripe banana skin...' Get there early – the clown service is always packed.

Joseph Grimaldi, the godfather of clowning

Joseph Grimaldi, who made his debut at Sadler's Wells aged three, pioneered many modern clowning techniques, from visual pranks to the dreaded audience participation. A blue plaque marks Grimaldi's former home at 56 Exmouth Market, Clerkenwell. His grave is largely overlooked in the grubby little Joseph Grimaldi Park on the corner of Pentonville Road and Rodney Street, Islington. With a happy and sad mask dangling from the iron railings, it's a rather forlorn tribute to the fools' hero, but every June a lively festival is held here in Grimaldi's honour.

MUSEUM OF CURIOSITIES

The beautiful and the damned

11 Mare Street, E8 4RP
0207 998 3617
www.thelasttuesdaysociety.org
Wed-Sun 12-10.30pm
Check website for admission prices
Cambridge Heath or London Fields rail, Bethnal Green tube

Those easily offended by death and decay should stay away.' Don't say you haven't been warned: the Museum of Curiosities is not for the faint-hearted. (Another sign on the door, pinched from druggie dandy Sebastian Horsley's Soho front door, reads: 'This is not a brothel. There are no prostitutes at this address.')

Descending a gold spiral staircase into the musty basement, it takes a while to adjust to the crepuscular gloom. Beasts, freaks and monsters gradually start swimming into view: a two-headed kitten, a unicorn's skull, a tongue-eating louse, a mummified pygmy, pickled babies in bottles. Alongside the taxidermy and totems peering from the walls and ceilings are glass cabinets crammed with erotica ('small pecker condoms'), juvenilia (celebrity poos) and occult paraphernalia (a sinister alchemist's toolkit). Perhaps the weirdest item of all is 'a casket containing some of the original darkness that Moses called down upon the earth'. There's a corner devoted to artist Stephen Wright (see p. 378) and a shrine to Horsley, including a red glitter suit and the nails he used to crucify himself.

Most objects are labelled with spidery black captions that might have been written by Prince Charles, but are in fact the handiwork of Viktor Wynd, the collector and curator of this singular 'Wunderkabinett'. A self-styled 'artist, author, lecturer, impresario and 'pataphysicist' (the apostrophe is deliberate; the quasi-philosophy is best defined as a bunch of pretentious provocateurs), Wynd made a name for himself on the London underground scene, hosting masquerade balls and literary salons. All the while, he was amassing this private collection of the grotesque and macabre, creepy and shocking, sublime and ridiculous.

It began as a curiosity shop and gallery, but achieved museum status thanks to a crowd-funding campaign. If you have anything at home you think Wynd might like, do post it to him at the museum.

The admission price includes a cup of tea at the bar upstairs, a faintly sleazy affair crammed with skeletons, skulls and stuffed animals. Absinthe cocktails, edible insects and chocolate anuses are consumed at your own risk. Occasionally, you might stumble into a taxidermy class or a seance, so it's probably best to ring ahead of your visit.

RAGGED SCHOOL MUSEUM

A Victorian lesson in East End history

46-50 Copperfield Road, E3 4RR
0208 980 6405
www.raggedschoolmuseum.org.uk
Wed and Thurs 10am-5pm, first Sunday each month 2-5pm.
Victorian lesson at 2.15 & 3.30pm on the first Sunday of every month; limited
places available on a first-come first-served basis
Admission free
Mile End tube or Limehouse DLR

Tower Hamlets is still one of the poorest boroughs in London, but in Victorian times it suffered poverty on an incomparable scale. Families were crammed into one-room flats and illiterate kids ran barefoot along the coal-blackened alleys. One third of all funerals in the area were for children under five. When Thomas Barnardo arrived in London in 1866 to train as a missionary, a cholera epidemic had swept through the East End. Barnardo set about founding the Ragged Schools to provide free education for London's poorest children. Today, kids can dress up like Oliver Twist at the Ragged School Museum, a Dickensian throwback aptly located on Copperfield Road in Mile End.

From 1887 to 1908, tens of thousands of children were educated at this school, housed in a former warehouse beside Regent's Canal. On the first Sunday of every month, a Victorian lesson is re-enacted by a suitably severe actress in period costume (accessorized with a forbidding cane) in one of the original classrooms. Scratched desks with inkwells, slate writing boards, and dunce hats create an evocative setting for this local history lesson. Kids are encouraged to be hands-on: sitting at the desks, climbing into the tin bath, or getting to grips with a mangle and carpet beater in the Victorian kitchen.

Downstairs is the small Museum of Tower Hamlets, which offers a potted history of local landmarks like the Bryant and May match factory, now converted into luxury flats. There are mementoes from the Blitz, including song sheets with jaunty titles like *In the Blackout Last Night*, designed to boost wartime morale. Visitors can learn about other well-meaning Victorian institutions like the Working Lads Institute, whose mission was to teach young workers to read and write, and The Factory Girls Club, run by 'refined Christian ladies' to teach girls 'feminine and domestic virtues' so they could become servants.

The promise of free meals led to overcrowding in the Ragged Schools, although school dinners were just as dire in those days: 'Breakfast was bread and cocoa. Dinner was lentil or pea soup and bread, varied occasionally by rice and prunes or haricot beans.' Threatened with demolition in the early 1980s, the building was converted into a museum after a campaign by local residents. Barnardo's is still one of the UK's biggest children's charities.

SUTTON HOUSE

The oldest house in Hackney

2 & 4 Homerton High Street, E9 6JQ
0208 986 2264
www.nationaltrust.org.uk/sutton-house-and-breakers-yard
Wed-Sun 12-5pm
Check website for current admission prices
Hackney Central rail

Once the last bastion of pre-hipster Hackney, even Homerton has been gentrified; soon there will be more flat whites than fried chicken shops. In Tudor times, Homerton was so upmarket that dozens of aristocrats built country estates here. Thomas Sutton, supposedly the richest commoner in Britain and founder of Charterhouse (see p. 94), lived in Homerton. This National Trust property is mistakenly named after Sutton; in fact, he lived next door in a mansion that has since been demolished.

Sutton House's mish-mash of architectural styles reflects its motley succession of residents since 1535. The original owner, Sir Ralph Sadleir, Henry VIII's Secretary of State, had 30 acres of gardens and orchards attached to Bryk Place, the only brick building in what was then a half-timbered village. The cellar contains stacks of 500-year-old bricks, hand-made in situ from blood red 'brickearth' drained from nearby Hackney Brook.

Sutton House has successively been occupied by a sheriff, a silk merchant, a girl's school (coyly known as The Ladies' University of Female Arts), a church institute, and trade union, until it was bought by the National Trust in 1938. Not much happened until the 1980s, when a bunch of punks squatted the derelict building – a perfect venue for underground gigs and raves.

Miraculously, many of the original Tudor features survived: oak-panelled rooms, carved fireplaces, a flagstone courtyard, and an authentically rudimentary kitchen. The Linenfold Parlour is the most impressive room, lined with wood panels carved to look like draped fabric. Bizarrely, this panelling was stolen in the late 1980s, but later sold back to the National Trust.

Visiting Sutton House is like going on a historical treasure hunt. You can lift floorboards, open panels, and peer inside cupboards to discover traces of the house's hidden past. Poke your nose into the Victorian garderobe, or toilet – people hung their clothes in the loo, believing the stench of ammonia would keep moths away. Kids can rummage through period costumes or explore a caravan retro-fitted like a stately home in Breakers Yard. Traces of a 17th-century trompe-l'œil mural are far more accomplished than the wall paintings daubed by punks in the attic, which contains what looks like the prototype of Tracey Emin's unmade bed. But the squatter's slogans couldn't be more topical: 'London belongs to the millions, not the millionaires.'

BANNER REPEATER

Platform for the arts

Platform 1, Hackney Downs Station, Dalston Lane, E8 1LA
www.bannerrepeater.org
Tues-Thurs 8-11am, Fri 8am-6pm, Sat 12-6pm, Sun 12-6pm (during exhibitions)
Admission free
Hackney Downs or Hackney Central rail

Commuting is one of the downsides of living in London. Overcrowded and overpriced trains, buses littered with half-eaten chicken wings, lairy drunks and bomb scares are occupational hazards these days. If you live anywhere near Hackney Downs, however, early morning rush hour can be a more inspiring experience. In 2009, two empty shops on Platform 1 of Hackney Downs train station were transformed into a non-profit, artist-run gallery and reading room.

Founded by artist Ami Clarke, this experimental project space focuses on text-based and digital art, monographs and printed publications. The reading room looks like a terribly trendy bookshop, but browsing is encouraged: there's a full archive of Artists' Publishing and an interactive digital archive in development. A regular reading group examines Object Oriented Ontology, if that's your thing. Even if it's not, you might find yourself reading about it: every morning, artists distribute free copies of in-house journal *Un-Publish* to some of the 4,000 passengers who trundle through Hackney Downs station on a daily basis.

The adjacent exhibition space is dedicated to new work by established and emerging artists – predominantly videos, photographs, performances and installations that explore the tensions between technology and art. Regular talks and events encourage heated debates of the issues and challenges faced by artists today.

Banner Repeater is named after a railway signal that foreshadows a stop signal further down the track, which might be obscured by buildings, bridges or bends. Presumably, the idea is that the arresting art on display will stop commuters in their tracks. For a gallery that makes a point of being accessible to the general public, the work has a surprisingly arcane and academic bent. Nevertheless, it's a vital platform for artists struggling to survive in an increasingly commercially-driven cultural and metropolitan landscape. Next time your train is delayed, put down your phone and look at some art instead.

NEARBY

The Record Deck   (24)

A few years ago, librarian Luke Guilford decided to give up his job and turn his passion for vinyl into a business. Unable to afford London rents, Guilford converted his houseboat into a floating second-hand record shop. Look out for the Record Deck as it drifts around London's waterways, mainly on the Lea River.

GODS OWN JUNKYARD

The light fantastic

Unit 12, Ravenswood Industrial Estate, Shernhall Street, E17 9HQ
0208 521 8066
godsownjunkyard.co.uk
Fri & Sat 11am-9pm, Sun 11am-6pm
Admission free
Walthamstow Central tube, Wood Street rail

Like so much of London, Soho is being sanitised. One by one, the salacious sex shops and seedy drinking dens are being swallowed up by bland restaurant chains and overpriced cocktail bars. Bar Italia is still hanging on, its neon clock luring late-night drinkers for a shot of espresso. And there are still a few peep shows on Brewer Street, their lurid signs advertising the presence, behind tinsel curtains, of GIRLS, GIRLS, GIRLS.

Soho's saucy signage is the legacy of lighting designer Chris Bracey, who died in 2014, aged 59. Bracey's dad, Dick, a Welsh miner, moved to London after the Second World War and landed a much less gloomy job as an electrical engineer for funfairs and amusement arcades. In 1952, he set up Electro Signs, London's first neon sign maker, in Walthamstow. Dick Bracey quickly spotted the commercial potential of Soho's red light district: he installed illicit signs outside sex shops in the dead of night, enlisting his young son, Chris, as his partner in crime.

Electro Signs is still in business. A few streets away, hidden on a drab industrial estate, Chris Bracey set up his own neon emporium in 2005. Squeezed between a car mechanic and a microbrewery, Gods Own Junkyard is part workshop, part showroom. As well as Bracey's own creations, it contains the biggest collection of vintage neon signs in Europe.

Like some kind of psychedelic discotheque, every inch of the shambolic warehouse is aglow. There are flaming lips and flickering hearts, flashing slogans ('Sex, drugs and bacon rolls') and retro signs for pawnshops and massage parlours. A wooden shed has been converted into a tongue-in-cheek shrine, with statues of Buddha and a Catholic priest framing a life-size Jesus with a fluorescent halo, packing a pair of blue neon pistols. The work is called *Son of a Gun*.

After vajazzling Soho's fleshpots, Bracey branched out to create brilliant backdrops for several blockbusters, including *Blade Runner* and *Batman*. Not surprisingly, Gods Own Junkyard – still a family concern, run by Bracey's wife, Linda, and sons, Marcus and Matt – has itself featured in fashion and film shoots. Discovering this technicolour wonderland in the depths of suburbia is still an eye-popping surprise. After admiring the eye candy, you can have tea and cake in the secret garden, where tiny tables are topped with giant toadstools.

LONDON MUSEUM OF WATER & STEAM

Vast feats of Victorian engineering

Green Dragon Lane, Brentford TW8 0EN
0208 568 4757
www.waterandsteam.org.uk
Daily 11am-4pm
Check website for admission prices and events schedules
Kew Bridge rail (South West trains from Waterloo, via Clapham Junction)

The Steam Museum lies directly across the river from Kew Gardens. Look for the Stand Pipe Tower as a landmark. Apparently based on a Florentine bell tower, it is an example of antique forms incorporated into industrial design that informs the rest of the museum. The museum is housed in what was once the Kew Bridge Pumping House, opened in 1838 as part of a system to provide West London with clean water. The Pumping House was largely driven by steam, and the museum's collection of pumping engines is the largest in the world. As in most industrial museums, there is an obvious educational intent in the displays. The first part of the museum is worthy: visitors walk through exhibits detailing the history of London's water supply. Very dull for the most part, with the occasional exception. Part of the sewer display blankly talks about 'toshers', scavengers for flushed valuables, who worked the sewers in gangs of three to protect against rat attacks and death by gassing. When you pass through to the engine rooms, things become more interesting. The engines themselves, mostly 19th-century, are flamboyant and functional at the same time. The Dancer's End engine (named for the Rothschild estate in Hertfordshire where it came from) is kitted out in bold red livery, the Waddon engine in chocolate brown.

The star of the collection is the Grand Junction 90-inch Cornish steam engine. Built in 1846, its scale is overpowering. Housed in a separate part of the museum, it fills the room and dominates the space. Standing beneath it is an overwhelming experience. Each stroke of the pump moved 2,142 litres of water; the beam alone weighs 52 tons. The engine is also beautiful, and of all the exhibits highlights the Victorians' taste for the introduction of antique forms into technology. The engine is supported on fluted Doric columns, which are echoed in the shape of the cylinders and on the valve housing. The edifice is painted a very dark brown, like mahogany; this, along with the Greek influence, lends it the air of a temple – many English church interiors are filled with similar woodwork on tombs or organ lofts. This sense of greatness is magnified when the engines are in operation; their movement is hypnotically beautiful. It is essential, however, to check on the website for the operation schedule. Cornish Engine weekends are the best times to visit, when the Grand Junction is working. The museum also operates a pretty little steam railway at weekends that currently loops around the car park.

THE MUSICAL MUSEUM

(27)

Feel the Mighty Wurlitzer

399 High Street, Brentford, TW8 0DU
020 8560 8108
www.musicalmuseum.co.uk
Tues, Fri, Sat, Sun 10.30am–5pm
Check website or call for guided tours & instrument demonstrations
Kew Bridge rail station

Music is something we take for granted these days; the stuff pours out of headphones, video games, restaurant toilets and lifts. We've reached this stage in a series of short, rapid steps, and this purpose-built museum is full of the baroque miracles that got us here. Founded by Frank Holland in 1963, this is one of the world's foremost collections of automated music systems. This means machines you might be familiar with – musical boxes, pianolas, iPods – and machines you might not. The Hupfeld Phonoslizst-Violina, anyone?

What's most impressive about the museum is that the trust responsible for it aim to get as much as possible of the collection up and running; for this reason, it's essential to check the timings for a guided tour with instrument demonstrations. Working highlights include a rudimentary German jukebox the size of a Transit van, a coin-operated violin player and king-sized gramophones. The ambition of the builders of these machines is impressive – an orchestrion, for example, was designed to replicate the sound of a small orchestra using actual instruments, and sounds like twenty musicians trapped in a box. The sophistication of what were almost entirely mechanical devices is amazing – some player pianos, which slid over a piano keyboard and were operated by foot, were able to reproduce the nuances of the artists who recorded the musical rolls they used. And the guide will let you have a go on one if you're good.

But the glory of the museum lies sleeping in its own hall on the second floor. One of the main uses of these instruments was to accompany silent films. The grander the cinema, the grander the accompaniment, and grandest of all was a Wurlitzer, a massive organ which not only played music, but also produced sound effects including rain, birdsong and storms. The museum's Wurlitzer came from the Regal Cinema in Kingston on Thames; it can play itself, but in its day was often played by leading cinema organists who were stars in their own right.

Monthly tea dances and silent films accompanied by the Wurlitzer

The museum runs monthly Tea Dances accompanied by the Wurlitzer, which include a free dance class and a glass of prosecco, as well as occasional concerts. More excitingly, it runs seasons of the type of silent films it was designed for. On these nights, the Mighty Wurlitzer is woken, and rises up from the floor, lights blazing and pipes howling, to thrill audiences all over again.

LONDON TRANSPORT MUSEUM DEPOT

London Transport's attic

118-120 Gunnersbury Lane, Acton Town, W3 9BQ
0207 565 7298
www.ltmuseum.co.uk/whats-on/museum-depot
The Depot runs two open weekends a year, but also offers guided tours that typically focus on one aspect of the collection. Check website for details
Check website for admission prices
Acton Town tube

This is a treasure trove for the train spotters, bus lovers and assorted public transport perverts who live in London, of whom there are a surprisingly large number. The London Transport Museum in Covent Garden is a restrained, well-thought-out collection of highlights from the city's history of public transport; the Depot, which houses over 320,000 items that make up the bulk of the museum's collections, is something else. It's hard to imagine that a warehouse of 6,000 square metres might be bursting at the seams, but the Depot – which contains full-length tube trains and a large collection of buses and trams, as well as all the ephemera that go with running them – certainly feels like it might pop at any moment.

There is a huge variety of things to see. Admittedly, some of this is fairly specialist – a large number of what could be electricity transformers from Frankenstein's laboratory at the entrance, for example – but much of it is immediately accessible. The extensive collection of architect's models includes the maze of passenger tunnels at Oxford Circus. There are, of course, hundreds of station signs using the famous roundel that show how it evolved, maps and even a cabinet containing the famous Johnston Sans typeface, displayed like a holy relic in a glass case. There are oddities, too – a fragment of the experimental spiral escalator at Holloway Road looks like a terrible idea, but it was built anyway.

At times, it feels a bit like a house-clearance sale, but the glory of the depot is the machinery. There are some recent tube trains – London Underground is in the middle of replacing rolling stock across its network – but the bulk are vehicles from the past. They include a first-class carriage from 1892 that spent many years as a chicken coop before being fully restored; it was used to carry passengers during the celebrations for the Underground's 150th anniversary in 2013. The enormous Leyland charabanc, a predecessor of the coach, is crying out to be driven. In fact, you walk around wishing that London Transport could bring most of the collection back into use – the trams, the buses with their conductors, the trolley buses. For a Londoner, what's interesting is the instant familiarity of much of the collection despite its being long out of use, presumably a reflection of innate style.

KELMSCOTT HOUSE

Crafty artist's residence

26 Upper Mall, Hammersmith, W6 9TA
0208 741 3735
http://williammorrissociety.org/our-museum
Thurs and Sat 2-5pm
Admission free
Ravenscourt Park or Hammersmith tube

In truth, there isn't a huge amount to see at this tiny museum, the headquarters of the William Morris Society. The pleasure of the place is the house itself and its riverside location. Morris believed strongly that a beautiful house was a work of art, with a beautiful book the next highest order of creation. In Kelmscott House, where he spent the last years of his life and set up the Kelmscott Press, he melded these two loves.

The house, which is stunning, sits on an upstream bend of the Thames where the river starts to look like countryside. Across the path is The Dove, a beautiful little pub with a riverside terrace, as well as the smallest bar in England. Find The Dove, which is more of a landmark, and you've found Kelmscott House. It is now privately owned, so only the basement and coach house are open for viewing. These contain a collection of Morris drawings for his famous wallpapers, his printing press, and some beautiful furniture. There are also a number of photos of Morris (unlike a lot of late Victorian portrait subjects, he looks like a lot of fun). The coach house was used as a meeting place for Fabians and the other socialist-inclined groups Morris was involved with; Keir Hardie, George Bernard Shaw and Prince Kropotkin all gave lectures here. There is also a small shop, selling reproductions of Morris' prints and woodcuts.

Morris was an astounding man – he died 'having done more work than most ten men' – and these three rooms radiate some of the energy he threw into being a designer, artist, craftsman, writer and socialist, all of which have an instantly recognisable style.

Other Arts and Crafts landmarks

A mere 600 yards up the river is 7 Hammersmith Terrace, the former home of Emery Walker, typographer, antiquary, and friend and mentor to William Morris. The Georgian exterior hides an Arts and Crafts gem of an interior, preserved as they were in the lifetime of Walker, who lived here from 1903-1933. (http://emerywalker.org.uk/)

The William Morris Gallery (Lloyd Park, Forest Road, Walthamstow), in another of his impressive Georgian homes, has a far larger collection of prints, rugs, carpets, wallpapers, furniture, stained glass and painted tiles designed by Morris himself, as well as works by Edward Burne-Jones, Philip Webb, Dante Gabriel Rossetti, and Ford Madox Brown. Left-wingers can admire the satchel in which Morris carried his socialist pamphlets. The pinnacle of Morris' aesthetic is the Red House in Bexleyheath, which Morris co-designed with his friend Philip Webb in 1859. Now run by the National Trust, the wonderful gardens and grounds of this iconic Arts and Crafts home make the perfect setting for a picnic. (www.nationaltrust.org.uk/red-house)

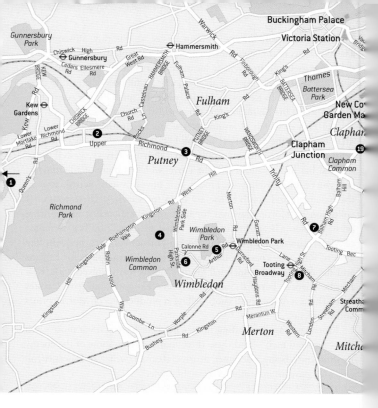

Greater London (South)

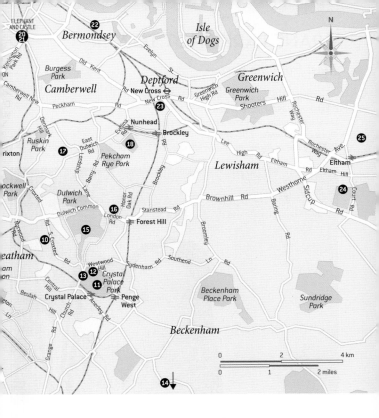

CRANE PARK SHOT TOWER

Blast from the past

Crane Park, Whitton, TW2 6AB
0208 755 2339/07702 669 888
www.wildlondon.org.uk/reserves/crane-park-island
Open every Sunday 1.30-4pm
Whitton rail or Richmond tube/rail, then H22, 110 or 111 bus

London was once full of munitions works, most of which were at a good distance from the centre, as they had a nasty habit of exploding. Standing alone in the middle of Crane Park is the last remnant of the Hounslow Gunpowder Mills – its shot tower. The mills once ran along the River Crane, a Thames tributary that flowed into the river at Isleworth. Its isolation was perfect for the frequently lethal manufacture of weapons.

The Hounslow Gunpowder Mills went up spectacularly at regular intervals, including one explosion in 1772 that blew out all the stained glass at Horace Walpole's country house, Strawberry Hill, over 4 miles away. There were plenty of fatalities over the years, and the last recorded explosion was in 1915.

The Shot Tower, built in 1826, is the last intact structure of the factory, which was in operation until 1927. The tower was used to make ammunition: lead was melted in a crucible at the top of the tower, forced through a copper form to gauge the bullet size, and then dropped down through the inside of the tower. As the drops fell, surface tension drew them into spheres. At the bottom, they were caught and cooled in water. Anything that failed to make the grade was returned to the top of the tower to start again.

The Crane Park tower is a small one, only capable of making bore shot. Some of the millstones used to grind saltpetre, an ingredient of gunpowder, lie at the foot of the tower. The millpond has been turned into a nature reserve, where, if you look carefully, you can still see some traces of the munitions industry, including blast mounds, sluice gates and engine beds. The Shot Tower, which contains information about the surrounding wildlife reserve, is only open to the public on Sunday afternoons.

Image source: http://www.heritage.vic.gov.au/admin/file/content2/c7/Coops_shot_tower.pdf

Ammunitions factories were once a huge industry supplying the British Empire. The biggest was the Royal Arsenal in Woolwich, which employed 80,000 workers during the First World War. The arsenal has, predictably, been converted into riverside flats, but you can explore its explosive history at the Greenwich Heritage Centre (https://www.greenwichheritage.org), housed in the old ordnance factory.

RICHARD BURTON'S MAUSOLEUM ②

A tent in a graveyard

St Mary Magdalen Roman Catholic Church
61 North Worple Way, Mortlake, SW14 8PR
Daily 9am–3pm
Mortlake rail

Richard Burton is buried in a tent near East Sheen. No, not that Richard Burton – the film star is still buried in Switzerland. This is the far more interesting, far stranger Richard Burton, the Victorian explorer, geographer, translator, writer, soldier, orientalist, cartographer, ethnologist, spy, linguist, poet, fencer, diplomat and reputed speaker of at least 29 languages.

Burton was one of those 19th-century supermen who seemed able to turn his hand to anything. He is best known as the translator and publisher of unexpurgated versions of *The Arabian Nights*, the *Kama Sutra* and *The Perfumed Garden* (the *Kama Sutra's* Arab equivalent) in English, scandalising Victorian England, and for his attempt to discover the source of the Nile, which almost killed him.

Although Burton sounds like the archetypal Victorian hero, in fact he was critical of the colonial policies of the British Empire, putting his career at risk. He was also pretty eccentric. While in the army (where he was nicknamed Ruffian Dick), he kept a troupe of monkeys in the hopes of learning their language. He had himself circumcised to sneak into Mecca in disguise. He challenged someone to a duel for making fun of his moustache. Later in life, he worked on a hypothesis that homosexuality was determined by geography. His interest in sexuality allegedly led him to measure the penises and record the sexual practices of the locals wherever he travelled. He wrote a monograph entitled "A History of Farting".

So, a live wire. His energy bursts out of the photographs of him, even in old age. His wife Isabel was no slouch either – a writer and philanthropist who learnt to fence in order to accompany him, she designed their tomb. The design is supposed to reflect Burton's deep

ties with the Arab world. It is (very) loosely modelled on a Bedouin tent, and is decorated with a frieze of Islamic stars and crescents, as well as a crucifix and Star of David. Unlike a Bedouin tent, you can go round the back, climb up a short ladder and peer into it through a window, where the couple's coffins are on display side by side.

The church itself is a bit hard to find – be careful not to confuse it with nearby St Mary the Virgin, a far likelier looking place for the Burtons' tomb.

THE ANTIQUE BREADBOARD MUSEUM

Look at my lovely bread

17 Lifford Street, SW15 1NY
020 8785 2464
theantiquebreadboardmuseum@gmail.com
Admission and availability: https://antiquebreadboards.com
Open most Tues and Sun, 2.30–4.30. Contact to make booking
Putney Bridge or East Putney tube

Y ou've heard of a micro-brewery? A small brewer, focused on lovingly made artisanal beer? Well, this is a micro-museum, one room in Madeleine Neave's home devoted to lovingly made wooden breadboards. A museum dedicated to the most ordinary item in a kitchen may sound dull, but nothing is ever really boring or ugly, it's all a question of how carefully you're prepared to look at it. And the Antique Breadboard Museum lets you look carefully, and as a result is very interesting.

Madeleine is the daughter of Rosslyn Neave, an antique dealer with a wide range of interests, but who became increasingly fascinated by breadboards. Dedicated boards for bread don't appear to have existed much before 1820. It seems that the Corn Laws drove the price of bread beyond the means of many British families, turning it into a status symbol. And of course, if you can afford bread, you want to let everyone know by showing it off on a lovely hand-carved breadboard.

Early boards were often true luxury items. George Wing of Sheffield produced exquisitely carved boards for the aristocracy, one of which was put up for sale for 16 guineas, roughly equivalent to £2,000 in 2020. These custom-made boards would have been at the heart of the gargantuan breakfasts and teas that characterised genteel country house living for wealthy Victorians.

Naturally, the next step was the breadboard's adoption by the middle classes, and by the 1860s there was a thriving mass market. Decorative themes focused on simple patterns, but the boards get most interesting when amateur carvers make their own boards or personalise them. One board, decorated with ears of wheat and a rose surrounding a shield with monogrammed initials, must have been a wedding gift; another, apparently commissioned for a Rev. Woodfin by a loving congregation, has a quote from Corinthians slap in the middle of it. Many of the boards are deeply worn, and because you're encouraged to handle them, you get an uncanny sense of their history. The museum contains related items such as a trencher, the wooden plate from where we get the word trencherman. There's also a collection of breadknives, which came into being alongside breadboards – after all, if you're showing off your lovely board, you need a lovely knife, right?

Entry to the museum includes a beautifully served cream tea.

WIMBLEDON WINDMILL MUSEUM ④

The daily grind

Windmill Road, Wimbledon Common, SW19 5NR
0208 947 2825
www.wimbledonwindmill.org.uk
End of March to end of Oct, Sat 2-5pm, Sun and public holidays 11am-5pm
Check website for admission prices, events and off-schedule openings.
Wimbledon tube/train, Putney train or East Putney tube, followed by 93 bus

Wimbledon Common is famous for being home to the Wombles – furry creatures who recycled rubbish in the eponymous 1970s TV series. Like all commons, Wimbledon is land with traditionally shared rights (it's where the word 'commoner' comes from). This common dodged 'enclosure' in 1864 by Earl Spencer, who wanted to develop luxury housing on it – sounds familiar – and has thus preserved its rural feel, including its windmill.

Although there are several watermills on the River Wandle, the local community wanted to produce their own flour. So in 1817, Charles March was granted permission to build the windmill 'upon this condition, that he shall erect, and keep up, a public Corn Mill, for the advantage and convenience of the neighbourhood'. The millers also had to keep watch for duellists, who liked to clash swords on the common.

The mill was closed in 1864 when Earl Spencer decided to build himself a new mansion on the site and fence off Wimbledon Common as his private garden. Understandably, the locals protested. The Earl's plan was shelved by the Wimbledon and Putney Commons Act of 1871, which gave the common back to the people. The mill was converted into living quarters for six families. One of the residents was Lord Baden-Powell, founder of the Boy Scout movement. Today, the windmill has been converted into a small museum. The entrance hall contains the Great Spur Wheel, which used to power it. There are countless models of windmills and interactive displays of working machinery. Kids can get to grips with grinding wheat, lifting sacks of flour, or changing windmill sails. A ladder leads up to the tower where you can see the machinery turning on windy days. The Windmill Museum also contains a small shop, which sells model windmills, honeycomb produced by bees on Wimbledon Common and, of course, Wombles.

NEARBY

Artesian Well   ⑤

In 1763, an earlier Earl Spencer built an artesian well in Arthur Road to provide water for his manor house nearby. A horse-driven mechanism pumped water up to the storage tank under the dome. The Earl decided to deepen the well in 1798, but it took over a year to strike more water – it gushed out with such force that the workmen almost drowned. The well soon dried up and in 1975 the domed tower was converted into a private home.

Buddhapadipa Temple   ⑥

14 Calonne Road, SW19
www.watbuddhapadipa.org
The first Thai Buddhist temple to be built in the United Kingdom, this elegant edifice is decked in murals and surrounded by 4 acres of gardens, in which sits an ornamental lake, a flower-garden and orchard. Open for visitors daily 9am-5pm. Check website for events and to make group bookings.

THE LONDON SEWING MACHINE MUSEUM ⑦

A stitch in time

308 Balham High Road, SW17 7AA
0208 682 7916
www.craftysewer.com
Open first Saturday of every month (except January) 2-5pm
Admission free
Tooting Bec tube

Rooting out this museum is like finding a needle in a haystack. You'd never guess that there's treasure buried between the discount and DIY stores on Balham High Road. The exterior – a grey slab of 1960s concrete with sky blue panelling – doesn't bode well either. As if to throw prospective visitors off the scent, the building is emblazoned with 'Wimbledon Sewing Machine Co. Ltd.' – even though it's in Tooting.

Inside it's like a Primark sweatshop without the child labour: a vast, strip-lit hangar filled with row upon row of sewing machines. New and used, domestic and industrial, overlockers and precision finish buttonhole machines, whatever tickles your fancy. But the really good stuff is upstairs: two huge rooms of antique sewing machines dating from the 1830s to the 1950s.

The prize exhibit is one of the first wooden prototypes designed by Barthélemy Thimonnier, the inventor of the sewing machine. Hardly any of his machines have survived because a mob of tailors burnt down the factory where they were introduced, fearing that mechanisation would destroy their livelihood. A close contender is the ornate machine that Queen Victoria had custom-made for her eldest daughter Vicky as a wedding present. Decorated with royal crests, crown-shaped ivory spools, carved oak treadles and a stitch plate engraved with Windsor Castle, it must have cost a fortune to manufacture in 1850. The owner of this and the other 700-odd sewing machines, Ray Rushton, paid £23,500 for it in 1997. Rushton has scored bargains, too: he snapped up an Edwardian sewing machine camouflaged as a cast iron lion from a rag-and-bone man for just £7.

A dapper cigar smoker, Ray Rushton has worked in the shop since he was a boy. After the Second World War, his father Thomas Albert Rushton would drag him around London picking up second-hand sewing machines. Father and son lugged up to six machines at a time. They repurposed and sold them for a pretty profit. Business was so brisk that in 1946 Rushton set up shop in Wimbledon; there's a replica of the original store in the museum. At one time, the family owned seven shops.

Ray began to stockpile vintage items that didn't have such good resale value during the lean post-war years, when it was cheaper to make than to buy clothes. He kept his collection under wraps for 40 years until he set up the museum in 2000. Now he does a nice sideline in props for period dramas. Every single sewing machine is in full working order.

GALA BINGO TOOTING

Chartres Cathedral meets Liberace

50 Mitcham Road, Tooting, SW17 9NA
0208 672 5717
Mon-Thurs 10am-11pm, Fri-Sun 10am-Midnight
Admission for members only; membership is free to anyone over 18
Tooting Broadway tube

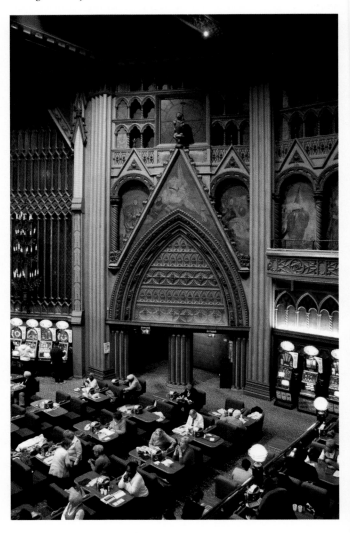

Now, alas, a Gala bingo hall, this was the first cinema in the UK to be listed as Grade I – the most rigorous preservation order a building can get. From the outside, the tall, square building doesn't look all that special, give or take a few columns; on the inside, it looks like Chartres Cathedral if it had been designed by Liberace. Opened in 1931, this palace to entertainment was commissioned by Sidney Bernstein, an exiled white Russian who later founded Granada TV, and designed by Fyodor Fyodorovich Kommisarzhevsky, a Russian director and set designer briefly married to actress Peggy Ashcroft.

The heavily gilded foyer is lined with Gothic mirrors and fake leaded windows, punctuated by a pair of sweeping marble staircases. But all this is relatively restrained: the auditorium – inspired by its namesake, the Alhambra Palace in Granada – is where Kommisarzhevsky went bananas. Under a coffered ceiling are cathedral porches, heraldic symbols, and glass chandeliers, now partly obscured by the bingo lighting and screens. The decoration intensifies as you approach the stage. All around the auditorium are arches filled with murals of troubadours and wimpled damsels – but underneath all this medieval madness, the bingo fans play on, eyes fixed on the cards. The combination feels like a weird early version of a themed Vegas casino deep in South London.

In its day, the Granada was the only suburban cinema in London to have its own 20-piece orchestra. The glamorous usherettes wore gold silk blouses with blue slacks, pill box hats, blue cloaks over one shoulder and white gloves, while the doormen wore a blue uniform with brass buttons, peaked caps, and gold epaulettes. On its anniversary, the cinema would serve every customer a slice of cake – wheeled in from the baker next door, it weighed over a ton. Over 2,000 people were turned away on opening night, and over three million viewers came to the pictures here every year. However, the arrival of the television sent audience numbers into a tailspin, and the cinema closed in 1973. It was revived as a bingo hall in 1991. You need to be a member to visit, though membership is free. Call the Granada for details.

Frank Sinatra, the Beatles, Little Richard, and the Rolling Stones all played to 3,000 shrieking fans at the Granada, which doubled as a music hall. The original Wurlitzer organ is still here, but its chambers are buried beneath the stage.

THE ROOKERY

The beauty of suburbia

Streatham Common South, SW16 3BX
Open 7.30am - 15 minutes before sunset
Admission free
Streatham rail

It is unlikely that Streatham features in many guide books. Despite spawning a diversity of talents, including supermodel Naomi Campbell, occultist Aleister Crowley (there's something about Streatham High Street that might turn anyone into a Satanist), and William Mildin, 14th Earl of Streatham and allegedly the model for Tarzan, it is an unlovely place. However, in the 18th century, Streatham was a rural haven close to the city, and thus the site of many large country houses.

The Rookery is an area of public gardens adjoining Streatham Common. First opened to the public in 1913, the gardens once belonged to a huge pile of a house that was demolished in the early 1900s. It is an extremely formal garden, quite out of character with the rest of the Common. A series of walks, including a pergola supporting a massive wisteria, radiate out from well-planted central beds. The segmentation of the garden provides ample possibilities for seclusion; this would be a good place for a really serious game of hide-and-seek. The garden slopes down a hill that offers extensive views – admittedly, these include Norbury, but you can't have everything. Other features include a garden with all-white blossoms (and even benches), modelled on Vita Sackville-West's grounds at Sissinghurst, a really good picnic area with fixed tables (very rare in London), and a little covered well in the middle of the garden.

In the summer, the sloping lawns of the Rookery are used to stage performances (a lot of Shakespeare). The park is part of the Capital Ring, a 78-mile walking route around London (https://tfl.gov.uk/modes/walking/capital-ring) – even if you just do one of the 15 sections, there's plenty to see in each of them.

Streatham's wells

The Rookery is laid out above Streatham's original mineral wells, which attracted huge crowds in the 17th and 18th centuries – it was common for coaches full of thirsty punters to queue for a mile along Streatham High Road. Presumably, Queen Victoria didn't have to wait in line when she came to drink her fill. The healing qualities of the waters were first discovered in 1659 when farm hands drank from the spring and experienced its 'purging effects'. This sounds like a reason not to drink the waters, but they were said to cure all manner of ills including rheumatism, gout, jaundice, bilious attacks and blindness.

BRITISH VINTAGE TELEVISION AND WIRELESS MUSEUM

Radiohead

23 Rosendale Road, SE21 8DS
0208 670 3667
bvwm.org.uk
By appointment only, though the Friends of BVTWM usually operate an open day on Fridays 12-6pm. Please call in advance to book a place
West Dulwich rail

Tucked away in leafy West Dulwich, this large Edwardian house was the lifelong home of Gerry Wells, whose collection of antique radios, televisions and related equipment makes up the museum's collection. Wells was the son of an insurance clerk who developed an early obsession with electricity and broadcast. He began collecting bits and pieces of electrical kit from bomb sites, as well as radios. His parents disapproved; his mother allegedly told him he'd never be satisfied until he'd filled the house with radios. Well, mother knows best.

The house and the sheds in the garden are crammed with radios – a conservative estimate is around 2,000 units. Since Wells' death in 2014, the museum, now run by trustees, has been trying to bring some sort of order to the collection, with pieces sorted by chronology, origin or manufacturer. The house was a little more chaotic before this – for example, Wells rescued the massive converter from the nearby Crystal Palace transmitter at one point and set it up in his bedroom.

The wireless was the centre of most British homes for years, but the arrival of television made it obsolete overnight. It was this sudden decline that helped build the museum's collection. Wells apparently never bought a wireless in his life; rag-and-bone men and other people who knew he had an interest would drop junked wirelesses off at the house. As a result, the collection is a real mixture: it includes Art Deco Bakelite wirelesses, a silver globe radio – looks amazing, sounds terrible – and a pair of Nazi wirelesses complete with swastikas. The collection also includes old televisions, a medium that Wells hated, but nonetheless collected. The TV sets are barely recognisable to modern eyes, yet the technology is recent.

The museum is trying to get as many of the wirelesses up and running as possible. Wells was a music lover and insisted that it sounded better through valve amps – when the wirelesses play, it's hard to disagree. For a while, he built and sold his own brand of Wadar valve amps for hi-fi that were a stylish blend of retro-futurism, like something from *Flash Gordon*, all from a shed in the garden. Other things to watch out for are the enormous horn amplifier in the front room, which gets surprisingly loud, and Gerry Wells' personal DJ booth, put together by the man himself to play music for his parties.

CRYSTAL PALACE DINOSAURS

Concrete monsters

Sydenham Hill, Crystal Palace Park, SE19 2GA
www.cpdinosaurs.org
Mon-Fri 7.30am, weekends & Bank Holidays 9 am – park closure one hour before dusk
Admission free
Penge West or Crystal Palace rail/Overground

One of the strangest pieces of Victoriana extant in London, these life-size concrete dinosaurs were built around a lake in Crystal Palace Park by the sculptor Benjamin Waterhouse Hawkins and unveiled in 1854.

The dinosaurs sparked some controversy at the time. Designed to educate the British public, their anticipation of Darwinism outraged many at a time when creationism rather than evolution was widely accepted. The study of dinosaurs was in its infancy: the word 'dinosaur' was only coined in 1842 by Richard Owen, curator of the Hunterian Museum (see p. 144), who acted as an advisor to Hawkins.

What must then have seemed like a white-hot fusion between art and science now looks a bit silly. The inaccuracy of the models isn't helped by their display, with the animals apparently domesticated around a duck pond. The dinosaurs just look plain weird; although in fairness to Hawkins, working with concrete, lead and iron rods must have been problematic. For many years, the dinosaurs were partially overgrown by the vegetation. Walking around the lake, concrete heads would loom suddenly out of a bush. The installation has since been fully restored, with the original colours re-applied as closely as possible and the addition of two new pterodactyls.

A dinner party in the stomach of an iguanodon

The night before the dinosaurs were unveiled, a dinner party was held on 31 December 1853, in the stomach of a half-built Iguanodon. The celebrations began with the toast: 'Saurians and Pterodactyls all! Dream ye ever, in your ancient festivities, of a race to come, dwelling above your tombs... dining on your ghosts'.

Victorian London was in love with the idea of itself as a beacon of enlightenment. Crystal Palace Park on Sydenham Hill embodied this notion. It was purpose-built to re-house the Crystal Palace, centrepiece of the 1851 Great Exhibition in Hyde Park, which was conceived to demonstrate the industrial, military and economic superiority of Great Britain. The park was also where inventor John Logie Baird developed television. After the Crystal Palace burned down in 1936, the park's popularity dwindled, but it remains full of the ghosts of its glorious past. Looming over the athletics stadium is a huge bust of Sir Joseph Paxton, best known for designing the Crystal Palace, and for cultivating the Cavendish banana, the most consumed banana in the western world.

CRYSTAL PALACE SUBWAY

Hidden brick beauty

Crystal Palace Parade, SE19 1LG
www.cpsubway.org.uk
Open House London weekend, plus events – check website for details
Admission free
Crystal Palace rail

This brickwork jewel of a tunnel is almost all that remains of the High Line station to the Crystal Palace. The Palace, a colossal prefabricated glass and iron structure that housed the Great Exhibition in 1851, was moved from Hyde Park to what was then called Penge Common in 1854. It was the tourist sensation of the day. Visitor numbers were so high that the original Low Line station couldn't keep up with demand. In 1856 the High Line was opened, which shortened the walk to the Palace.

The station was designed by Charles Barry Jr, son of the architect of the Houses of Parliament, and little expense was spared. From the station, first-class passengers entered the subway, which runs under Crystal Palace Parade, now a busy main road, but more of an elegant boulevard in its day. The subway is made up of terracotta and cream brick arches, supported by 15 octagonal columns. It could be a Byzantine crypt rather than a public underpass. Going through a vestibule roofed with glass and iron, visitors would then walk straight into the Palace.

Glory fades, however. In 1936, the Crystal Palace burnt down and the station went into a steep decline. The subway was used as an air raid shelter in the war, with ticketed accommodation for 192 sleepers or 360 standers. After the war, rail traffic ground to a halt and the station fell into disrepair – one local remembers it as being 'very, very creepy'. It finally closed in 1954 and was demolished in 1961, although Ken Russell shot the short film *Amelia and the Angel* there in 1957.

Only the subway survived. It was used by children as a playground, and in the 1990s for raves, but was eventually sealed for safety reasons. Luckily, it now has supporters – the Friends of Crystal Place Subway – who are working to widen public access and get as much use from the space as possible.

NEARBY

Crystal Palace Museum ⑬

www.crystalpalacemuseum.org.uk

Just round the corner from the subway, at the top of Anerley Hill, is this little museum. Only open on Sundays from 11am to 4pm, it contains large-scale models of Crystal Palace and assorted remnants and items associated with the Exhibition. The museum also offers tours of the ruins of the Palace on the first Sunday of every month during the summer.

BETHLEM MUSEUM OF THE MIND ⑭

Asylum for the arts

Monks Orchard Road, BR3 3BX
0203 228 4227
www.bethlemgallery.com; museumofthemind.org.uk
Wed-Fri 10am-5pm (last entry 4.30pm) and first and last Saturday of the month
Admission free
Eden Park rail, then 356 bus; or East Croydon rail, then 119 or 198 bus

Bethlem Royal Hospital, once notoriously known as Bedlam, was founded in 1247 at a site now under Liverpool Street Station. (Thousands of inmates' skeletons were unearthed during recent Crossrail excavations.) The mental hospital subsequently moved to Moorfields, London's first public park. It moved south of the Thames (to the site now occupied by the Imperial War Museum) in 1815, before relocating to the south-eastern suburbs of London in 1930.

Straight ahead of the present hospital's main gate is a large brick building that has housed a museum and gallery since 2015. The Museum of the Mind, on the upper floor, is a collection of art and objects relating to Bethlem's past, and the history and treatment of mental illness. These include relics of Bedlam's chequered past – sections of padded wall, restraints (including a 'strong dress') and an early, bulky ECT machine, as well as Caius Cibber's statues of *Melancholy* and *Raving Madness*, which originally topped the gates at Moorfields. However, this is not a museum for ghouls; the displays are carefully crafted to engage contemporary as well as historical issues in mental healthcare.

The museum's art collection spans 200 years. At its core is the Guttman-Maclay Art Collection, named after two doctors who collected work by trained artists who had experienced mental distress or disorder. As a viewer, it is difficult not to pick over the work for signs of mental illness. Sometimes the link is explicit and painful: Marion Patrick's matt grey figure studies don't need titles like *Depression II* to show us their meaning. But the collection is by no means without hope. As an inmate in 1953, Canadian painter William Kurelek produced *The Maze*, a dark expression of his personal trauma, but later donated a sequel, *Out of the Maze*, as a thank you to the hospital. This companion piece, showing a family picnicking under blue, blue sky, suggests recovery. Louis Wain's cat paintings may look a bit manic, but they're also joyful. Who knows?

Downstairs, the Bethlem gallery shows work from current or former patients of the hospital. The ceramic frieze that fronts the nearby studio is well worth the short walk from the museum. Bethlem sits in 290 acres of well-tended parkland that are open to visitors – ask at reception for guides to some of the walks.

SYDENHAM HILL WOODS

Woodland, wildlife, and old masters

Start at Sydenham Hill station, SE21 7ND
Sydenham Hill rail

This is a good walk. Exit Sydenham Hill station via College Road, cross the road, and head up the broad path to the top of the hill, where the refurbished Dulwich Wood House Inn does very good pub lunches. At the gate, turn left and walk 500 metres along Crescent Hill Road to the upper entrance to Sydenham Hill Woods. The left hand fork descends to the disused line of the High Level railway, built in 1865 to service the Crystal Palace (or Screaming Alice in rhyming slang, if you insist).

Follow the abandoned railway track for a kilometre – diversions in the adjoining woods include seasonal outdoor art installations and a ruined chapel that was once a folly in someone's garden. Eventually, a bench across the path invites you to climb a set of wooden steps leading up to the left. A metal fence separates the woods from a golf course with sweeping city views denied to non-members. Follow the path to an old footbridge, turn left through a metal gate, and descend Cox's Walk to Dulwich Common. Turn left and after a kilometre you will see the stone gates to Dulwich Park. There is a good café in the middle of the park, where you can take your ease. Press on to College Road, where you should stop at the Dulwich Picture Gallery.

You can either walk back up College Road to Sydenham Hill station or turn left up Gallery Road to the entrance of Belair Park, and walk through the park to West Dulwich Station on Thurlow Park Road. This part of London is especially green, a legacy of the swathes of land bought by John Alleyn, a major figure of the Elizabethan theatre and founder of Dulwich College. Alleyn made a couple of very successful marriages, and was proprietor of several profitable playhouses, bear-pits and brothels. The college still owns the land, which has very tight development regulations.

Dulwich Picture Gallery

Built by John Soane, Dulwich Picture Gallery was the first purpose-built gallery in the world. Its solid collection includes works by Poussin, Claude, Rubens, Murillo, Van Dyck, Rembrandt, Watteau and Gainsborough, originally assembled for the King of Poland in 1790 as an 'instant' national collection. When Poland was wiped off the map in 1795 after a series of disastrous wars, the King's collection became available and was eventually housed in Dulwich in 1811.

College Road is named after Dulwich College, one of the country's grander schools. The school motto is 'God's Gift'. Oddly enough, it is the alma mater of Raymond Chandler, author of *The Maltese Falcon* and *Farewell, My Lovely*; but it is hard to imagine this as the birthplace of Sam Spade.

16

THE HORNIMAN MUSEUM

A balloon with tusks

100 London Road, Forest Hill, SE23 3PQ
0208 699 1872
www.horniman.ac.uk
Daily 10.30am-5.30pm. Gardens open Mon-Sat 7.15am-sunset,
Sun 8am-sunset
Admission free, except for major temporary exhibitions
Forest Hill rail

The Horniman Museum is another creation of a Victorian philanthropist. Opened in 1901, it was commissioned to hold tea merchant Frederick John Horniman's collections of natural history, anthropology, and musical instruments. Like many Victorian collections, what's in the museum looks eccentric because of its apparently random nature. There are some extraordinary objects here, well worth the journey into deepest Forest Hill.

The Horniman's most famous exhibit is probably its stuffed walrus. Taxidermists assembled this from the skin alone, without having any idea of what a walrus actually looked like. Not knowing that the walrus is wrinkled, they stuffed it to the limit, so the finished item looks like a balloon with tusks, and is the size of a small car. Happily, the museum has never corrected this error.

The real jewels of the collection are in the ethnography collection, generally reckoned to be third in importance after the British Museum and the Pitt Rivers collection in Oxford. There is a large amount of fine African statuary – an estimated 22,000 objects, not all of them on display – including systematic collections from the Sua of Zaire and the Hadza of Tanzania.

Best of all is the musical gallery, which was completely renovated between 1999 and 2002. The room is lined with glass cabinets holding instruments from all over the world, and interactive tables allow you to play recordings of any of them. Refurbishment also included the opening of a small aquarium, and converted the entire museum to a more child-friendly format. This means that weekends see herds of haggard, hung-over South London parents with their kids, staring blankly at the fish. Weekdays are probably the best for a serious visit.

Other things to look out for include a stuffed mermaid (the marriage of a dead monkey and a fish by a perverted taxidermist), a glass-walled beehive, and a disconcerting life-size statue of Kali, trampling some very serene heads. The museum café is a bit hit and miss, but the shop is full of quirky little presents. The museum also lays on a very large number of events.

The analemmatic sundial

The museum is set in 16 acres of gardens with good views across London. The gardens contain an eclectic collection of ten sundials, including a butterfly, a stained-glass window, and an analemmatic sundial, where you can tell the time using your own shadow. So make sure you visit on a sunny day.

HOUSE OF DREAMS

17

Artist in residence

45 Melbourne Grove, East Dulwich, SE22 8RG
www.stephenwrightartist.com
Open 6 days a year (check website for details) or by appointment
Check website for admission prices
East Dulwich rail

In gentrified East Dulwich, one house stands out from its suburban neighbours. Roses and mosaics frame a bright blue door with a hand-painted sign that reads: 'House of Dreams'. Entering is like tumbling down a rabbit hole into a wonderland of wild colour, a fantastical world made from flotsam and jetsam. Plastic dinosaurs, disembodied dolls, plaster saints and rubber ducks gaze at you from every inch of wall and ceiling. False teeth, bottle tops, tinsel garlands, wigs and watering cans are fashioned into giant sculptures that strike exotic poses. Even the floors are elaborate mosaics made from a kaleidoscope of broken tiles, stained glass and baubles.

Artist in residence Stephen Wright greets visitors with a huge smile and a warm hug. A successful textile, stationery and interior designer, Wright began transforming his home into a work of art in 1998, after developing an interest in outsider art. When his partner and his parents died in quick succession, the work became a form of catharsis. 'It's a sort of shrine made from other people's rubbish,' Wright laughs. 'It's also the diary of my life.' Huge black and white 'memory boards' record moments that have marked Wright's life – some wryly amusing, others searing accounts of bullying and bereavement.

'When my mother died, I discovered safety pins inside all her clothes. Little notes in her handbags. You find all these mysterious secrets about a person you loved after they're gone,' says Wright. 'So I started making sculptures out of my parents' clothes because I wanted to create a family to comfort me.' He obsessively hunts for material in flea markets and junk shops on his frequent travels, from old photographs of strangers to religious votives. The rear garden is filled with plants from his favourite places, a depository of living memories. Increasingly, visitors bring their own memento mori to incorporate into the house – glasses, buttons, ashes, hair.

'By sharing the house with so many people, I want to share the message of freedom of spirit,' Wright explains. 'Our society is becoming more controlled; there are less opportunities for creativity. The House of Dreams is a reaction against that. I want to go back to being a child, where you don't have to explain anything you make. You don't have to follow rules, you can do what you want.'

The house will never be finished. But Wright has bequeathed it to the National Trust, so it will never be lost either.

NUNHEAD CEMETERY

Gothic nature reserve

Linden Grove, SE15 3LP
www.fonc.org.uk
Daily, 1 April-3 Oct 8.30am-7pm; 4-31 Oct 8.30am-5pm; 1 Nov-28 Feb
8.30am-4pm; 1-31 March 8.30am-5pm
Tours generally start from the Linden Grove entrance – check website for details
Admission free, but donations gratefully received
Nunhead rail

Nunhead Cemetery was the second of the seven commercial cemeteries built in a ring around London in the middle of the 19th century to alleviate 'overcrowding' in the graveyards of the City churches. Highgate Cemetery, burial site of Karl Marx – who lived a bourgeois life north of the river in Hampstead – is probably the most famous, but Nunhead, opened in 1840, is possibly the most attractive. Its formal avenues of lime trees still survive, but they enclose a jumble of fallen stone and wilderness. The cemetery covers 52 acres, rising to 60 metres above sea level, thus offering extensive views over the City of London and St Paul's Cathedral between the trees.

In the early 1970s, the United Cemetery Company abandoned Nunhead because a lack of space meant it stopped making money: there was no room for new tenants. After an extensive restoration project the cemetery was reopened in 2001. Now almost completely overgrown, the place is effectively a wildlife reserve, where South Londoners can find songbirds, owls, woodpeckers and around 16 types of butterfly.

The cemetery is typically Victorian, obviously built by a city at the height of its economic power. Wealthy families commissioned mausoleums that are still magnificent today. Of course, like all Victorian developments, the cemetery was a model of efficiency – its circular drive meant that the turnover of services in the chapel could be kept brisk while remaining seemly. The chapel itself has a covered porch for the efficient disembarking of mourners in bad weather; it still stands above a crypt, and looks like a set from a Dracula film. Large monuments, unsettled by root growth, loom out of the trees at strange angles; beseeching stone angels lie surrounded by flowers.

The Friends of Nunhead Cemetery (FONC) offer guided tours starting from the Linden Grove gates at 2.15pm, usually on the last Sunday of every month. In addition, there are often specialist tours – these might include Music Hall Artistes, Military Connections or a Plant Walk. Monumental inscription recording is carried out by the Friends – volunteers are welcome.

Look for the Scottish Martyrs' obelisk on Dissenters Row, a memorial to five men transported to Australia in 1792 for advocating political reform. The Anglican Chapel designed by Thomas Little in 1843 was recently restored after arson in the 1970s.

GROWING UNDERGROUND

Future farming

1a Carpenter's Place, Clapham, SW4 7TD
020 7627 1027
Book tours via http://growing-underground.com
Or email tours@growing-underground.com
Clapham Common tube

Deep below the fleshpots of Clapham High Street lies an urban farm, silently growing micro-greens in a network of tunnels using LED lighting and a hyper-efficient hydroponics system. It looks more like a spaceship than a farm. Ever seen *Silent Running*, where Bruce Dern is an ecologist tending greenhouses in outer space in order to reforest a post-apocalyptic Earth?

Originally one of eight deep air-raid shelters built across London in the early 1940s (you can still see their drum-shaped entrances at locations including Goodge Street and Stockwell), these forgotten tunnels offered a perfect environment for a particular type of farming. When entrepreneurs Steven Dring and Richard Ballard were looking for a site to grow micro-greens (seedlings, basically) in a sustainable, carbon-neutral way, they thought about disused office blocks, but it turns out

that 65,000 square feet of inaccessible tunnels 33 metres underground were just what they needed. The site offers a perfectly controlled micro-climate that is unaffected by weather or seasonal changes.

However, the place feels strange. Entrance is via an elderly lift, and the descent to the farm is like passing through an airlock. Keeping the operation pest and disease free is essential, and everyone has to undergo a decontamination process and put on the kind of white coveralls and rubber boots you might associate with a nuclear power plant before going in. This all adds to the sci-fi feel of the place, which is reinforced when you visit the growing tunnels. These are painted white and lined with row upon row of growing mats, stretching out into the distance on shelving.

Much of the site remains unused, and the contrast between the fresh green smell of the farm and the dust and dereliction of the rest of the tunnels adds to the weirdness. The original plan for the shelters was to convert them into part of London's transport system – the Northern line runs parallel to the farm and you can hear its trains rumbling past. This conversion never happened, and for years the tunnels were used for storage, although the nearby shelter at Clapham South was famously used to house the first wave of Jamaican immigrants who sailed to the UK on the SS *Windrush*. Growing Underground is nowhere near using the full capacity of the place yet, although this is the long-term plan. Business is good, and visitors get to sample the produce fresh from the farm.

MICHAEL FARADAY MEMORIAL

It's a metal box

Elephant and Castle, SE1 6TG
Elephant & Castle tube/train

This ... thing, which was previously marooned on a roundabout on the gyratory road system of the Elephant and Castle, has now been enclosed in the pedestrianised area surrounding the shopping centre as the area's redevelopment picks up speed. It's an abandoned disco. It's a storage unit for frozen food. No, in fact, it's a monument to the Victorian scientist Michael Faraday.

The stainless steel box was designed by architect Rodney Gordon in 1959 and built in 1961. The design is not wholly artistic – it contains an electrical substation for the Northern and Bakerloo lines, appropriately enough for a memorial to one of the great pioneers of electricity. It was originally designed to be built of glass to display the workings of the transformer. However, fear of vandalism prevented this, so it was changed to a metal casing. In truth, nothing about the memorial explicitly suggests Faraday, although an inscription in the concrete paving nearby explains that it is his memorial.

The structure aims to stress Faraday's importance as a scientist (Einstein kept a picture of him on his study wall). Born in 1791 in nearby Newington Butts, Faraday came from a poor family and was largely self-taught. Aged 14, he was apprenticed to a bookbinder and spent the next seven years reading at every possible opportunity. In 1831, after years working at the Royal Institution, he discovered electromagnetic induction, the principle behind the electric transformer and generator.

NEARBY
Elephant and Castle Shopping Centre ㉑

Repeatedly threatened with demolition, this eyesore at the heart of the Elephant somehow manages to stagger on. Opened in 1965, and sold as Europe's first covered shopping mall, the centre is worth a look. Its hideousness appears to have put off large chains – as a result, it is full of independent outlets, including Colombian cafés and shops on the upper floor and a budget bowling alley in the attic. In the concrete moat that surrounds the building – what were architects Boissevain and Osmond thinking? – are a huge range of stalls, with especially good juice bars and Caribbean food. The people who work here seem convinced it has a future – it probably doesn't – but the friendly chaos of the place is a refreshing alternative to the mall developments that are rising all over the city.

THAMES PATH CAT

City of cats

Bermondsey Walk, SE16 4TT
Bermondsey tube

This one's for all the cat lovers. London has a surprising number of cat sculptures, from the monstrous black and white mouser looming over Catford market (Cat-ford – you see?) to the small bronze statue of Samuel Johnson's cat Hodge outside the great man's house in Gough Square. Cats crop up throughout the city's past, most famously in the tale of Dick Whittington, a medieval success story who rose from nothing to become mayor of London three times, and who supposedly made his first fortune by selling his cat to a rat-infested country. This iconic London cat has two statues, appearing once curled round the feet of Whittington in front of the Guildhall Art Gallery, and another sat on the Whittington stone at the bottom of Highgate Hill.

The Thames Path Cat is a comparatively new addition to this clowder of cats. Part of a group of four statues known as *Dr Salter's Daydream*, the cat lies flat along the Embankment wall, staring at a young girl. They are watched from across the path by a man and a woman, Dr Salter and his wife Ada, who both dedicated their lives to helping the poor of Bermondsey at the end of the 19th century, then one of the roughest and least healthy parts of the capital. Unfortunately, his 8-year-old daughter Joyce contracted scarlet fever, common in deprived areas, and died. This is the little girl who leans smiling against the wall; the cat was her pet, Gorvin.

Originally there were just three statues, but in 2014, Ada was added to the group when it was relocated, creating the first public sculpture of a female politician in London – she was London's first female mayor, elected to Bermondsey in 1922. Lean over the wall for a good view up to Tower Bridge, or drop into the Angel pub next door.

The remains of Edward III's moated manor house

Just south across the road from the statues is a small park that contains the remains of Edward III's moated manor house. All that is left of the building is a low wall, but originally this was a small royal residence built on an island in the river, which the king seems to have used as a base for falconry when he wasn't beating up the French or watching everyone drop dead from the Black Death. The Thames was originally full of islands that have since been absorbed from the river into the city, including Bermondsey and the Isle of Dogs, as well as Thorney Island, where Westminster Abbey now stands.

THE GIANT SCRIBBLE

A squiggle on the skyline

Ben Pimlott Building, St James's, SE14 6AD
New Cross rail

This purpose-built extension of the visual arts department at Goldsmiths College is largely unexceptional: a seven-storey building clad in metal with windows punched through to provide daylight and ventilation for the artists within. But architect Will Alsop has created a landmark in New Cross – one of the least lovely parts of the city – by draping the roof terrace with a giant metal scribble.

British architects tend to be fiends for function over form, but the main purpose of this playful anomaly, highly visible on the South London skyline, seems to be to lift the spirits of travellers driving along the dreary A2. The super-sized scribble has 72 twists and weighs over 25 tonnes. If stretched out, it would be 534m long – over twice as tall as Canary Wharf tower.

The fire escape on the south side, a jagged edge of self-supporting, prefabricated steel, is equally dramatic. The studios at the front of the building are glazed from floor to ceiling, so passers-by can spy on aspiring artists at work. At night, the building is illuminated by industrial lights, creating mysterious pools of light and shadow on the metallic surface.

The alma mater of high-flying British artists such as Damien Hirst, Gillian Wearing, and Anthony Gormley (see p. 294), Goldsmiths College prides itself on a certain edginess, but like the rest of London, the area is starting to see creeping gentrification. Rubbish & Nasty, the clothes and record shop on New Cross Road, is long gone, but the area surrounding the college is still worth exploring.

Will Alsop's London landmarks

Modern architecture in London tends to be associated with Richard Rogers or Norman Foster, so a day spent trailing Will Alsop's playful work would be one well-spent. Most notable are the Peckham Library (122 Peckham Hill Street), an upturned L-shape inspired by an open book, resting on seven wonky columns, and the off-kilter Palestra office block, opposite Southwark tube station. The Blizard Building at Queen Mary University (Turner Street, Whitechapel), wrapped in multicoloured glass and containing moulded pods modelled on giant molecules, is also worth a look.

ELTHAM PALACE

A maximalist's wet dream

Court Yard, Eltham, Greenwich, SE9 5QE
0370 333 1181
Mon, Tue, Wed, Sun 10am–5pm
Check website for admission prices
Eltham rail, then a half-mile walk or 161 or 126 bus

A little trouble to get here, but worth the effort, Eltham Palace is one of the most bizarre buildings in London. The original palace was given to King Edward II by Bishop Bek in 1305. King Edward IV added the Great Hall, the only part of the medieval structure still standing. In the 1530s, Henry VIII added royal lodgings and gardens, complete with a bowling green and archery range. It was the only royal palace large enough to contain all Henry VIII's 800 courtiers. The scattered Tudor remains suggest the palace must have been a monster in its prime.

During the 18th and 19th centuries the palace fell into disrepair, but this only heightened its attraction for the Romantic artists of the age and their lust for Gothic ruins. This was a period when wealthy aesthetes actually purpose-built ruins to flit around – lunacy, of course, but popular among the super-rich.

In 1933, the palace was leased by the extravagant socialites Sir Stephen and Lady Virginia Courtauld. The arrival of the Courtaulds (whose relatives founded the famous Courtauld Galleries) marked the palace's renaissance. They instantly ran into controversy by appointing architects Seely and Paget to design a new Art Deco residence incorporating the restored Great Hall. Stately homes in England are too often blighted by an obsession with pseudo-heritage – inglenooks, Palladian bathrooms, half-timbered Tudor garages, and the like. To their credit, the Courtaulds chose a bold, modern design with lashings of English eccentricity.

The exterior of the house is not especially interesting, but the interiors are unexpectedly insane. Dripping with 1930s opulence, the place is a maximalist's wet dream – walls are dressed with exotic veneers and the sunken baths have onyx trimmings. The couple even built a miniature palace filled with jungle murals for their pet ring-tailed lemur, Mah-Jongg, whom they purchased from Harrods. Try to spot the Courtald's yacht moored in the mural of Venice that adorns the entrance hall.

The house was also a showcase for the latest technological wizardy: a centralised vacuuming system, synchronised clocks, and concealed ceiling lights.

A circular motif runs riot throughout – domed ceilings, round lights, and portholes. Virginia Courtauld's curved bedroom with a circular ceiling creates the impression of a classical temple. But the snazzy leather map of Eltham in her boudoir bears little resemblance to the Eltham of today, an anonymous suburb of London.

SEVERNDROOG CASTLE

A folly in the forest

Castle Wood, Shooters Hill, SE18 3RT
0800 689 1796
www.severndroogcastle.org.uk
April-Oct: Thurs, Fri and Sun 12.30-4.30pm; Nov-March: Thurs, Fri and Sun
11am-3pm
Check website for admission prices
North Greenwich tube, then 486 bus, alighting at the Memorial Hospital; or
train to Welling rail, then 486 or 89 bus

Tucked away in the woods of Shooters Hill, high above South London, sits the folly of Severndroog Castle. Built in 1784 by the widow of naval commander Sir William James, the triangular Gothic-style tower has three rooms sitting on top of one another, with a viewing platform for ten on the roof. On a clear day, you can allegedly see seven counties from the top, although because the platform is high in the treetops, the view can be restricted. But no matter – the tower is built on one of the highest points in London, and the views are spectacular.

The folly was built to commemorate Sir William's life, and in particular his most famous exploit when he destroyed the fleet and fortress of Survarnadurg (hence Severndroog) in India in 1755. According to the British, this was a nest of pirates preying on the East India Company's shipping out of west India; according to the locals, it was the base of the admiral of the Maratha Empire's navy.

Sir William retired to London to work for the East India Company, and died wealthy. The castle passed into private hands, survived a plan to build a 10,000-catacomb cemetery in terraces on the site, and was then used by General William Roy in his trigonometric survey of London, linking the nearby Royal Greenwich Observatory with the Paris Observatory. Next, it served as a lookout for German bombers in both World Wars. It then passed into the hands of the local council, which boarded it up in 1986. After lying derelict for 28 years, it was restored and reopened in 2014.

As well as regular visiting hours, the castle can be privately hired, so check the website before undertaking your journey. There's a tea room on the ground floor.

The castle sits on the Green Chain Walk (www.greenchain.com), a linked system of open spaces between the River Thames and Crystal Palace Park, as well as the Capital Ring, a series of continuous walks beginning in nearby Woolwich. A bit much to do in one day, but a good project if you live here.

Nearby Oxleas Wood contains some of the last remaining ancient woods that once circled the capital. Oxleas Meadow, in the middle of the woods, has a very good traditional British café with views down the hill, across a buried water reservoir and far into Kent.

ALPHABETICAL INDEX

ACKNOWLEDGEMENTS

Our thanks to:

Gaby Agis, Etta Lisa Basaldella, Carole Baxter, Frédéric Court, Adam Curniskey, Nigel Dobinson, Alain Dodard, Benjamin & Maider Faes, Mattie Faint, Patrick Foulis, Ronald Grant, The Greenwich Phantom, Jaco Groot, Charlotte Henwood, John Hilton, Rose Jenkins, Ludovic Joubert, Xavier Lefranc, Islington Local History Centre, Robert Jeffries, Zoe Laughlin, Caoimhe Nic a' Bháird, Alex Parsons-Moore, Valérie Passmore, Clare Patey, David Phillips, Ellis Pike, Jeremy Redhouse, Jane Rollason, Michael van Rooyen, Muffin van Rooyen, avv. Renato Savoia, Chris Slade, Amélie Snyers, Angelos Talentzakis, Boz Temple-Morris, Christopher Wade, David Walter, Harriet Warden, Clem Webb, David White, Shazea Quraishi.

PHOTOGRAPHY CREDITS

Stéphanie Rivoal: BFI mediatheque, Bevis Marks Synagogue, British Optical Association Museum, Bunhill Fields, Cab Shelters, Doctor Johnson's House, Guildhall Yard, Horseman's Sunday, Leighton House, Little Angel Theatre, London Library, London Silver Vaults, London Stone, Notre Dame de France, Queen Alexandra Memorial, St. Bartholomew's the Greater, St Dustan in the East, the Golden Boy of Pye Corner, The Monument, The Old Operating Theatre, The Petry Museum

Jorge Monedero: 2 Willow Road, Alexander Fleming Laboratory Museum, Ben Pimlott Building, British Dental Association Museum, Brixton Windmill, Broadgate Ice Skating, Brunel Museum, Burgh House and the Hampstead Museum, Cable Street Mural, Canonbury Tower, Canal Museum, Clerk's Well, Creekside Discovery Centre, Crystal Palace Dinosaurs, Circus Space, Clown's Gallery & Museum, Chumleigh Gardens, Dead House, The Ferryman's Seat, Fetter Lane Moravian Burial Ground, First Drinking Fountain, Fan Museum, Gala Bingo Hall, HandleBar Moustache Club of Great Britain, Hunterian Museum, John Wesley's House, Joe Orton's Library Books, Kelmscott House, Kew Bridge Steam Museum, London's First Drinking Fountain, London's Living Room, The London Scottish Regimental Museum, Marylebone Cricket Club, Masonic Temple, Newgate Cells, New River Walk, Nunhead Cemetery, Princess Caroline Sunken Bath, Ragged School Museum, Rudolph Steiner House, Slice of Reality and Quantum Cloud, Sutton House, Sydenham Hill Woods, Thames River Police Museum, The Cherry Tree at The Mitre, The Serpentine Solarshuttle, The Cinema Museum, The Coade Stone Caryatids, The Execution Dock, The Executioner's Bell, The Horniman Museum, The Royal Hospital of Chelsea, The Rookery, The Tent, Twining Tea Museum, West Reservoir, Wimbledon Windmill Museum, Whitechapel Bell Foundry

Peter Scrimshaw: Crossness

Adam Tucker: Anaesthesia Heritage Centre, Boris Anrep's Mosaics, British and Vintage Television Museum, Solarshuttle, Crossbones Graveyard, Faraday Memorial, Finnish Church, Florence Nightingale Museum, Fountain Court, Kensal Rise Cemetery, Longplayer, London Bridge Model, Marx Memorial Library, Monsters of Trafalgar Square, Novelty Automation, Old Globe Theater, Parkland Walk, Sherlock Holmes Room, Strand Tube, Thames Barrier, Tower Subway, Tyburn Convent, West London Bowling

Auto-icon of Jeremy Bentham © University College of London - Barts Pathology Museum © Carla Valentine - Bleigiessen © Thomas Heatherwick Studio - Camley Street Nature Reserve © Anna Guzzo London Wild Trust - Crane Park Shot Tower © Marathon - Crossness Pumping Station © Crossness Trust Crystal Palace Subway © James Balton - Dennis Severs house © James Brittain - Eltham Palace © English Heritage Photo Library - Fenton House © Jenna Garrett - Fitzroy House © Fitzroy House - Garden Museum ©Gavin Kingcome - Geffrye Museum © Chris Ridley - Grant Museum © Fred Langford Edwards & UCL - God's Own Junkyard © God's Own Junkyard - Horse Hospital © Horse Hospital - Institute of Making © Institute of Making - Japanese Roof Garden © Brunei Gallery, SOAS University of London - Kirkaldy Testing Museum © Lars Plougmann - London Sewing Machine Museum © London Sewing Machine Museum - London Transport Museum © Transport for London - London Wall © Fremantleboy, Drallim - London zoo bird house Clock © Tim Hunkin - Museum of Brands, Packaging and Advertising © Museum of Brands, Packaging and Advertising - Museum of Curiosities © Oskar Proctor - Roman amphitheatre © Guildhall - Roots & Shoots © Roots & Shoot - St Paul Triforium © St Paul - St Stephen Church © David Iliff - Severndroog Castle © Severndroog Castle - Sky Garden © Sky Garden - Sir John Soane Museum © Lewis Bush - Shri Swaminarayan Mandir © Shri Swaminarayan Mandir - The Banner repeater © Holly Whittaker - The Foundling Museum © Richard Bryant Arcaid - The Magic Circle Museum © the Magic Circle - The National Theatre © The National Theatre - Tower Bridge Bascule Chamber © Tower Bridge - Two Temple Place © Peter Dazeley - 575 Wandsworth Road © National Trust Images/Cristian Barnett - Westminster Undercroft Abbey Museum © Dean & Chapter of Westminster

Maps: **Cyrille Suss** - Layout design: **Coralie Cintrat** - Layout: **Stéphanie Benoit** - Proofreading: **Jana Gough** and **Kimberly Bess**

© JONGLEZ 2020

Registration of copyright: April 2020 – Edition: 10

ISBN: 978-2-36195-364-5

Printed in Bulgaria by Dedrax

Thomas Jonglez

It was September 1995 and Thomas Jonglez was in Peshawar, the northern Pakistani city 20 kilometres from the tribal zone he was to visit a few days later. It occurred to him that he should record the hidden aspects of his native city, Paris, which he knew so well. During his seven-month trip back home from Beijing, the countries he crossed took him in Tibet (entering clandestinely, hidden under blankets in an overnight bus), Iran and Kurdistan. He never took a plane but travelled by boat, train or bus, hitchhiking, cycling, on horseback or on foot, reaching Paris just in time to celebrate Christmas with the family.

On his return, he spent two fantastic years wandering the streets of the capital to gather material for his first "secret guide", written with a friend. For the next seven years he worked in the steel industry until the passion for discovery overtook him. He launched Jonglez Publishing in 2003 and moved to Venice three years later.

In 2013, in search of new adventures, the family left Venice and spent six months travelling to Brazil, via North Korea, Micronesia, the Solomon Islands, Easter Island, Peru and Bolivia. After 7 years in Rio de Janeiro, he now lives in Berlin with his wife and 3 children.

Jonglez Publishing produces a range of titles in nine languages, released in 30 countries.

FROM THE SAME PUBLISHER

PHOTO BOOKS
Abandoned America
Abandoned Australia
Abandoned Asylums
Abandoned Cinemas of the world
Abandoned France
Abandoned Italy
Abandoned Japan
After the Final Curtain - The Fall of the American Movie Theater
After the Final Curtain - America's Abandoned Theaters
Baikonur - Vestiges of the Soviet space programme
Chernobyl's Atomic Legacy
Forbidden Places - Vol. 1
Forbidden Places - Vol. 2
Forbidden Places - Vol. 3
Forgotten Heritage
Private Islands for Rent
Unusual Hotels - Europe
Unusual Hotels - France
Unusual Hotels of the World
Unusual Hotels - UK & Ireland
Unusual Wines

'SECRET' GUIDES
New York Hidden bars & restaurants
Secret Amsterdam
Secret Bali - An unusual guide
Secret Barcelona
Secret bars & restaurants in Paris
Secret Belfast
Secret Brighton - An unusual guide
Secret Brooklyn
Secret Brussels
Secret Buenos Aires
Secret Campania
Secret Cape Town
Secret Copenhagen
Secret Dublin - An unusual guide
Secret Edinburgh - An unusual guide
Secret Florence
Secret French Riviera
Secret Geneva
Secret Granada
Secret Helsinki
Secret Istanbul
Secret Lisbon

Secret Liverpool - An unusual guide
Secret London - Unusual bars & restaurants
Secret Madrid
Secret Mexico City
Secret Milan
Secret Montreal - An unusual guide
Secret Naples
Secret New Orleans
Secret New York - An unusual guide
Secret New York - Curious activities
Secret Prague
Secret Provence
Secret Rio
Secret Rome
Secret Tokyo
Secret Tuscany
Secret Venice
Secret Vienna
Secret Washington D.C.
Unusual Nights in Paris
Unusual Shopping in Paris

'SOUL OF' GUIDES
Soul of Athens - A guide to 30 exceptional experiences
Soul of Barcelona - A guide to 30 exceptional experiences
Soul of Lisbon - A guide to 30 exceptional experiences
Soul of Los Angeles - A guide to 30 exceptional experiences
Soul of New York - A guide to 30 exceptional experiences
Soul of Rome - A guide to 30 exceptional experiences
Soul of Tokyo - A guide to 30 exceptional experiences
Soul of Venice - A guide to 30 exceptional experiences

Follow us on Facebook, Instagram and Twitter